THE CUBAN MISSILE CRISIS
IN AMERICAN MEMORY

THE CUBAN MISSILE CRISIS IN AMERICAN MEMORY

Myths versus Reality

Sheldon M. Stern

STANFORD UNIVERSITY PRESS
Stanford, California

Stanford University Press
Stanford, California

Printed in the United States of America on acid-free, archival-quality paper

Library of Congress Cataloging-in-Publication Data
Stern, Sheldon M., author.
    The Cuban Missile Crisis in American memory : myths versus reality /
Sheldon M. Stern.
    pages cm. — (Stanford nuclear age series)
Includes bibliographical references and index.
ISBN 978-0-8047-8376-7 (cloth : alk. paper) —
ISBN 978-0-8047-8377-4 (pbk. : alk. paper)
1. Cuban Missile Crisis, 1962—Historiography. 2. National Security Council
(U.S.). Executive Committee. 3. United States—Foreign relations—Soviet Union.
4. Soviet Union—Foreign relations—United States. 5. United States—Foreign
relations—1961–1963. I. Title. II. Series: Stanford nuclear age series.
E841.S7575 2012
972.9106'4—dc23   2012014300

Typeset at Stanford University Press in 10/14 Minion

Contents

Foreword

I T HAS NOW BEEN MORE THAN EIGHT YEARS since the publication
of *Averting 'the Final Failure': John F. Kennedy and the Secret Cuban
Missile Crisis Meetings* (2003) and more than six since *The Week the World
Stood Still: Inside the Secret Cuban Missile Crisis* (2005), both in the Stanford
University Press Nuclear Age Series. During that time, in many discussions
about the missile crisis, I have often been asked about the historical reliability
of Robert Kennedy's *Thirteen Days* as well as the published recollections of
other key participants in the Executive Committee of the National Security
Council (ExComm), such as Robert McNamara, Ted Sorensen, and others.

Unfortunately, it became apparent as the decade progressed that many historians writing about those participants' accounts were unwilling to make the
commitment of time required to listen to the missile crisis recordings of the
ExComm. Some chose instead to rely on the extremely flawed 1997 Harvard
Press transcripts or the more reliable 2001 Miller Center/Norton transcripts.
Nonetheless, despite the availability of the often revelatory and incontrovertible evidence on the tapes, many of the myths that had taken root before the
recordings became available continued to flourish. No myth is more resilient than the notion that RFK saved the peace by persuading the president
to accept the terms in Khrushchev's private offer to remove the missiles for
a U.S. pledge not to invade Cuba, and later to ignore the terms of the Soviet
leader's public offer to remove the missiles in Cuba if the U.S. withdrew its
missiles from Turkey.

This book builds on my own narrative account of the ExComm meetings to expose the misconceptions, half-truths, and outright lies that have shaped the still dominant but largely mythical version of what happened in the White House during those harrowing two weeks of secret deliberations. A half century after the event, it is surely time to document, once and for all, that RFK's *Thirteen Days* cannot be taken seriously as a historical account of the ExComm meetings.

It is equally essential to explore the specific role of key individuals (Dean Rusk, McNamara, McGeorge Bundy, Llewellyn Thompson, etc.) in those meetings, the details of which often conflict directly with RFK's memoir, and with their own published recollections. Finally, it is necessary to make clear that only one person at the ExComm meetings consistently and persistently resisted the advocates of military escalation from the ExComm, the Joint Chiefs, and the Congress: President Kennedy himself.

I am especially indebted to my son, Dr. Jeremy A. Stern, a historian in his own right, for urging me to write this book in order to close a critical gap in the historiographical record about the most dangerous crisis of the Cold War era. Special thanks as well to my wife Helen and my daughter Jennifer, and for the memory of my brother Marty (1935–2012).

Sheldon M. Stern
Newton, Massachusetts
March 2012

THE CUBAN MISSILE CRISIS
IN AMERICAN MEMORY

1 History: From Reel to Real

> The Cuban missile crisis remains a strange enigma—one of the
> most dramatic and well-documented events of modern history,
> yet one of the most thoroughly misunderstood.
>
> —Fred Kaplan, 2003

The New Evidence

With the fiftieth anniversary of the Cuban missile crisis fast approaching, some scholars have questioned whether there is really anything new to say about the nuclear superpower confrontation of October 1962. The answer, of course, is quite simple: if there is additional evidence then there must be something new to say. And, in fact, a great deal of extraordinary and unprecedented evidence has recently become available. This material has substantially redefined the early understanding of the crisis (based almost entirely on American sources) that had prevailed for the first quarter century after 1962. Nonetheless, the importance of much of this new evidence has not been fully recognized or absorbed.

First, a series of international conferences brought together scholars and government participants from the U.S., the U.S.S.R., and Cuba and produced extraordinary new documents and personal recollections. (The conferences were held in Hawk's Cay, Florida, March 1987; Cambridge, Massachusetts, October 1987; Moscow, January 1989; Antigua, January 1991; and Havana, January 1992. A follow-up conference in Havana was held to mark the fortieth anniversary of the crisis in 2002.) These discussions revealed, for example, that Nikita Khrushchev had indeed sent nuclear warheads (never located by the U-2 spy planes) as well as medium-range and intermediate-range ballistic missiles to Cuba; however, wary of a "Dr. Strangelove" scenario, Khrushchev had ordered the missiles and warheads to be stored miles apart; the declassified crisis correspondence between Khrushchev and Fidel Castro revealed that the latter had urged the former to initiate a nuclear strike against the U.S. in the event of an invasion of Cuba—which the Soviet leader interpreted as a call for a nuclear first-strike and refused; and, most startling of all, Khrushchev had managed to covertly send more than 42,000 Red Army troops to Cuba to repel an American invasion and had also shipped battlefield tactical nuclear warheads to the island, authorizing on-site commanders to decide when or if to fire them.

Second, the ebbing, and then end, of the Cold War brought forward significant archival evidence from Communist sources about the missile crisis, or "Caribbean crisis" as it was termed in Moscow, or "October crisis" as it was (and is) called in Havana. These primary sources resulted in valuable additions to, and corrections of, the historical record, which previously had an unavoidable Washington tilt since essentially all the primary source evidence had come from the American side. The new documents, which historians never imagined they would see, confirmed, for example, that JFK's instinct was right when he refused on October 27 to order an attack on the Soviet surface-to-air missile (SAM) site that had brought down a U-2 plane over Cuba (which he had agreed to do a few days before); Soviet officers on the ground had fired the missiles on their own initiative, and Khrushchev was appalled by their recklessness. Also, in the event of American bombing or invasion, Soviet forces in Cuba had nuclear cruise missiles in place to destroy the U.S. naval base at Guantánamo—which would almost certainly have ignited a nuclear war. In addition, evidence from the Soviet archives suggested that Khrushchev's original explanation for his dangerous gamble in Cuba had been fundamentally true: despite the firm convictions of JFK and his advisers, tensions over Berlin were not a decisive factor in the chairman's decision to ship nuclear missiles and warheads to Cuba. Nor did he intend these missiles as an aggressive threat to the security of the United States. From the perspective in Moscow, the missiles were meant to provide a beleaguered Cuban ally with deterrence against covert or overt U.S. attacks and to give the Americans "a little of their own medicine" after JFK's decision to activate the Jupiter missiles in Turkey.[1] Khrushchev was also anxious to conceal the inadequacy of Soviet intercontinental ballistic missiles (ICBMs)—giving the U.S.S.R. at least the public appearance of relative parity in the nuclear balance of terror. Finally, he was also determined, in response to harsh criticism from Red China, to shore up his standing as the leader of the communist world. It was a colossal political misjudgment, however, to assume that the Americans would understand or accept the Kremlin's perspective.

Third, and the most recent, has been the declassification of the one-of-a-kind 43-plus hours of White House missile crisis tape recordings (just over half from the iconic thirteen days and the remainder from the November postcrisis). Not even the difficult-to-access archival documents from the Kremlin have influenced our understanding of the missile crisis quite as much as Kennedy's secret tape recordings. The tapes are the closest thing imaginable to a verbatim record of the crisis. In the famous formulation of nineteenth-century historian Leopold van Ranke, the tapes promise the tantalizing prospect of history *wie es eigentlich gewesen ist*—as it really was.

The once-secret tapes of the Executive Committee of the National Security Council (ExComm) have been available for just over a decade; nonetheless, some writers, likely put off by the demanding and labor-intensive effort required to listen to these technically primitive (initially reel-to-reel) recordings, have chosen instead to use the extremely inaccurate 1997 Harvard Press transcripts, the more reliable 2001 Miller Center/Norton transcripts, or my own 2003 narrative of the meetings.[2] This volume will substantiate, once and for all, that there is no substitute for listening to these tapes. No secondary source (transcripts or a narrative), no matter how reliable, can stand in for this unique primary source—now universally available, at no cost, from the Presidential Recordings Program on the website of the Miller Center of Public Affairs at the University of Virginia (http://millercenter.org/academic/presidentialrecordings).

It is hard to imagine, for example, that David Talbot could have made the demonstrably false claim that JFK "could count on only his brother and Robert McNamara for support" in the ExComm meetings and that RFK had "matured from a kneejerk hawk to a wise and restrained diplomat," or that Michael Dobbs could declare that the younger Kennedy "was a chastened man" by October 27, if they had listened to these recordings (Chapters 2–4).[3] Dobbs also contends that on the evening of that decisive day, McNamara, when asked if he wanted dinner, "snapped, 'Eating is the least of my worries.'" In fact, the defense secretary muttered, almost inaudibly, "You don't have to worry, eating is the least of my worries." McNamara's dismal tone, lost in even the best transcript, momentarily exposed the raw depths of exhaustion, fear, and anxiety which he and his colleagues had endured around the clock since October 16.[4]

Many of the pervasive misconceptions about the missile crisis derive, of course, from the initial "heroic" interpretation—created and promoted by JFK, RFK, and key members of the administration, eagerly swallowed by gullible journalists in the first years after the event, popularized by the selective and manipulative writing of administration insiders like Arthur Schlesinger Jr. and Theodore Sorensen, and reaching near iconic status in Robert Kennedy's *Thirteen Days*—not to mention wide currency in dramatizations such as *The Missiles of October* (1974) and *Thirteen Days* (2000). The latter concocts a crucial role in the ExComm meetings for JFK aide Kenneth O'Donnell; this claim is pure fiction. The film does not reveal that President Kennedy was taping the discussions, ignores U.S. covert actions against Castro and Khrushchev's motives for placing the missiles in Cuba, and casts Robert Kennedy as a consistent dove—in line with RFK's *Thirteen Days*, but *not* with the tapes.

In this "heroic" but historically one-dimensional rendering, the courageous and determined young American president, always cool under fire, successfully resisted the aggressive intent of the Soviet Union and its puppet regime in Cuba and won a decisive victory over international communism. And even more important, having learned sobering lessons on the nuclear brink, Kennedy reached out to the Soviet Union and Cuba in his last year in office and began the process of détente—as reflected in his June 1963 American University speech, the Moscow-Washington Hot Line, and the Limited Nuclear Test Ban Treaty, as well as a series of cautious and secret diplomatic initiatives aimed at achieving a rapprochement with Castro's Cuba.

This heroic consensus did not go unchallenged for very long despite the best efforts of JFK loyalists. In the 1970s and 1980s, in the wake of the Vietnam war and the expanding documentary record on national security issues from the 1960s, revisionist and New Left historians zeroed in on the Kennedy administration's "secret war against Cuba," which encompassed sabotage and subversion against the Cuban economy, plots to overthrow or assassinate Castro, and "contingency plans" to blockade, bomb, or invade Cuba. These historians accused Kennedy of reckless brinksmanship and condemned him for turning down Khrushchev's entirely reasonable proposal to resolve the nuclear standoff by removing missiles from both Cuba and Turkey. They concluded that JFK's "heroic" management of the crisis, measured against this newly available evidence, was little more than a self-serving fabrication.

One prominent New Left historian, for example, told me in the early 1980s that JFK had been the ultimate macho cold warrior and that the historical record would eventually prove that in foreign relations Kennedy had been the most dangerous of the Cold War presidents. However, as Kennedy Library historian, I had already listened to the tapes. The library was preparing for their declassification, and I was the first nonmember of the ExComm, and certainly the first professional historian, to hear all the recordings and learn exactly what had happened at these meetings. As a result, I knew that JFK had actually accepted the missile trade despite strenuous opposition from essentially all his advisers. I could only reply, "You may be in for some major surprises when these tapes are declassified."

However, the story is unfortunately not that simple, and the crisis is still widely misunderstood despite the availability of this definitive primary source. An entirely mythical Cuban missile crisis remains alive and well. And ironically, the most pervasive and enduring myths about the crisis revolve around the very core event—the secret White House meetings—for which these verbatim tape recordings exist.

There is, of course, nothing new about historical participants manipulating the evidence and inventing "truths" to suit their purposes. In 1984, as a case in point, the Kennedy Library sponsored a conference to mark the centenary of the birth of Harry Truman. The keynote speaker was Clark Clifford—the ultimate Washington insider and power broker—who had served in the Truman White House. Clifford was an imposing figure in every sense: not a single strand of his silver-white hair was out of place, and he seemed almost royal in his immaculately tailored suit. At the conclusion of his talk, which included his personal recollections of the day FDR died and Truman became president, he took questions from the audience.

A rather scruffy, bearded young man politely but firmly contradicted several of the important details in Clifford's account of the events of April 12, 1945. Clifford looked down at him from the rostrum and with a rather lordly gesture admonished the student, "Young man, I was there." The audience spontaneously erupted into applause for the distinguished speaker. In fact, the student's version was correct (and I told him so), and later I decided to check the details of Clifford's recollections. I discovered that Clark Clifford was in the navy, stationed in San Francisco, on that historic day. He did not even meet Truman for the first time until later that summer.

Many of the enduring myths about the Cuban missile crisis can likewise be traced back to the Kennedy administration's own initial spin on the events of October 1962—especially to Robert Kennedy's personal (and until recently, unverifiable) version in *Thirteen Days*. These misconceptions, of course, also have their own curious and rather circuitous history.

McGeorge Bundy, JFK's special assistant for national security, worked at the Kennedy Library in the early 1980s researching his memoir (published in 1988).[5] During that period, he was granted special access to some of the ExComm recordings and listened to the meetings from the first day (October 16) and the last day (October 27). He usually brought a brown-bag lunch, and I often sat and talked with him in the staff lunchroom. Bundy knew that the tapes were going to be declassified but seemed very surprised when I told him that I had already listened to them. He admitted that he was having problems identifying some of the voices of his former colleagues; one afternoon we listened together, and I was able to persuade him that the voice he thought was John McCloy's was actually John McCone's. However, he was particularly interested in my contention that the Black Saturday tapes revealed that the president had accepted Khrushchev's missile trade proposal; he insisted that it was an understanding, not an actual deal. He seemed evasive, if not hostile, when I referred to the stubborn and all but unanimous resistance to the trade by the ExComm—including Bundy himself—on that final Saturday of the crisis.

A quarter of a century later, in October 2007, I shared the platform with Ted Sorensen at a Princeton University conference marking the forty-fifth anniversary of the missile crisis. Sorensen was scheduled to speak first, but his driver called to say that they were stuck in traffic and I was moved up to that spot. About five minutes into my remarks, the door to the theater was opened, and Sorensen entered on the arm of his assistant (a severe stroke had left him legally blind). The crowd gave him a standing ovation. He listened attentively as I discussed my findings from the meeting tapes—backed up with verbatim quotes.

However, when he stepped to the microphone, Sorensen emphatically rejected my conclusions on the grounds that he was the only person on the panel "who was actually there"—even claiming, much like Bundy in those earlier lunchroom chats, that there had never been a missile trade deal. And again like Bundy, he objected to my findings about the strident and all but unanimous opposition to the trade on that final day. Sorensen did, in fact, attend most of the ExComm meetings but rarely contributed to the discussions. His most important role was behind the scenes in drafting JFK's October 22 speech and the letters to Khrushchev. When he did speak up, his views generally paralleled those of RFK. For example, he urged the seizure of an East German passenger ship because it would demonstrate that the U.S. response was "not a soft one at all"; recommended that the Organization of American States declare Cuba's possession of nuclear weapons a violation of the Rio Pact in order to give the U.S. "greater grounds" for attacking Cuba; opposed Khrushchev's Cuba-Turkey missile trade offer; and declared on the final evening of meetings, "I think in some ways it's a sign of weakness if we just keep responding [to Khrushchev] in messages."

These key participants in the White House meetings were clearly working to spin and shape the evidence in an effort to minimize their own opposition to the secret agreement that in the end avoided nuclear war—an agreement which had to be imposed on the ExComm by the increasingly irritated and intractable President Kennedy. This last-ditch effort, in light of the availability of the tapes, seems to be little more than tilting at windmills. Notwithstanding, Sorensen did not budge from this position in his personal memoir, published only months after the Princeton conference.[6]

There are many conflicting Cuban missile crises in American historical memory. Unfortunately, the mythic crisis, shaped largely by manipulation and half-truths, has gained far more attention than the crisis rooted in hard and often irrefutable evidence. The White House tape recordings offer scholars the rare opportunity to forge a fresh, accurate, and in-depth understanding of this unique historical event. This volume, therefore, building on my previous narrative version of the ExComm recordings, exposes and analyzes a series of pervasive and lingering myths and misconceptions which continue to cloud our understanding of the most dangerous two weeks in human history.

The Historical Authenticity of the Missile Crisis Tapes

The Kennedy White House tapes present historians with a unique opportunity to accurately assess both the process and substance of presidential leadership during the most perilous event of the Cold War. Many presidents have faced extremely grave crises, but never before or since has the survival of human civilization been at stake in a few short weeks of extremely dangerous deliberations, and never before or since have their unique and secret discussions been recorded and preserved. And given the end of the Cold War and the breakup of the Soviet Union, the Cuban missile crisis will hopefully remain, for policy makers and scholars, the only "case study" of a full-scale nuclear showdown between military superpowers.

These tape recordings are a one-of-a-kind historical source because they transcend the limitations of human memory and the inevitable selectivity of notes taken at the time or memoranda written after the fact. They allow us to know, with very few exceptions resulting from their sometimes poor quality or preservation, exactly what the meeting participants said and heard. They highlight, as never before possible, the thought processes that influenced and shaped decision-making. And perhaps most important, the tapes allow us to glimpse the real people behind the political mask worn by all public figures.

Inevitably, in our increasingly cynical era, some analysts have questioned or even dismissed the historical value of the Kennedy administration tapes because only the president and his brother, Attorney General Robert Kennedy, knew they were being recorded. The Kennedy taping system has been particularly suspect because it was manually activated (not voice activated like Nixon's) and easily derailed by human carelessness or error. JFK, like any person in similarly stressful circumstances, often forgot to turn the machine on until after a meeting had begun and sometimes neglected to turn it off, so that the tape ran out. He also failed to record his critical October 18 confrontation with Soviet foreign minister Andrei Gromyko as well as the decisive Oval Office meeting, with only eight advisers, on the evening of October 27. In at least one case, the tape was left running after a meeting ended and recorded the chatter of the White House cleaning crew.

Presumably, therefore, JFK (and perhaps RFK as well) could have manipulated the outcome during the taped meetings in order to enhance his historical reputation. This view has been and continues to be repeated, again and again—often by people who should know better. JFK seemed "open and straightforward," but the value of the tapes "can only be diminished by the fact that the two key players of the crisis [JFK and RFK] knew they were being recorded." The apparent neutrality of the tapes is doubtful because "we can never determine how much either man tailored what he said in order to control the historical record." The tapes are "selective and somewhat misleading because the President could turn his tape recorder on and off at will." Even the editors of the 1997 edition of published transcripts seemed concerned about "the President selectively choosing what to record for posterity."[7]

William Safire, columnist, author, and one-time aide to President Nixon, pushed this argument much further in a specific response to the 1997 publication of transcripts of the missile crisis tapes. Safire declared that "the [JFK] tapes inherently lie. There pose the Kennedy brothers knowing they are being recorded, taking care to speak for history—while their unsuspecting colleagues think aloud and contradict themselves the way honest people do in a crisis." The ExComm tapes, Safire insisted, "do not present pure, raw history" since JFK knew the tape was rolling and could "turn the meetings into a charade of entrapment—half history-in-the-making, half-image-in-the-manipulating. And you can be sure of some outright deception [by] the turning-off of the machine at key moments."[8]

These arguments, however, are plainly nonsense:

First, perhaps, in a recorded phone conversation between two people, it might be possible to manipulate the discussion somewhat to shape the outcome.[9] But in a meeting of some fifteen people, operating under enormous stress and tension, it would be tactically and physically impossible. JFK could turn the tape machine on and off in the Cabinet Room—the switch was under the table in front of his chair—but how would he have kept the participants from seeing what he was doing? Of course he would have had no way of knowing when to stop since there was no visible counter and he could not have seen one anyway unless he stuck his head under the table.

Second, JFK would never, even in his most vivid imagination, have conceived of the possibility that we, the public, would *ever* hear these tapes. He thought of them, quite correctly, as private property—*which they were legally at the time*—and of course he could not foresee the Freedom of Information Act, "Watergate," and the Presidential Records Act, which ultimately facilitated the opening of these confidential materials. He might then have picked and chosen freely from the tapes when he wrote his memoirs—omitting the frequent references to classified national security material and the potentially compromising personal and political remarks (especially on the recorded telephone conversations). Why would he need to "control" the content of the tapes when he was certain that historians and the public would never hear them unless he or his estate granted special access to this unique portion of his personal property?

Third, Safire seems to have forgotten that the president he had worked for, Richard Nixon, knew that he was being recorded but nevertheless did *not* try (with one possible exception) to tailor his remarks for the tapes. As we all know, Nixon repeatedly incriminated himself. Why? Because even well into the Watergate investigation and hearings, he never thought that he would or could be compelled by the courts to release these personal, private, and confidential recordings. If he had believed it early enough, he might easily have destroyed the tapes and likely have saved his presidency.

The fourth and most critical point, however, demonstrates that Safire's argument is fatally flawed by what historians call "presentism." JFK and the other missile crisis participants, we should never forget, did not know the outcome of the crisis when they were in the middle of dealing with it. Even if President Kennedy had tried, as Safire puts it, to "pose" for history, how could he have known which position taken during the discussions would ultimately be judged favorably by historians? What if, for example, the Russians had responded to the blockade, just as the Joint Chiefs of Staff (JCS) had warned, by carrying out low-level bombing raids in the southeastern U.S. or by launching the operational nuclear missiles in Cuba at the American mainland? Historians today would still be listening to the same tapes (assuming any tapes or historians had survived), but with a radically different outlook. It would then be the Chiefs who had turned out to be right: the blockade would have proven to be, as they had predicted, a feeble and inadequate measure, and air strikes—which we credit Kennedy for resisting—to neutralize the missile sites and airfields would appear to have been the correct course after all. In other words, *if the outcome had been different*, the same tapes could then be interpreted to make Kennedy look appallingly negligent rather than diplomatically cautious and reasonable.

Alternatively, what if Khrushchev had not agreed on October 28 to remove the missiles, and the bombing and invasion tentatively planned for later that week had gone forward? Even assuming that Kennedy and Khrushchev could have avoided using nuclear weapons, a shaky assumption at best, there would still have been substantial casualties on both sides before some kind of cease-fire was *perhaps* reached through a neutral third party like the United Nations. Today, some scholars would denounce JFK for failing to demonstrate American firmness and grit by immediately attacking the missiles and "drawing a line in the sand," which presumably would have deterred the Soviets from risking a military response. Again, the same tapes could then be interpreted to make Kennedy look weak and indecisive on the one hand, or irresponsible and reckless on the other—*if the outcome had been different*.

Robert Kennedy's words on the tapes further highlight the fact that the participants could not know what position would seem "right" in the 20/20 vision of hindsight. Clearly, RFK knew of the taping system; but he took a persistently hawkish stance, pushing for a tough strategy that would remove Castro and demonstrate American resolve to the Soviets. Yet when he decided to write a book on the missile crisis meetings and to run for president in 1968, he downplayed his aggressive posture (never imagining that the tapes would one day be made public), painting himself as a persistent dove and conciliator. RFK knew only *after* the crisis had been resolved that the dovish position was politically more useful, and that having pursued a peaceful solution in 1962 would later seem very appealing to a nation divided by the war in Vietnam. He could not have manipulated his image on the tapes any more than his brother since neither of them knew what was going to happen the next day or even the next hour.

The editors of the 1997 Harvard Press transcripts eventually revised their position: "Kennedy could not know how the crisis or discussions would come out, so he would not know what to say that would make him look good." Similarly, in the 2001 Norton edition, they concluded that JFK had no way of knowing which 1962 viewpoint "would look good to posterity."[10]

As President Kennedy told the ExComm when the perilous naval quarantine around Cuba was about to be implemented, "What we are doing is throwing down a card on the table in a game which we don't know the ending of." JFK and the ExComm, notwithstanding their Cold War ideological convictions and blinders, had no choice but to deal with the stress and danger in the situation at hand to the best of their abilities—with no guarantee of success, or even survival.

JFK and Nuclear War: The Impossible Choice

In the spring of 1960, journalist Hugh Sidey sat down with John F. Kennedy in the Massachusetts junior senator's office. JFK was struggling to capture his party's presidential nomination, and Sidey was trying to size him up. "What do you remember about the Great Depression?" Sidey asked in an effort to gauge Kennedy's grasp of economics. JFK replied with "absolute candor [that] surprised us both. 'I have no first-hand knowledge of the depression,' he answered. 'My family had one of the great fortunes of the world and it was worth more than ever then. . . . I really did not learn about the depression until I read about it at Harvard.'" Senator Kennedy then leaned forward and added, "'My experience was the war. I can tell you about that.'"[11] He then lectured Sidey for much of an hour:

> He had read the books of great military strategists—Carl Von Clausewitz, Alfred Thayer Mahan, and Basil Henry Liddell Hart—and he wondered if their theories of total violence made sense in the nuclear age. He expressed his contempt for the old military minds . . . Kennedy chortled over the boasts of those who developed new military technology, claiming the new weapons rarely lived up to their billing—at first. But they were almost always perfected and then stockpiled—and then used. War with all of its modern horror would be his biggest concern if he got to the White House, Kennedy said. . . If I had to single out one element in Kennedy's life that more than anything else influenced his later leadership it would be a horror of war, a total revulsion over the terrible toll that modern war had taken on individuals, nations and societies, and the even worse prospects in the nuclear age. . . It ran even deeper than his considerable public rhetoric on the issue.[12]

This "deep core of realism about the world," Sidey concluded, came out of Kennedy's own unique and personal past—"a past . . . that was serious much of the time and was focused on understanding the events and people that drove nations, the preparation of a young man for what was still an ill-defined and distant challenge. . . Policy at the top comes out of the heart and mind of the President, or at the very least is tempered by his personality. And his convictions and passions are almost always linked to early impressions gained from family and school and youthful experience."

During the tense summer of 1961, just halfway into the first year of the Kennedy administration, Sidey recalled that JFK observed gloomily, "'Ever since the longbow, when man had developed new weapons and stockpiled them, somebody has come along and used them. I don't know how we escape it with nuclear weapons.'" "Domestic policy," he sometimes mused, "can only defeat us; foreign policy can kill us."[13]

"There are, I have found, many compartments within the souls of men who rise to great power," Sidey concluded, an assessment that can be vividly documented in the formative years of John Kennedy.[14] The twenty-two-year-old Kennedy, writing a month after the outbreak of World War II, warned that the war would be "beyond comprehension in its savage intensity, and which could well presage a return to barbarism."[15]

Four years later, the letters written by the twenty-six-year-old junior naval officer from the South Pacific confirm that he was an acute observer of events around him and more dubious than ever about the logic and results of war. He told his Danish lover, Inga Arvad:

> I would like to write you a letter giving in a terse sharp style an outline of the war situation first hand . . . in which I would use the words global war, total effort and a battle of logistics no less than eight times each . . . I refrain from this for two reasons . . . the first being I know you don't give a damn, and the second being that frankly I don't know a god-damned thing, as my copy of the Washington Times Herald arrives two months late, due to logistical difficulties . . . and it is pretty hard to get the total picture of a global war unless you are sitting in New York or Washington, or even Casablanca. . . .
>
> I understand we are winning it, which is cheering, albeit somewhat hard to see, but I guess the view improves with distance . . . I know mine would . . . I wouldn't mind being back in the States picking up the daily paper, saying 'Why don't those bastards out there do something?' It's one of those interesting things about the war that everyone in the States . . . want[s] to be out here killing Japs, while everyone out here wants to be back. . . . It seems to me that someone with enterprise could work out some sort of an exchange, but as I hear you saying, I asked for it, honey and I'm getting it.[16]

JFK's cynicism about the war erupted regularly: "When I read that we will fight the Japs for years if necessary," he told his parents, "and will sacrifice hundreds of thousands if we must—I always like to check from where he is talking—it's seldom out here." He poignantly told Inga that the "boys at the front" rarely discussed the war that threatened to engulf them every day, but instead talked endlessly about "when they are going to get home." These impressions never faded: "That whole story was fucked up," he told journalist Robert Donovan years later about the war in the Solomon Islands. "You know the military always screws up everything."[17]

The insights of this son of wealth and privilege in 1943 point directly to his "deep core of realism about the world" during the Cuban missile crisis meetings a generation later:

> The war goes slowly here, slower than you can ever imagine from reading the papers at home. The only way you can get the proper perspective on its progress is to put away the headlines for a month and watch us move on the map, it's deathly slow. The Japs have dug deep, and with the possible exception of a couple of Marine divisions are the greatest jungle fighters in the world. Their willingness to die for a place like Munda gives them a tremendous advantage over us, we, in aggregate, just don't have the willingness. Of course, at times,

an individual will rise up to it, but in total, no . . . Munda or any of these spots are just God damned hot stinking corners of small islands in a part of the ocean we all hope never to see again.

We are at a great disadvantage—the Russians could see their country invaded, the Chinese the same. The British were bombed, but we are fighting on some islands belonging to the Lever Company, a British concern making soap . . . I suppose if we were stockholders we would perhaps be doing better, but to see that by dying at Munda you are helping to insure peace in our time takes a larger imagination than most men possess. . . . The Japs have this advantage: because of their feeling about Hirohito, they merely wish to kill. American energies are divided, he wants to kill but he is also trying desperately to prevent himself from being killed . . .

This war here is a dirty business. It's very easy to talk about the war and beating the Japs if it takes years and a million men, but anyone who talks like that should consider well his words. We get so used to talking about billions of dollars, and millions of soldiers, that thousands of casualties sound like drops in the bucket. But if those thousands want to live as much as the ten that I saw [his PT boat crew], the people deciding the whys and wherefores had better make mighty sure that all this effort is headed for some definite goal, and that when we reach that goal we may say it was worth it, for if it isn't, the whole thing will turn to ashes, and we will face great trouble in the years to come after the war . . .

There was a boy on my boat, only twenty-four, had three kids, one night two bombs straddles [sic] our boat, and two of the men were hit, one standing right next to him. He never got over it. He hardly ever spoke after that. He told me one night he thought he was going to be killed. I wanted to put him ashore to work, he wouldn't go. I wish I had. . . . He was in the forward gun turret where the destroyer hit us . . . I don't know what this all adds up to, nothing I guess, but you said that you figured I'd . . . write my experiences—I wouldn't go near a book like that, this thing is so stupid, that while it has a sickening fascination for some of us, myself included, I want to leave it far behind me when I go.[18]

JFK's observations belie the fact he was barely two years older than Andrew Kirksey, the twenty-four-year-old "boy on my boat" killed on PT-109.

John Kennedy's aversion to war became even more pronounced after his navy service. In the spring of 1945, as a reporter for Hearst newspapers, he covered the San Francisco conference establishing the United Nations and was disillusioned by the "inadequate preparation and lack of fundamental agreement" between the former Allies. He also speculated about "the eventual discovery of a weapon so horrible that it will truthfully mean the abolishment of all the nations employing it."[19]

Two years later, the twenty-nine-year-old freshman congressman, gripped by the escalating suspicions of the Cold War, warned of the potential for nuclear apocalypse: "The greatest danger is a war which would be waged by the conscious decision of the leaders of Russia some 25 or 35 years from now. She will have the atomic bomb, the planes, the ports, and the ships to wage aggressive war outside her borders. Such a conflict would truly mean the end of the world."[20]

All his life JFK had a high regard for personal courage and toughness, but at the same time, he loathed the brutality and carnage of war. He had also recognized a profound historical paradox: human beings had never been capable of building a stable and peaceful world, but at the same time, war, especially between nations possessing nuclear weapons, was no longer a rational option. Kennedy was as passionately anticommunist as any of his missile crisis advisers, but he understood that once military conflict was unleashed between the nuclear superpowers, all bets were off.

One colleague recalled a briefing by Soviet specialists at which JFK had revealed "a mentality extraordinarily free of preconceived prejudices, inherited or otherwise. . . . He saw Russia as a great and powerful country, and it seemed to him there must be some basis upon which the two countries could live without blowing each other up." Kennedy once remarked at a White House meeting, "It is insane that two men, sitting on opposite sides of the world, should be able to decide to bring an end to civilization." He was convinced "that there was nothing more important to a President than thinking hard about war."[21] "We should bear in mind," he wrote early in 1960, "a few impressive lines of advice from [Sir Basil Liddell] Hart's book: 'Keep strong, if possible. In any case, keep cool. Have unlimited patience. Never corner an opponent, and always assist him to save his face. Put yourself in his shoes—so as to see things through his eyes. Avoid self-righteousness like the devil— nothing is so self-blinding.'"[22]

JFK was profoundly impressed by a reported exchange between a former German chancellor and his successor after the outbreak of World War I. "How did it all happen?" the ex-chancellor asked. "Ah, if only one knew," was the reply. "If this planet is ever ravaged by nuclear war—" President Kennedy remarked in 1963, "if the survivors of that devastation can then endure the fire, poison, chaos and catastrophe—I do not want one of those survivors to ask another, 'How did it all happen?' and to receive the incredible reply: 'Ah, if only one knew.'"[23]

Nonetheless, JFK never lost his detached and ironic sense of humor about such potentially fatal realities in human affairs. After nuclear scientist Edward Teller testified against the Nuclear Test Ban Treaty at 1963 Senate hearings, Senator J. William Fulbright told the president, in a recorded phone conversation, that Teller's arguments had been quite persuasive and may have changed some votes. Kennedy replied with a bemused tone of resignation reflecting that deep core of realism about the world, "There's no doubt that any man with complete conviction, particularly who's an expert, is bound to shake anybody who's got an open mind. That's the advantage of having a closed mind."[24] The Cuban missile crisis provided the supreme test of John Kennedy's capacity to have an open mind and, at the same time, to hold fast to his core beliefs about nuclear war in the face of unyielding pressure from the "experts" around him.

It is not an exaggeration to say—because it is incontrovertibly backed up by the verbatim missile crisis recordings—that John F. Kennedy was the only person at the ExComm meetings who genuinely understood that nuclear war could *never* be a viable or rational choice. Nuclear weapons had altered the very meaning of war itself, and everything—anything—had to be done to avert a nuclear apocalypse.

That is why, despite the fact that his own administration had contributed significantly to creating the crisis, and after absorbing the initial shock and anger about the discovery of the missiles, he realized during the initial meetings that there was no safe or "manageable" military option in the nuclear era. In these private discussions, the president frankly acknowledged that even America's allies felt that "we've got this fixation about Cuba," "that we're slightly demented on this subject," and that attacking this small island nation would be a "mad act by the United States." JFK recognized that even though the U.S. had far more nuclear missiles than the U.S.S.R., "we can't use them," because "the decision to use any kind of a nuclear weapon, even the tactical ones, presents such a risk of it getting out of control so quickly."[25]

He alone among the ExComm consistently grasped that keeping the Jupiter missiles in Turkey in order to preserve the unity of NATO was not worth the risk of global nuclear war. That is also why he told the Joint Chiefs of Staff that using military force in Cuba could escalate to the firing of nuclear weapons and that it was "a hell of an alternative" to "begin a nuclear exchange" which in the United States alone would mean "80–100 million casualties" and "the destruction of a country." That is likewise why he told his congressional critics that attacking the nuclear installations in Cuba was "one hell of a gamble" and questioned whether that was "a gamble we should take?"[26]

Khrushchev himself later confirmed that if the missile sites had been strafed or bombed, he would have had to retaliate: "I knew that the United States could knock out some of our installations, but not all of them. If a quarter or even a tenth of our missiles survived—even if only one or two big ones were left—we could still hit New York, and there wouldn't be much of New York left."[27] JFK finally imposed the Cuba-Turkey trade on his recalcitrant advisers and even approved a fallback plan (Chapter 5) to make the secret missile deal public if that was the political price that had to be paid to secure Soviet agreement and prevent a nuclear war.

As McGeorge Bundy, one of the president's most persistent critics at the ExComm meetings, eventually conceded, "Twenty-five years have passed and I find myself less impressed by my own insistence on the reality of NATO sentiment than I am by the President's unwavering recognition that the basic interest of all concerned was to find a peaceful end to the crisis, and that the Turkish missiles, whatever the opinion of allies, did not justify bloodshed in Cuba" and the very real likelihood of nuclear war.[28]

Major Participants in the ExComm Meetings

George W. Ball (1909–1994)
Under Secretary of State

Ball supported a blockade and was among the first to condemn proposed surprise air attacks as an American "Pearl Harbor." However, he also advocated a declaration of war in the early meetings, and during the crucial October 27 discussions initially opposed the Cuba-Turkey missile trade but switched sides after the shooting down of an American U-2 spy plane over Cuba.

McGeorge Bundy (1919–1996)
Special Assistant to the President for National Security

Bundy initially urged military action against the missiles alone because of concern about Soviet reprisals in Berlin. He was always eager to stand up for his personal policy choices and sometimes irritated the president. Bundy eventually supported extensive air strikes in Cuba and, in the later meetings, forcefully resisted JFK's willingness to "trade" Soviet missiles in Cuba for U.S.

missiles in Turkey because he believed this choice would divide the NATO alliance and undermine American credibility.

C. Douglas Dillon (1909–2003)
Secretary of the Treasury

Dillon initially supported air strikes on just the missile sites as the course of action least likely to provoke Soviet retaliation, but eventually he went along with the blockade as the first step in isolating and eventually ousting Castro. He vigorously resisted the proposal to remove American missiles from Turkey in exchange for the withdrawal of Soviet missiles from Cuba.

Roswell Gilpatric (1906–1996)
Deputy Secretary of Defense

Gilpatric generally supported the JCS view that the missiles represented a military rather than a diplomatic threat and was sympathetic to their proposals to eliminate them by bombing and/or invasion.

Lyndon B. Johnson (1908–1973)
Vice President of the United States

Johnson, despite his initial reluctance to speak at the ExComm meetings, especially when JFK was present, and his ambivalence about the use of force, did eventually make some important contributions to the crucial discussions on October 27.

U. Alexis Johnson (1908–1997)
Deputy Under Secretary of State for Political Affairs

Johnson, like most members of the ExComm, first supported surprise air strikes against the missile sites but ultimately endorsed the blockade. He was not an active participant in the discussions but worked behind the scenes drafting policy papers for the meetings.

John Fitzgerald Kennedy (1917–1963)
President of the United States

Kennedy's determination to seek a political rather than a military solution, in order to avert nuclear war, stands in sharp contrast to the Cold War rhetoric and policies which had helped propel him into the White House, and the covert actions against Cuba which he had pursued since 1961 and would continue to support in his final year as president. He guided the ExComm discussions without ever appearing overbearing, patiently listened to all points of view, and was remarkably tolerant of harsh criticism.

Robert F. Kennedy (1925–1968)
Attorney General of the United States

If JFK temporarily left the room or did not attend an ExComm meeting, the participants instinctively recognized that RFK served as the president's stand-in. But unlike his brother, RFK was one of the most consistently hawkish and confrontational members of the ExComm—contrary to his claims in *Thirteen Days.*

John McCone (1902–1991)
Director, Central Intelligence Agency

McCone regularly briefed the ExComm on Soviet moves in Cuba and updated former president Eisenhower on JFK's behalf. He advocated removal of the missiles by whatever means necessary, including the use of military force. He did, however, break with most of his ExComm colleagues, after a U-2 was shot down on October 27, by supporting the president's determination to consider a Turkish missile trade.

Robert S. McNamara (1916–2009)
Secretary of Defense

McNamara initially broke with the Joint Chiefs and argued that the Soviet missiles in Cuba posed a political rather than a military threat to the United States. However, he eventually became far more hawkish and vigorously opposed the president's support for a direct trade of the Cuban and Turkish missiles. He was one of the most articulate and outspoken members of the ExComm.

Paul H. Nitze (1907–2004)
Assistant Secretary of Defense for International Security Affairs

Nitze was one of the ExComm's most consistent hawks. His tense exchange with President Kennedy about tightening JCS procedures so that U.S. missiles in Turkey would not be fired at the U.S.S.R. is one of the most dramatic moments of the ExComm meetings (see Epilogue). He was a resolute opponent of the Cuba-Turkey missile trade.

Dean Rusk (1909–1994)
Secretary of State

Rusk has been criticized for lack of leadership in the ExComm discussions. The tapes prove otherwise. He contributed detailed and thoughtful analyses of diplomatic policy choices throughout the meetings and, like most ExComm members, shifted positions several times; he generally resisted surprise air strikes, endorsed the blockade, and advised against seizing Soviet ships that had turned away from Cuba. However, he opposed a deal involving U.S. missiles in Turkey. Late on the evening of October 27, Rusk collaborated with JFK on a secret diplomatic effort, through the U.N., to prevent the outbreak of war (see Chapter 5).

Theodore C. Sorensen (1928–2010)
Special Counsel to the President

Despite the fact that Sorensen was not a foreign policy specialist, Kennedy relied on his judgment and invited him to participate in the ExComm discussions. Sorensen spoke rarely but did join the majority in resisting a Turkish missile swap. He also wrote several important policy option memos during the crisis and was the principal author of JFK's October 22 speech to the nation.

Maxwell D. Taylor (1901–1987)
Chairman of the Joint Chiefs of Staff

Taylor generally represented the hawkish views of the Chiefs, but he did favor bombing over invasion in the early meetings, and eventually accepted the quarantine. He also opposed the Cuba-Turkey missile deal. Taylor always displayed respect for the president and avoided the condescending tone adopted by several members of the JCS.

Llewellyn E. Thompson (1904–1972)
United States Ambassador-at-Large

Thompson had served as ambassador to the Soviet Union from 1957 to 1962 and was the only member of the ExComm who knew Khrushchev personally. As a result, the ExComm listened with special interest to his assessments of Soviet thinking and Khrushchev's motives. Despite initially endorsing the blockade, he later supported a declaration of war and the ouster of Castro and strenuously resisted a trade of U.S. missiles in Turkey for Soviet missiles in Cuba.

Concise Summary of the Meetings of the Executive Committee of the National Security Council (ExComm), October 16–27, 1962

Tuesday, October 16, 11:50 A.M.

The fifteen men gathering in the Cabinet Room that morning were stunned that the Soviets had deceived the administration about their intentions in Cuba. Analysts from the National Photographic Interpretation Center explained that the medium-range ballistic missile (MRBM) sites thus far discovered were still under construction. It quickly became clear that any attempt to destroy the sites with air attacks had to be carried out before they became fully operational. However, there was no way to be certain when the sites would become operational, and bombing was also unlikely to destroy all the missiles. The Soviets might retaliate by seizing West Berlin or by firing the missiles that survived the bombing at the U.S. mainland—initiating a nuclear world war. Three principal options were on the table: air strikes against the missile sites, a naval blockade of Cuba, and/or a full-scale invasion. By the end of the meeting, the president had all but decided in favor of the air strikes.

October 16, 6:30 P.M.

Several participants suggested that the presence of the Soviet missiles in Cuba did not really alter the strategic balance of nuclear power. "It doesn't make any difference," the president argued, "if you get blown up by an ICBM flying from the Soviet Union or one that was ninety miles away. Geography doesn't mean that much. . . . After all this is a political struggle as much as military." The president admitted to being puzzled by Soviet motives in Cuba. There was some awareness that Khrushchev might be reacting to the presence of U.S. missiles in Turkey and Italy; but no one in the room seriously considered the possibility that he had acted defensively, to protect his Cuban ally. The morning meeting had ended with a consensus for the use of force—particularly for a limited air strike on just the missile sites. During the evening, however, there was a growing awareness of the dangers raised by any military action in Cuba. If the U.S. attacked the island nation, especially without warning, where would it end?

Wednesday, October 17, 8:30 A.M.

The ExComm met at the State Department without the president (who was campaigning for the November congressional elections).[29] There was still a great deal of uncertainty and vacillation, but support seemed to be coalescing around some combination of air strikes, a blockade, and diplomatic approaches to the U.S.S.R. Former secretary of state Dean Acheson, invited by the president, insisted on immediate air strikes to eliminate the nuclear threat and demonstrate American resolve to the Soviets.

Thursday, October 18, 11:00 A.M.

Early that morning, U-2 photos turned up evidence of intermediate-range ballistic missile sites in Cuba. The IRBMs had a range about twice that of

MRBMs and carried far deadlier warheads. Soviet strategic bombers, with the capacity to carry nuclear payloads, were also discovered. The ExComm reconvened with a renewed momentum for military action—especially an invasion. Support for a surprise bombing attack had begun to erode because it seemed reminiscent of Pearl Harbor. But the president resisted the pressure for an invasion, insisting that many people would regard such an attack as "a mad act by the United States." He also made two tentative references to the possibility of a deal involving the U.S. missiles in Turkey. There was particular concern that Khrushchev would order Soviet troops into West Berlin if the U.S. attacked Cuba—likely leading to nuclear war. "Now the question really is," the president declared, "what action we take which lessens the chances of a nuclear exchange, which obviously is the final failure." The blockade option began to look more and more advantageous.

October 18/19, midnight

President Kennedy returned to the Oval Office alone at midnight to record his recollections of an unrecorded meeting just held in the White House living quarters. He observed that there had been a consensus for a blockade, which he described as a limited action "for a limited purpose." "I was most anxious," he stressed, that the blockade proclamation should not include a declaration of war.

Friday, October 19, 9:45 A.M.

The president met with the Joint Chiefs of Staff to reveal his decision to blockade rather than bomb or invade Cuba. He explained that a limited first step might persuade the Soviets not to retaliate in Berlin—reducing the chance of nuclear war. General Curtis LeMay, air force chief of staff, countered that only an invasion would deter Khrushchev in Berlin and called the blockade "almost as bad as the appeasement at Munich." The navy, army, and marine chiefs of staff agreed that the only solution in Cuba was "the full gamut of military action by us." The president insisted that a Soviet nuclear strike on American cities would result in 80–100 million casualties: "you're talkin' about the destruction of a country." The point, he contended, "is to avoid, if we can, nuclear war by escalation. . . . We've got to have some degree of control."

October 19, afternoon and evening

The ExComm met at the State Department (the president had left to campaign in the Midwest) and remained deeply divided about taking military action against Cuba. The tentative consensus for a blockade also began to erode. Robert Kennedy contacted his brother in Chicago and the president, claiming to have a cold and fever, promptly returned to Washington.

Saturday, October 20, 2:30 P.M.[30]

Defense secretary Robert McNamara endorsed the blockade but admonished the president that "there were differences among his advisers." JCS chairman General Maxwell Taylor insisted that attacking the missiles was less dangerous than allowing the sites to become operational. RFK argued that this might be the last chance "to destroy Castro." The president finally made his position clear: a blockade was the least provocative first step. He again suggested that it might be necessary to remove U.S. missiles from Turkey "if this issue were raised by the Russians." He also ordered that American personnel in Turkey be instructed not to fire the Jupiter missiles, even if attacked, without a direct presidential order. Kennedy directed Ted Sorensen to prepare a speech to the nation announcing the blockade.

Sunday, October 21, early morning and 2:30 P.M.

The discussions turned to the implementation and enforcement of the blockade, defined as a "quarantine of offensive missile equipment." The president expressed the hope that the Soviets would "turn their ships back rather than submit to inspection." But he still feared that Khrushchev might instead rush the missile sites to completion, announce that "Soviet rockets will fly" if the U.S. attacked Cuba, and move to force the U.S. out of Berlin. Kennedy also ordered the evacuation of U.S. dependents from the Guantánamo naval base within twenty-four hours; 2,500 military family members were given fifteen minutes to pack one bag each before boarding navy transport ships for Norfolk, Virginia.

Monday, October 22, 11:00 A.M.[31]

The principal purpose of the meeting was to finalize the president's speech to the nation (scheduled for early that evening) and the letter to Khrushchev, which would be handed to the Soviet ambassador just before airtime. Secretary of State Dean Rusk proposed a possible U.N. role in neutralizing nuclear missiles in any country that was not a nuclear power—in effect, Cuba, Turkey, and Italy. "Why don't we go all the way?" the president responded. "That gives us an excuse to get 'em out of Turkey and Italy." However, he rejected any proposal to lift the quarantine until the missiles were removed from Cuba. There was also discussion about how to handle the press and public relations after the speech, perhaps by making some U-2 photos public.

October 22, noon

The president asked if American personnel in Turkey had been instructed (as he had ordered two days earlier) not to fire the Jupiter missiles without direct presidential authorization. Assistant defense secretary Paul Nitze strenuously resisted, claiming that the JCS had already issued instructions to cover that eventuality; he also reminded the president that an attack on Turkey meant immediate execution of the European Defense Plan—"which is nuclear war." "I don't think," JFK pronounced sharply, "we ought to accept the Chiefs' word on that one, Paul." Nitze finally agreed to make sure the JCS understood the president's orders (for a more complete account of this exchange, see Epilogue).

October 22, 3:00 P.M.

The president met with the full National Security Council, including the Joint Chiefs, to formalize his decision to blockade Cuba. "Khrushchev," he grimly predicted "will not take this without a response, maybe in Berlin or maybe here. But the choices being one among second best—I think we've done the best thing at least as far as you can tell in advance." He conceded that if work continued on the sites or a U-2 was shot down then additional steps would be considered. He seemed confident that a convincing case could be made in the court of world public opinion that the blockade was not comparable to the 1948 Soviet blockade of Berlin: "This is not a blockade in that sense. It's merely an attempt to prevent the shipment of weapons there." Kennedy did not want to hand Khrushchev a propaganda plum by revealing that surprise air attacks had even been discussed and was anxious to manage the news in order to preserve this cover story. "So I think," he ordered, "we oughta just scratch that from all our statements and conversations. . . . I can't say that strongly enough."

October 22, 5:00 P.M.

Only two hours before going on national television to reveal the crisis in Cuba, the president met with the bipartisan leaders of the House and Senate—summoned from across the country since Congress was not in session. The leaders, aware that they were being informed, not consulted, sat in stunned silence during a detailed intelligence briefing. Finally, two of the most senior Senate Democrats (Richard Russell of Georgia, chairman of the Armed Services Committee, and J. William Fulbright of Arkansas, chairman of the Foreign Relations Committee) vigorously attacked the blockade decision as inadequate and demanded a full invasion (for a more complete account of this exchange, see Epilogue). The president tried to defend his decision, arguing that an attack on Cuba could result in the loss of Berlin or the possible firing of nuclear missiles at the U.S., which he described as "one hell of a gamble." He predicted that attacking the missile bases and killing thousands of Russians would be far more dangerous than stopping their ships. But he also admitted, "Now, who knows that? . . . We just tried to make good judgments about a matter on which everyone's uncertain. But at least it's the best advice we could get. So we start here."

Tuesday, October 23, 10:00 A.M.

The latest U-2 photos revealed that several MRBM launchers were no longer visible and could have been moved. JFK urged stressing the mobility of the missiles in order to defuse charges that they should have been discovered earlier: "Let's get that on the record." The president also seemed surprised to learn that "There is a question about whether these things really exist?" and finally agreed to display some of the photos at the upcoming U.N. debate. Soon after JFK left the meeting, Secretary Rusk arrived with the news that the Organization of American States (OAS) would unanimously endorse the blockade later that afternoon. His colleagues were thrilled that "our diplomacy is working"; but Rusk cautiously observed, "Well, my God! . . . I think it was very significant that we were here this morning." It appeared that the Soviets were not going to respond to the blockade with a sudden, irrational nuclear strike on the United States.

October 23, 6:00 P.M.

A vigorous debate developed over whether the navy should stop and search Soviet ships that had reversed course before reaching the quarantine line. The president argued that a ship carrying offensive weapons would most likely turn around to avoid capture. "We've had no indications," Rusk explained, "of any Soviet instructions . . . to pull away. . . . Just the converse." Kennedy also expressed serious concerns that the Soviet crews might resist boarding and that machine-gun fire could result in dozens of casualties on both sides. In addition, the defense department's civil defense director all but admitted that there was not much that could be done to protect civilians, especially in rural areas, from radiation exposure in the event that "ten or fifteen missiles" were fired at the U.S. from Cuba.

October 23, 7:00 P.M.

Shortly after the conclusion of the 6:00 P.M. meeting, the president and his brother Bobby talked alone in the Oval Office. "It looks like it's gonna be real mean, doesn't it?" JFK declared. "If they get this mean on this one—Jesus Christ! What are they gonna fuck up next?" "There wasn't any choice," RFK responded; "I mean you woulda been impeached." "Well, that's what I think," JFK replied. They agreed that OAS support would be invaluable in legitimizing the blockade but also recognized that no one could forecast events at the quarantine line the following morning.

Wednesday, October 24, 10:00 A.M.

The ExComm gathered in the Cabinet Room at virtually the moment that the quarantine proclamation became legally effective. The discussion initially focused on the ships approaching the quarantine line; however, an unconfirmed message arrived claiming that "all six Soviet ships currently identified in Cuban waters have either stopped or reversed course." There was, nonetheless, great concern that Soviet submarines near Cuba might sink a U.S. Navy vessel. The president (at RFK's suggestion) ordered all navy ships to have a Russian-speaking officer on board. When confirmation arrived that the Soviet ships had indeed reversed course, the president instructed that they should not be stopped, boarded, or harassed: "You don't wanna have word goin' out from Moscow, 'Turn around,' and suddenly we sink their ship."

October 24, 4:30 P.M.

The president chatted briefly in the Oval Office with a few advisers. He was shown photos that revealed Soviet efforts to camouflage the missile sites during the night and remarked: "I think the irony will be that the Russians led us into a trap." Bundy recommended using the photos to "back our claim," and JFK approved making them available to the press.

October 24, 5:00 P.M.

The president met for the second time with the bipartisan leaders of Congress. Rusk explained that the situation was still fluid and that the Soviets had not yet decided on their next move. President Kennedy suggested several possible scenarios: the Soviets might turn back some ships carrying weapons; they might choose a ship "for a test case, either to have us sink it, or disable it, and have a fight about it"; or they might allow the inspection of ships not carrying offensive weapons. Senators Russell and Fulbright, his toughest critics at the first congressional meeting, asked why conventional weapons (e.g., rifles) were not being interdicted. The president explained that "the first collision with the Soviets" should be on offensive missiles "for political reasons . . . this puts us in a much stronger position around the world." But he added, "if they accept the quarantine, we will not permit these rifles to go through." The congressional leaders agreed to remain on eight-hour standby for another meeting.

October 24, 6:00 P.M.

After the congressional meeting, the president talked informally with several advisers in the Oval Office. Former defense secretary Robert Lovett endorsed the blockade because it gave the Soviets "a couple of days while they make up their own minds what their intentions are." He was, like the president, suspicious of military overconfidence, especially the "congenital habit of overstating the ease as well as the results of an air strike." The views of the sixty-seven-year-old Lovett dovetailed with those already expressed by the forty-five-year-old commander in chief: "There's no such thing," he explained, "as a small military action. . . . Now the moment we start anything in this field, we have to be prepared to do everything." He urged the president to wait until Soviet intentions had become clear. JFK expressed concern that work on the missile sites would continue regardless of the United Nations proposal for a joint suspension of the quarantine and arms shipments to Cuba. McCone stressed, and Kennedy agreed, that any deal had to include a halt to work on the missile sites and assurances that no missiles would be placed on launchers, to be verified by on-site U.N. observers.

Thursday, October 25, 10:00 A.M.

McCone reported that work on the missile sites was proceeding rapidly. McNamara recommended immediately establishing "a pattern of boarding" ships. The defense chief confirmed, however, that fourteen ships had already "turned back as a result of the quarantine." The president reflected grimly "that we're gonna have to grab a Russian ship and that he [Khrushchev] says he's not gonna permit it." Bundy speculated that U.N. secretary general U Thant might convince the U.S.S.R. to avoid challenging the quarantine. "In that case," JFK finally decided, "we might as well wait." But the president cautioned not to make too much of the ships that had reversed direction: "I don't want a sense of euphoria passing around," he counseled. "That message of Khrushchev is much tougher than that." In response to several demands for more stringent enforcement of the quarantine, Kennedy concluded, "I think we could grab us one of these things anytime. I don't think it makes a hell of a lot of difference what ship it is. . . . This is not the appropriate time to blow up a ship. . . . So let's think a little more about it."

October 25, after 5:00 P.M.

The intelligence briefing confirmed again that the Soviets were working quickly to complete construction of the missile sites. McNamara recommended that a Communist bloc (East German) passenger ship carrying 1,500 civilians should not be stopped. Robert Kennedy, however, urged the president to downplay a confrontation at sea and instead bomb a missile site "as the first step" in order to demonstrate American resolve. Four days earlier, the president had decided that air strikes were too risky because all the missiles could not be destroyed. Now, in response to his brother's suggestion, he revived the air attack option *if* a stalemate at sea gave the Russians time to finish the missile sites. The president nonetheless decided not to intercept the passenger ship as long as the U Thant initiative held out "a chance of easing this." "If you try to disable it," he argued, "you either sink it or have it catch fire." JFK was willing to give Khrushchev more time, but he edged closer to RFK's uncompromisingly tough stance: "I think if the work continues, we . . . have to do this air business . . . because otherwise the work's going on and we're not really doin' anything else."

Friday, October 26, 10:00 A.M.

At that very moment, McNamara revealed, the navy was on board a Soviet-chartered Lebanese freighter, chosen because it could be boarded "with the least possible chance of violence." Rusk declared that the U.S. must demand an end to arms shipments and work on the bases, as well as making the missiles and warheads inoperable—backed up by on-site U.N. inspectors from neutral nations. "We have to insist upon that very hard." The president turned to Adlai Stevenson, who had been asked to join the meeting in order to discuss U Thant's proposal to halt weapons deliveries to Cuba and suspend the quarantine. The U.N. ambassador endorsed the U Thant plan but ran into harsh criticism because the proposal did not include making the missile sites inoperable. Stevenson held his ground and also endorsed a Cuba-Turkey missile trade. The president was becoming increasingly concerned about being trapped in long-drawn-out negotiations while the missile sites were rushed to completion.

October 26, 3:00 P.M.

The president met with CIA director McCone and a technical analyst to review the latest photography of the missile sites. McCone expressed alarm about the fast pace of the work and argued that any negotiations must "ensure that these missiles are immobilized." The president replied that everything depended on Soviet intentions: the missiles could be fired before, during, or after an American attack. The CIA chief warned that an invasion would be very difficult because of the "very lethal stuff" deployed in Cuba. "What course of action does this lead you to?" the president asked. McCone answered bluntly, "Well, this would lead me to moving quickly on an air strike."

Saturday, October 27, 10:00 A.M.

The ExComm convened with the expectation of discussing the letter from Khrushchev that had arrived the previous evening—proposing to withdraw the missiles in exchange for a U.S. pledge not to invade Cuba. Instead, news arrived that the Soviet leader had made a new offer—publicly on Moscow Radio—to withdraw the missiles in exchange for the removal of U.S. missiles in Turkey. Kennedy's advisers demanded rejection of the new offer. The president argued, however, that since the proposal had been made publicly, the U.S. had to assume that it represented Khrushchev's most recent position. He predicted that the U.S. would lose international support if such a reasonable offer were rejected, and seemed quite angry that his previous statements about exploring such a deal had been ignored by the State Department. "Let's not kid ourselves," he reiterated three times. The ExComm, notwithstanding, lined up all but unanimously against the new offer and urged the president to focus on Khrushchev's Friday letter—warning that even discussing Turkey would wreck NATO and destroy U.S. credibility.

October 27, 4:00 P.M.

The disagreement over how to respond to the conflicting proposals from the Kremlin continued unabated. The ExComm all but unanimously warned that America's allies would feel betrayed if the U.S. removed the Jupiter missiles from Turkey, and pressured the president to accept Khrushchev's Friday offer and ignore the Saturday offer. But JFK insisted that the Friday proposal was no longer relevant. A report arrived that a U-2 had been shot down over Cuba by a Soviet SAM missile—and the pilot killed. Several hours later, the news that a low-level reconnaissance plane had been hit by an artillery shell further intensified the disagreement. JFK continued to argue that a deal on the Turkish and Cuban missiles had to be arranged as soon as possible—preferably with, but if necessary without, the agreement of NATO. He also rejected ExComm demands to implement his earlier decision to destroy the SAM site that had fired the fatal missile. The president finally agreed to a pro forma acceptance of the offer in Khrushchev's Friday letter, but continued to insist that this strategy was a waste of time. Instead, he decided to send his brother later that evening to offer the missile trade, covertly, to the Soviet ambassador. After Khrushchev accepted the secret agreement the following morning, the claim that the crisis had been resolved by accepting the offer in the Friday letter became the basis of the cover story that later became known as the Trollope ploy.

October 27, 8:00 P.M.

After the 4:00 ExComm meeting had dispersed, Ball, Bundy, Gilpatric, RFK, McNamara, Rusk, Sorensen, and Thompson met with President Kennedy, at his invitation, in the Oval Office. "The best available evidence," Barton Bernstein has concluded, "indicates that the president was the dominant person at that small session. He called the meeting, selected the participants, and excluded about another eight men." JFK revealed that his brother was about to hand deliver the new letter for Khrushchev to Ambassador Anatoly Dobrynin in a potentially decisive private meeting at the Justice Department.

The president continued to press for a deal on the Turkish missiles. Finally, Dean Rusk suggested that RFK should advise the ambassador that although a public quid pro quo for the missiles in Turkey was unacceptable, the president was prepared to remove them once the Cuban crisis was resolved. "The proposal was quickly supported by the rest of us," Bundy wrote decades later, "and approved by the president. It was also agreed that knowledge of this assurance would be held among those present and no one else." The "private deal undoubtedly met the objections of some of the serious opponents of a public deal. But the central fact was that the president made clear that he cared deeply about this issue, he chose the policy, and nobody would resist him. They were the president's men, and he was the president."[32]

October 27, 9:00 P.M.

When the exhausted and anxious ExComm reconvened later that evening, only half of its members were aware of RFK's fateful meeting with Dobrynin and the secret proposal to remove the Jupiter missiles from Turkey. The president agreed to call up "twenty-four air reserve squadrons [fourteen thousand men] and roughly three hundred troop carrier transports." But most of his attention was focused on making sure that the members of the NATO Council, scheduled to meet the following morning, understood the risks involved in keeping the Jupiter missiles in Turkey. No one would have predicted at that point that Khrushchev would essentially resolve the crisis in less than twelve hours. As a result, the meeting ended with a discussion of setting up an interim civilian government for Cuba and letting the Soviets know that U.S. military power might soon be unleashed against Cuba.

2 The Template:
Robert F. Kennedy's *Thirteen Days*

New testimony [from the recordings of the ExComm meetings]
supplements and reinforces Robert Kennedy's account in
Thirteen Days.

—Arthur M. Schlesinger Jr., 1999

O N MONDAY, OCTOBER 29, 1962, just a day after Nikita Khrushchev had announced on Moscow Radio that he had ordered the
removal of Soviet nuclear missiles from Cuba, President Kennedy met with
General David Shoup (marine commandant) and Admiral George Anderson
(chief of naval operations) in the Oval Office. The tone of the discussion was
unusually relaxed and informal—in sharp contrast to the meetings of the
previous two weeks, which had routinely begun with an intelligence briefing
on the ominous and continuing Soviet nuclear missile buildup in Cuba.

The president speculated that the Soviets might continue a conventional
(nonnuclear) arms buildup in Cuba once the missiles were removed. But after
some light-hearted banter about college football, he raised the possibility that
the resolution of the Cuban crisis might create a chance for a breakthrough
in Europe: "Berlin really is a paralyzing" problem. "Because everything you
want to do, you say, 'Oh, well, it will screw us in Berlin.' And I think if we can
ever get any kind of a decent deal in Berlin . . ." "I certainly agree," Anderson
replied. "It really gives them the initiative all the time." JFK cited General
George Marshall's prediction that Berlin would "become an impossible situation over the years," and concluded, "So that's what I think what we oughta
do now while we've got some initiative here."

Soon after the JCS officers left the Oval Office, the president placed a call to a White House staffer:

> I want to get a President's commemorative for the Executive Committee of the National Security Council who've been involved in this matter. What I thought of is something that would have the month of October on it and the 10 days, and have a line drawn around the calendar days. In other words, you see, just like a page out of a calendar. How could you get that so it wouldn't be too expensive? It's about twelve [days], about 12, a line drawn around it. It's the 29th actually today, so it would be the 28th. . . . Thank you.[1]

It is not especially surprising that even in its immediate aftermath JFK did not recall the exact number of days in which his administration, and later the world, had been totally absorbed by the most dangerous crisis of the nuclear era. Any such ambiguity was permanently erased by the 1969 publication of Robert Kennedy's *Thirteen Days*.[2] (Theodore Sorensen edited and completed the manuscript after the New York senator's assassination in June 1968.) Derived from RFK's personal diary and papers, the book has become the template, if not the cast-iron die, for all discussions of the secret Cuban missile crisis meetings. Most writers either endorse its perspective or make revisionist arguments against it; either way, the truth is often obscured and *Thirteen Days* continues to frame the discussion. The book has never been out of print in the forty-plus years since its publication and is the only specific account of the ExComm meetings by one of the actual—and in this case, principal—participants. The very term "Thirteen Days" has now become indelibly identified with the events of October 1962.

The scholars who wrote the lengthy Afterword to the 1971 edition of *Thirteen Days* assumed, quite reasonably and naturally, that RFK's version would remain the most definitive source on the ExComm meetings: "Even with the aid of Robert Kennedy's account," they concluded, "reconstruction of this process [of decision-making by the president and his ExComm advisers] can only be tentative."[3] (The existence of the ExComm tapes was not revealed by the Kennedy Library until two years *after* the publication of the 1971 Afterword.) RFK's sketchy and extremely general recollections (a total of only eighty pages) thus remained for several decades the core source—if not the iconic source—for most journalistic and scholarly writing on the missile crisis meetings.

The ExComm tapes, however, fundamentally and irrefutably contradict many of RFK's most important recollections. Indeed, those verbatim records offer a much more complex, interesting, and subtle understanding of the event. The tapes also expose *Thirteen Days* as not just selective or slanted history, which is the common affliction of personal diaries and memoirs, but rather as the capstone of an effort to manipulate the history of the missile crisis to Robert Kennedy's perceived political advantage.

In 1978, Arthur M. Schlesinger Jr., "a great admirer and devoted friend" of Robert Kennedy, published a thousand-plus-page biography of his friend: a remarkable and poignant tribute to a man whose career in public office had spanned less than eight years. Schlesinger received special access to the classified portions of the Robert Kennedy papers at the Kennedy Library "through the generosity of Ethel Skakel Kennedy and the Kennedy family"; this privilege included access to RFK's private diaries. Most of these papers remain closed to researchers; however, some sixty boxes may be opened in 2012.[4]

Schlesinger's conclusion about Bobby Kennedy's role in the missile crisis meetings was unequivocal: "Robert Kennedy was the indispensible partner. Without him, John Kennedy would have found it far more difficult to overcome the demand for military action. . . . It was Robert Kennedy . . . who stopped the air strike madness in its tracks. . . . Within the closed meetings of the so-called Executive Committee of the National Security Council, Robert Kennedy was a dove from the start." Schlesinger backs up this judgment with a quote he found in the RFK papers from October 16, the first day of the ExComm meetings: "'If you bomb the missile sites and the airports,' he [RFK] said on the first day, 'you are covering most of Cuba. You are going to kill an awful lot of people and take an awful lot of heat on it.'" The attorney general also warned that the Soviets would respond to U.S. bombing of the missile sites by simply sending in more missiles and by doing "the same thing [bombing U.S. missiles] in Turkey."[5]

In fact, this ostensibly dovish quote from RFK's private papers was profoundly misleading, if not out-and-out deceptive. Bobby Kennedy was actually arguing that bombing the sites was a weak and inadequate response; he was instead demanding *a full-scale invasion*. Even Joint Chiefs of Staff chairman General Maxwell Taylor had cautioned against an invasion only minutes before when he warned the president "as to whether we invade or not. I think that's the hardest question militarily in the whole business and one that we should look at very closely before we get our feet in that deep mud of Cuba." Of course, readers must remember that in 1978—before the opening of the

ExComm tapes—Schlesinger could not have known the full context of the RFK quote. (See Chapter 3 for a full analysis of RFK's role in the ExComm meetings.)

The general accuracy of the quotes from RFK's private papers scattered throughout *Thirteen Days* is almost certainly explained by a document discovered at the Kennedy Library in the late 1990s. On August 9, 1963, JFK's secretary Evelyn Lincoln sent eighteen missile crisis transcripts to attorney general Robert Kennedy's secretary in the Justice Department—raising the fascinating possibility that RFK, and perhaps President Kennedy himself, read some transcripts or (much less likely) listened to some tapes.[6]

RFK's memoir had clearly been based on something more solid than mere memory or incomplete notes. However, the actual content of the disingenuous quote discussed above also underscores the possibility that Bobby Kennedy may have used the transcripts or tapes selectively to shape and manipulate his place in the historical record. The draft manuscript of *Thirteen Days*, which may initially have been intended for release in time for the president's 1964 reelection campaign, was so tightly held within the Kennedy inner circle that many senior White House officials did not even know about its existence. Special assistant and confidant Kenneth O'Donnell, commenting on a version he read about six months after JFK's assassination, reportedly remarked to RFK, "I thought Jack was President during the missile crisis." Bobby is said to have replied, "He's not running, and I am." (RFK ran successfully for a U.S. Senate seat from New York in 1964.) Another version has RFK replying, "Jack wouldn't mind."[7]

However, in 1973, in the wake of the Watergate hearings that revealed the existence of the Nixon tapes, the Kennedy Library publicly acknowledged the existence of the ultimate historical deus ex machina: the secret recordings of the ExComm discussions. The first meeting tapes were declassified in the early 1980s, and all the tapes from the now legendary thirteen days were released by 1997. The tapes from the November postcrisis were released between 1999 and 2001. The recordings from October 16 to 28, plus those through the lifting of the naval quarantine on November 20, total about forty-three hours.

As King's College London historian Lawrence Freedman succinctly acknowledged in 2005, "The discovery that President John F. Kennedy had installed a system for taping conversations in the Oval Office transformed the historiography of the Cuban missile crisis."[8] Arthur Schlesinger's foreword to the 1999 edition of *Thirteen Days* was published right on the cusp of that historiographical transformation. Nonetheless, he continued—much like in his 1978 RFK biography—to uncritically accept many of RFK's published assertions despite the fact that they were, *for the first time*, open to corroboration by the tape recordings or to a lesser degree by the 1997 publication of a set of complete ExComm transcripts. Schlesinger's dust-jacket blurb had hailed the new transcripts as "a historical triumph!" and a "remarkable [and] unprecedented illumination" of the ExComm meetings. Nonetheless, he *completely ignored* both the aural and written substance of these new sources of information. His foreword, as a result, is shot through with what we can now prove are demonstrably manipulative and erroneous conclusions.

Schlesinger claimed, for example, contrary to the unequivocal evidence on the tapes, that

- "The American Joint Chief of Staff (*not McNamara, however*) had been all-out for invasion"(p. 9, emphasis added).
- The new evidence and scholarship, including the 1997 published transcripts of the ExComm recordings, "supplements and reinforces Robert Kennedy's account in *Thirteen Days*" (p. 10).
- "Robert Kennedy led the fight against military intervention" (p. 11).

Schlesinger also repeatedly manipulated and obscured the facts:

- He claimed correctly that JFK regarded "a trade of American missiles in Turkey for Soviet missiles in Cuba as a possible way out" and that "It was a deal most of his advisers opposed" (pp. 12–13). He did not mention, however, that RFK was the most influential and outspoken member of the ExComm opposed to the trade.
- He insisted that the Kennedy brothers were not obsessed about Cuba, as demonstrated by the progress on détente in 1963 (the American University speech, the Limited Test Ban Treaty, and the establishment of the Washington to Moscow hotline) (pp. 11, 14). Soviet-American relations did indeed improve in 1963, but Cuban-American relations remained essentially unchanged. Schlesinger ignores the fact that despite the lessons JFK had allegedly learned from the missile crisis and the cautious approaches to Castro in 1963, covert operations against Cuba continued and even escalated throughout the last year of the Kennedy administration. Thirteen covert CIA operations against Cuba were launched in just the last few months of 1963.[9]
- He endorsed RFK's contention that "if any one of half a dozen of them

[ExComm participants] were President, the world would have been very likely plunged into catastrophic [nuclear] war" (p. 15). But Schlesinger fails to acknowledge the by then indisputable fact that Bobby Kennedy himself was the most persistent and surely the most influential of that half dozen. If RFK had been president, and the views he expressed during the ExComm meetings had prevailed, nuclear war would have been the nearly certain outcome.

It is now clear as well that many of RFK's own most important and still widely accepted contentions in *Thirteen Days* contradict the incontrovertible evidence on the ExComm tapes. RFK claimed, for example, that

- Some members of the ExComm, "because of the pressure of events, even appeared to lose their judgment and stability" (p. 25). There is absolutely nothing on the tapes to support this claim (see Chapter 5).
- "Secretary McNamara, by Wednesday [October 17], became the blockade's strongest advocate" (p. 27). On the contrary, McNamara continued to call for "nothing short of a full invasion" and strenuously opposed the Cuba-Turkey compromise (see Chapter 4).[10]
- "I supported McNamara's position in favor of a blockade" (p. 29). RFK actually continued to press for an invasion as "the last chance we will have to destroy Castro." Indeed, late in the second week of deliberations, he revived the dormant bombing option by declaring, "rather than have a confrontation with the Russians at sea . . . it might be better to knock out their missile base as the first step" after warning "Soviet personnel to get out of that vicinity in ten minutes" (see Chapter 3).[11]
- "We spent more time on this moral question [whether a powerful nation like the U.S. should attack a small nation like Cuba without warning] during the first five days than on any other single matter" (p. 30). RFK did express concern about the impact of a Pearl Harbor-type attack on Cuba on "our moral position at home and around the globe"; but his claim that this ethical argument dominated the first week's discussions is absurd. Sorensen took this argument one step further on the final page of *Thirteen Days*: "It was Senator Kennedy's intention to add a discussion of the basic ethical question involved: what, if any, circumstance or justification gives this government or any government the moral right to bring its people and possibly all people under the shadow of nuclear destruction?" (p. 98). These sentiments may have accurately reflected Robert Kennedy's perspec-

tive in 1968, but they have little or no relevance to his consistently hawkish views in 1962 (see Chapter 3).

- "We all spoke as equals. There was no rank, and, in fact, we did not even have a chairman. Dean Rusk—who, as Secretary of State, might have assumed that position—had other duties during this period of time and frequently could not attend our meetings" (p. 36). In fact, Rusk was one of the ExComm's most regular attendees and contributors, and the only participant to openly challenge RFK's confrontational recommendations (see Chapter 5).

- President Kennedy "had asked the State Department to conduct negotiations" for the removal of the Jupiter missiles from Turkey, "and he had ordered their removal some time ago" (pp. 39, 83). JFK had discussed removing the Jupiter missiles but never made a formal decision or issued a presidential order. He actually decided to go ahead with the activation of the missiles in Turkey, and one site had even been scheduled to be turned over to Turkish control during the very month of the missile crisis.[12] That activation of the Jupiter missiles was, in fact, a key reason for Khrushchev's decision to send nuclear missiles to Cuba (see Chapter 9).

- During the first weekend of discussions (October 20–21), U.N. ambassador Adlai Stevenson proposed "that we make it clear to the Soviet Union that if it withdrew its missiles from Cuba, we would be willing to withdraw our missiles from Turkey." RFK asserted that President Kennedy "rejected Stevenson's suggestion" because "this was not the appropriate time to suggest this action" (p. 39). In fact, the president had already raised that possibility earlier that week and that is exactly what he finally did (see Chapters 8 and 9).

- RFK acknowledged the importance of the unanimous vote of the Organization of American States in support of the blockade (p. 47). However, he did not mention Dean Rusk's extraordinary diplomatic success in securing that result (see Chapter 5).

- The president received a "very formal letter" on Saturday, October 27; it "was obviously no longer Mr. Khrushchev personally who was writing, but the Foreign Office of the Kremlin" (p. 71). This assumption, which originated during the ExComm meetings that day, has been refuted by documents from the archives of the former Soviet Union (see Chapter 9).[13]

- "I suggested, and was supported by Ted Sorensen and others," that they ignore Khrushchev's October 27 letter demanding a Turkey-Cuba missile trade and respond instead to the October 26 message in which he had offered to remove the missiles in return for an American pledge not to invade Cuba (p. 77). This myth, which came to be called the Trollope ploy, was originally intended to conceal the fact that the administration had compromised and struck a deal with the Soviets to secretly remove the Jupiter missiles from Turkey within a few months. The immense and lingering impact of this historical distraction is thoroughly discussed in Chapter 9.

- Soviet ambassador Anatoly Dobrynin was explicitly told that "there could be no quid pro quo" for removing the missiles from Turkey and Cuba (p. 83). Even after the release of the tapes, which conclusively demonstrate that an explicit agreement was indeed reached, Bundy, McNamara, and Sorensen continued to press this half-truth in public appearances and memoirs (see Chapter 9). The claim in Sorensen's 2008 memoir is particularly puzzling since he acknowledged the facts at the 1989 missile crisis conference in Moscow: "I have a confession to make. . . . I was the editor of Robert Kennedy's book. . . . And his diary was very explicit that this [trade] was part of the deal; but at that time it was still a secret even on the American side. . . . So I took it upon myself to edit that out of his diaries."[14]

- Former ambassador to the Soviet Union Llewellyn Thompson's "advice on the Russians and predictions as to what they would do were uncannily accurate" (p. 89). Thompson's advice was actually erratic, inconsistent, and contradictory, and he was one of the most persistent opponents of the Cuba-Turkey missile trade (see Chapter 6).

In addition, many other critical aspects of the ExComm meetings are all but ignored or obfuscated in *Thirteen Days*. These distortions, as this book will document, extend well beyond RFK's personal role in the discussions. In fact, in and of itself, *Thirteen Days* is an enormous, if inadvertent and unintended, testament to the validity of the secret ExComm tapes as an objective historical source. The claim that "I was there" should, if anything, be regarded as a warning about historical inaccuracy rather than accepted as a special form of validation. History based on personal recollections rarely transcends the author's motives in writing it. This flaw has been particularly striking among the small, closed, and inevitably dwindling group of ExComm participants, who until the release of the tape recordings had successfully promoted their unique authority to shape our understanding of those historic deliberations.

3   The Real Robert Kennedy

> I'd like to take Cuba back. That would be nice.
> —Robert F. Kennedy, October 27, 1962

ROBERT F. KENNEDY played a unique role in the missile crisis meetings because he was the president's brother and his most trusted adviser and confidant. A different attorney general would likely not even have been asked to participate in these discussions. Indeed, the loyalty and trust between the Kennedy brothers was and will likely remain unique in the history of the American presidency. I can vividly recall, for example, first listening to their recorded telephone conversations and initially finding it difficult to even understand what they were talking about. Typically, as soon as the connection was made, the brothers, without so much as a hello or "how are the kids," would burst into a staccato exchange of barely coherent verbal fragments and exclamations before abruptly concluding with "OK," "Good," or "Right" or just hanging up. Their intuitive capacity to communicate often transcended the limits of conventional oral discourse. They *always* understood each other.

If the president temporarily left the room or did not attend an ExComm meeting, the participants instinctively recognized RFK as his brother's stand-in—despite his persistent disagreements with the president. Roswell Gilpatric later confirmed that "in a passive but clearly recognized sense [RFK was accepted by the ExComm as] the President's alternate." At one meeting, RFK may even have turned on the tape recorder after the president had turned it off and left the room. "You always had the feeling in dealing with Bobby," U. Alexis Johnson remembered, "that he was the fearless watchdog on behalf of the President. He had enormous possessive pride in the President, and he was looking after the President's interests in a way which, he felt, the President could not do."[1]

The ExComm, of course, was also aware that RFK chaired the Special Group (Augmented), which was in charge of covert operations in Cuba. Bobby Kennedy was an unswerving hawk on the Cuban question, the administration's point man on Operation Mongoose, and an ardent supporter of plots to oust or assassinate Castro. Mongoose was no fly-by-night scheme run by ultra right-wing extremists, as depicted in Oliver Stone's film fantasy, *JFK*. It became one of the largest clandestine operations in CIA history, "involving some four hundred agents, an annual budget of over $50 million and a variety of covert, economic, and psychological operations." Even Richard Bissell, CIA director of operations, who had been working on the Cuban "problem" since 1959, considered RFK "a wild man" on the subject of Castro. And the Cubans clearly knew about "at least some of the assassination attempts."[2]

Sam Halpern, a former CIA Operation Mongoose planner, later recalled, "As Dick Helms [CIA deputy director for operations] was fond of saying: 'If anybody wants to see the whiplashes across my back inflicted by Bobby Kennedy, I will take my shirt off in public.'"[3] RFK's stance during the ExComm meetings, which can only be fully understood in the context of his role in Mongoose, turns out to be very different from the idealized and romanticized view he consciously created for *Thirteen Days*. Indeed, in sharp contrast to his brother, RFK was one of the most consistently hawkish and confrontational members of the ExComm.

JFK had immediately summoned RFK to the White House after learning that the Soviets were constructing missile sites in Cuba. "Oh shit!, Shit!, Shit! Those sons a bitches Russians," RFK exclaimed upon seeing the U-2 pictures. Bobby Kennedy, clearly representing his brother, had tried dozens of back-channel contacts with Georgi Bolshakov, an official at the Soviet embassy who was also a colonel in Soviet Military Intelligence (the GRU), in an effort to "cajole, flatter, and deter Khrushchev." These efforts, as a result of calculated Soviet deception, had come to nothing, and RFK's personal sense of anger and betrayal was unmistakable during the ExComm discussions.

∼

On the first morning of the ExComm meetings, Tuesday, October 16, the discussion quickly established that the missile sites were still under construction and that the nuclear warheads had yet to be located and photographed. Initially, the most attractive military option seemed to be surprise bombing raids to destroy the missile sites alone; but there was also support for more comprehensive bombing of the SAM sites and Cuban airfields as well, followed, Robert McNamara advised, by an invasion. It became increasingly clear, however, that it was technically impossible to determine if the missiles were operational before attacking them and that all the sites would not be destroyed by air strikes. As the risks in all the military options became increasingly plain, JFK and his advisers recognized that there might not be a quick military fix in Cuba. The idea of a limited first step—a naval blockade—gradually began to pick up support.

Robert Kennedy, clearly distressed by the talk of a naval blockade, spoke up for the first time well into the first hour of the meeting. Speaking directly to his brother, RFK warned that any military action short of an all-out invasion would be ineffectual: "you're droppin' bombs all over Cuba if you do the second [comprehensive air strike]. . . . You're covering most of Cuba. You're gonna kill an awful lot a people, and we're gonna take an awful lot a heat on it." In addition, he predicted, the Russians would retaliate for the air strikes by supplying Cuba with additional missiles; and in the event of further air strikes, they would very likely attack the U.S. Jupiter missiles in Turkey. There was a more effective option, he insisted, "which is the invasion." That was the only choice that justified the military and political costs resulting from so much destruction and loss of life.

From these first remarks through the entire thirteen days of deliberations, RFK never seemed to connect the dots between U.S. military action against Cuba and the real possibility of escalation to full-scale nuclear war with the Soviet Union. (Ted Sorensen later claimed that Robert Kennedy had been "particularly good" during the first week of ExComm meetings: "Never stating a position of his own, he was persistent in trying . . . to get people to agree" on alternatives and consequences. On the contrary, as demonstrated by the views cited above, RFK staked out his own very provocative positions from the very first day.[4])

The president, obviously impressed by his brother's reasoning, asked how long it would take to mount an invasion. McNamara stated that it could be done in seven days. "Is it absolutely essential," RFK demanded contentiously, "that you wait seven days after you have an air strike?" Joint Chiefs chairman General Maxwell Taylor explained patiently that the movement of troops to Florida might sacrifice the element of surprise, but RFK suggested that tension over Berlin could be used to create a public cover story. It would be better, he demanded, "If you could get it in, get it started, so that there wasn't any turning back." He seemed oblivious to the fact that once military action got started it might be difficult, if not impossible, to turn back.

Despite concerns about Soviet retaliation in Berlin, as the meeting began to wrap up a consensus for military action at least against the nonoperational missile sites seemed solid. JFK was also willing to consider attacking the Soviet fighter planes in Cuba in order to prevent bombing reprisals in the Florida area. He assumed, however, that the Russians would use conventional bombs if they launched these raids. Why, he asked, would they want to start a nuclear war in "that sort of half-assed way?"

"We're certainly gonna . . . take out these missiles," JFK concluded, also agreeing to move forward with planning for wider air strikes and an invasion. "How long would it take to take over the island?" Robert Kennedy persisted yet again. General Taylor explained that it was "very hard to estimate, Bobby," suggesting that resistance could be contained in five or six days, but months would be needed to clean up the loose ends. The meeting broke up with an agreement to reconvene at 6:30 P.M.

That evening (October 16), JFK quickly returned to the key issue of the readiness of the missiles to be fired. General Marshall Carter, deputy director of the CIA, assured the president that the bases were in an early stage of construction. General Taylor, however, reported that the Joint Chiefs unanimously favored bombing the missile sites and the Soviet fighter planes. But the pugnacious Robert Kennedy still had no interest in air strikes alone. He predicted again that Khrushchev would simply reintroduce the missiles after the bombing. In that event, a blockade would have to be established. "Then we're gonna have to sink Russian ships," he declared fervently. It was better to stand up to Khrushchev now and take the consequences: "we should just get into it, and get it over with and take our losses if he wants to get into a war over this. Hell, if it's war that's gonna come on this thing, you know, he sticks those kinds of missiles in after the warning, then hey, he's gonna get into a war six months from now or a year from now." RFK seemed unable to grasp that a decision to "get into it" would not necessarily "get it over with." The result, instead, could easily have sparked out-of-control escalation culminating in the unthinkable.

The attorney general also warned that Cuba could try nuclear blackmail against other Latin American nations and suggested that the president should put planes in the air over Cuba so that the missiles could be attacked if the

Soviets or the Cubans tried to move them out of sight. JFK finally decided that plans should move forward for options one and two—the limited and the comprehensive air strikes; RFK pressed him again, "Does that encompass an invasion?" "No," the president responded firmly, "I'd say that's the third course." Bobby Kennedy did not reply.

RFK, however, was not dissuaded, and boldly suggested using the American naval base at Guantánamo Bay to stage an incident that would justify military intervention: "You know, sink the *Maine* again or something!" This proposal was entirely in character for Robert Kennedy. In June 1961, after the assassination of the Dominican Republic's brutal strongman Rafael Trujillo, RFK, still smarting from the Bay of Pigs disaster, pressed for American intervention to prevent a Castro-inspired communist takeover of the Dominican government. He had even suggested blowing up the U.S. consulate to create a pretext for sending in American troops.[5] Now, in urging the president to invade Cuba, he warned that a blockade could become "a very slow death" over a period of months and would still require dangerous military steps such as "the examination of Russian ships, shooting down the Russian planes that try to land there. You have to do all those things."

Later, in the evening meeting, Bobby Kennedy retreated somewhat from his belligerent posture and endorsed George Ball's suggestion that Cuba and the Soviet Union should be warned before bombing began. Such a move would affirm "what kind of a country we are." For fifteen years, RFK avowed, the U.S. had worked to prevent a Russian first strike against us. "Now, in the interest of time, we do that to a small country. I think it's a hell of a burden to carry." He also recommended sending a personal emissary to inform Khrushchev before the air attacks began.

Two days later, on October 18, the president had yet to make a final decision on the diplomatic or military options. RFK, however, was still fuming about false Soviet promises not to do anything politically damaging to the administration before the midterm elections; he urged the president to try to trap Soviet foreign minister Andrei Gromyko when they held their planned meeting later that day: "I suppose the other way is to do it rather subtly [!] with me saying [to Gromyko], 'What are you doing in Cuba? This is embarrassing in this election. What kind of missiles are you sticking in?'" Sorensen seconded the suggestion as "a pretty good gambit."

RFK even tried to reassure the president that "it's not really that bad," since a decision to invade did not have to be made for a few days. The president was, notwithstanding, becoming convinced that a blockade was the least provocative way to gauge Soviet intentions. However, private discussions between the brothers may have temporarily softened RFK's opposition. When JFK met with Robert Lovett later that day, the former defense secretary endorsed the blockade and seemed surprised that RFK was "of the same opinion" that it was reasonable to start with "a less violent step." Lovett also recalled that JFK was furious at, but rather amused by, Gromyko's "bare-faced lies."[6]

Despite Lovett's account, Robert Kennedy continued to be drawn to an invasion. If air attacks took place on Monday, October 22, he asked later at the October 18 meeting, "How many days after that would you be prepared to invade?" "Seven to ten days," McNamara told him. As the meeting wound down, there was some speculation about whether the blockade "has a chance of bringing down Castro." RFK countered scornfully, "Has a blockade ever brought anybody down?" He also reiterated that a blockade would not force the Soviets to stop construction of the existing missile sites. The blockade amounts to telling them, Bobby complained caustically, that "they can build as many missiles as they want?"

On the following day, the president met with the Joint Chiefs of Staff and revealed, to their dismay, that he had decided to start with a blockade. Anxious to avoid alerting the press about the evolving crisis, JFK then left Washington for a previously scheduled campaign trip to the Midwest. Meetings were held at the State Department on October 19, and RFK, essentially standing in for his brother, pointedly mentioned that he had spoken to the president only a few hours earlier and argued for the blockade because a sneak attack on a small country was not in the American tradition. However, it did not take long for his more aggressive personal stance to bubble to the surface. Later in the same meeting, in response to persistent opposition to the blockade, he declared that "it would be better for our children and grandchildren if we decided to face the Soviet threat, stand up to it, and eliminate it, now. The circumstances for doing so at some future time were bound to be more unfavorable, the risks would be greater, the chances of success less good."[7]

JFK, claiming that he had a cold and a fever, returned to Washington, and the ExComm meetings resumed later on the weekend of October 20–21. Robert Kennedy promptly renewed his tougher stance, asserting that "now is the last chance we will have to destroy Castro and the Soviet missiles deployed in Cuba." He did concede, however, that a combination of a quarantine and air strikes "was very attractive to him." If the Russians failed to halt missile construction once the blockade was in effect, air attacks could then begin without the stigma of a Pearl Harbor-type attack. By the end of the weekend, the president, increasingly doubtful about opening the Pandora's box of military escalation, had decided to start with a blockade, inform the leaders of Congress, and deliver an address to the nation on Monday, October 22. He did agree, nonetheless, with RFK's insistence that preparations for a possible invasion of Cuba would move forward as well.

Several meetings were held on Monday, October 22, essentially to finalize the wording of both JFK's speech and the letter to Khrushchev that would be handed to Ambassador Anatoly Dobrynin just before the president went on the air. When the ExComm discussions resumed on October 23, the crisis had entered a new phase: it was no longer secret. RFK's doubts persisted. He again expressed concern that the blockade would be perceived as too little, too late, and in a worried tone of voice suggested that the president might be accused of "closing the barn door after the horse is gone." JFK requested a CIA analysis of "what the effects of a blockade of everything but food and medicine would be on Cuba." "Do we want that," RFK quickly added, "on Berlin too?" JFK, always preoccupied with Berlin, agreed that it would be valuable to know "what the effect would be of a blockade in Berlin by them." "Of the same kind," RFK muttered.

That evening the discussion turned to the management of the soon-to-be implemented blockade, particularly what to do if Soviet ships were hailed, refused to stop, and turned and headed away from Cuba. McNamara suggested that any ship that turned around should not be boarded or searched and the president quickly agreed, "'cause they'd be grabbing stuff that might be heading home." RFK dissented vigorously and maintained that it would be "a hell of an advantage" to seize a vessel believed to be carrying missiles in order to examine and get pictures of the weapons. "Maybe you don't want to do it for the first 48 hours," he conceded, but it would be "damn helpful" to examine any secret Soviet equipment. Dean Rusk pointedly disagreed, arguing that seizing Soviet weapons would violate the stated, limited purpose of the blockade: to prevent these weapons from reaching Cuba.

Later on the evening of October 23, the Kennedy brothers talked alone in the Oval Office. "How's it look?" Bobby asked point-blank. "Well, it looks like it's gonna be real mean, doesn't it?" JFK snapped. "But on the other hand, there's really no choice. If they get this mean on this one—Jesus Christ! What are they gonna fuck up next?" "No choice," RFK echoed, "I mean you woulda been impeached." "Well, that's what I think," JFK replied; "I woulda been impeached." RFK emphasized that press reaction to the president's speech thus far, "is pretty good." "Till tomorrow morning," JFK retorted pessimistically, and RFK agreed, "it's gonna get unpleasant" after the blockade begins.

Early the following morning, Wednesday, October 24, as the quarantine went into effect, and certainly with JFK's full knowledge, RFK met with Ambassador Dobrynin in his Soviet embassy office. The attorney general made no effort to hide his own and the president's fury over Soviet duplicity. Dobrynin cabled the Kremlin that "The President felt himself deceived and deceived deliberately." He wanted his superiors in Moscow to understand that the Kennedys' anger was personal as well as official and emphasized that RFK appeared to be emotionally and physically exhausted and had not been home for six days and nights. Nevertheless, the ambassador told the attorney general that he had no personal knowledge of Soviet offensive missiles in Cuba and added ominously that he had not received any indication that Soviet ships heading for Cuba had been instructed to change course.

The ExComm met again on October 25—twenty-four hours after the implementation of the blockade. Reports, as yet unconfirmed, had been received that some of the ships approaching the blockade line had reversed course and were heading home. "My God," RFK declared testily, it would be better to grab a ship believed to be carrying missiles, even if it had turned around. "The point is to . . . intercept a ship that had something rather than a lot of baby food for children." (The administration had agreed to ship baby food to Cuba as part of the agreement for the release of the Bay of Pigs prisoners.) Immediate concern, however, focused instead on an East German passenger ship which was approaching the quarantine line, and a consensus quickly developed against risking the loss of civilian lives by stopping and boarding that type of vessel.

Robert Kennedy, however, tried to "give another side of it." Reaffirming his persistent concerns about being trapped in a stalemate, the attorney general suggested impassively that "rather than have the confrontation with the Russians at sea . . . it might be better to knock out their missile base as the first step." Echoing his tough stance at the early ExComm meetings, RFK sidestepped the issue of an American Pearl Harbor by proposing to warn Soviet personnel "to get out of that vicinity in ten minutes [!] and then we go through and knock [off] the base." The administration, he reasoned, should put air strikes back on the table, thus demonstrating "that we're not backing off and that we're still being tough with Cuba. That's really the point we have to make." He also expressed concern about waiting to stop a ship: "The only weakness in my judgment, is the idea to the Russians that you know . . . backing off and that we're weak."

The president nonetheless ruled out intercepting the passenger ship: "if you try to disable it, you're apt to sink it." He also decided to give Khrushchev more time. But JFK also edged closer to his brother's tougher stance: "I think if the work continues," we have to reconsider "this air business . . . because we got to begin to bring counter pressure because otherwise the work's going on and we're not really doin' anything else." RFK, evidently heartened by the president's renewed determination, added, "And we've got to show them that we mean it." He acknowledged that the Soviets might be backing away from challenging the blockade, but he remained unconvinced: "We retreat an inch and he [Khrushchev] says, 'six feet to go.'"

By the following morning, Friday, October 26, RFK had begun to pressure CIA director McCone to expand the activities of Operation Mongoose in order to deal with the increasingly urgent situation in Cuba. He was especially angry because it appeared that these efforts had become bogged down in turf wars between the CIA, Mongoose operations chief Edward Lansdale, and the Pentagon.

Later that evening the ExComm's attention was diverted from the quarantine when Khrushchev made a startling proposal in a secret letter to JFK: he would withdraw the missiles from Cuba if the U.S. would publicly promise not to invade or support an invasion of the island nation.

However, when the meetings resumed on Saturday morning, a report soon arrived that Khrushchev had made a new proposal—publicly over Moscow radio—that the U.S.S.R. would remove its missiles from Cuba if the U.S. would withdraw its missiles from Turkey. The reaction from the ExComm was one of shock, anger, and betrayal.

Eventually, a consensus developed that the Politburo and/or the Soviet military had seized the initiative in the Kremlin and decided to up the ante. The advice to the president was essentially unanimous—stick to the Friday message and ignore the latest offer. But JFK countered that a public offer could not be rejected: "you're going to find a lot of people thinking this is rather a reasonable position. . . . Let's not kid ourselves . . . they've got a very good proposal, which is the reason they've made it public with an announcement."

RFK made his disagreement very plain. "I don't see how we can ask the Turks to give up their defense." The first order of business had to be the removal of the threat to the U.S. and Latin America posed by the missiles in Cuba—which required making "doubly clear that Turkish NATO missiles were one problem and that Cuba was an entirely separate problem." "We can have an exchange with him [Khrushchev] and say, 'You've double-crossed us and we don't know which deal to accept.' . . . In the meantime, he's got all the play throughout the world."

The attorney general also warned about the possible deterioration of the U.S. position if talks with the Soviets dragged on for weeks or even months and the Cubans refused to allow inspections to verify that the missiles were inoperable—but, he added with obviously ongoing interest, "we could then decide to attack the bases by air." Later, when the president was out of the room, Bobby tried to explain that the public would soon learn about Khrushchev's new radio offer and that the president was simply trying to "take the initiative away" from the U.S.S.R.

The ExComm nonetheless continued to resist JFK's readiness to respond to Khrushchev's public offer, and RFK was consistently one of the most outspoken leaders of the hawkish side. The president soon returned and suggested calling a meeting of the NATO Council so that the allies could be directly involved in any decision about the Turkish missiles. JFK had already concluded that Khrushchev's public offer had made removal of the Turkish missiles unavoidable, and his immediate concern was to prevent the Turks from issuing an uncompromising statement rejecting a trade. The Turks had to understand, he warned, that if the U.S. took military action in Cuba, the Soviets could retaliate against the Jupiter missiles, exposing Turkey to great danger and putting enormous pressure on the U.S. to respond militarily. And once the military tit for tat began, would anyone be able to stop it short of a nuclear exchange?

RFK remained determined to link any U.S. noninvasion pledge to an equivalent commitment from the Cubans not to support military aggression or subversion in Latin America—especially since Khrushchev had asked for assurances that "the USA itself would not participate in an attack on Cuba and would restrain others from actions of this sort."[8] "I mean, all bets are off on this, I would think," he demanded, if Cuba supplied arms to Latin American insurgents. The president objected to the "bets [are] off" wording and lectured his brother, "I don't think we can use this language" in our letter to Khrushchev. JFK instead proposed dangling the possibility of the Turkish missile deal mentioned in the chairman's new letter. He recommended writing, "'As I was preparing this letter . . . I learned of your [new message].'" But the real crisis was in Cuba, and "'When we get action there [a cessation of work], I shall certainly be ready to discuss the matters you mentioned in your public message.' You see, that's more forthcoming. . . .I think our message oughta be that we're glad to discuss this [Turkey] and other matters but we've gotta get a cessation of work." "And," the disgruntled attorney general added, "the dismantling of the bases that are already there."

Bobby Kennedy made no effort to conceal his persistent doubts about showing any signs of taking Khrushchev's public offer seriously. Once the U.S. initiated a NATO meeting, he noted, that "blows the possibility of this other one, of course, doesn't it?" "Of what?" JFK replied impatiently. "Of getting an acceptance," RFK explained, "of the [Friday] proposal." "The advantage of the [NATO] meeting," the president reiterated, "is that if we reject it [the Turkey deal], they've participated in it. And, if we accept it, they've participated in it." Bobby was not persuaded and urged keeping the pressure on so that "We don't look like we're weakening on the whole Turkey complex."

The president recapitulated irritably: "You see, they [NATO] haven't had the alternatives presented to them. They'll say, 'Well, God! We don't want to trade 'em off!' They don't realize that in 2 or 3 days we may have a military strike [on Cuba] which would bring perhaps the seizure of Berlin or a strike on Turkey. And then they'll say, 'By God! We should have taken it!'"

Ultimately, JFK acquiesced to pressure from RFK and others urging him not to "abandon" Cuba to the communists: "Send this letter," RFK pleaded, "and say you're accepting his [Friday] offer. He's made an offer and you're in fact accepting it . . . God, don't bring in Turkey now. We want to settle [Cuba first]." Khrushchev "must be a little shaken up," he stressed, "or he wouldn't have sent the [Friday] message to you in the first place." "That's last night," JFK retorted yet again. "But it's certainly conceivable," Bobby replied, "that you could get him back to that. I don't think that we should abandon it."

JFK halfheartedly agreed that there was no harm in trying. "All right," he finally conceded, "Let's send this" letter dealing with Cuba first. But he stressed once again that the key question remained: "what are we gonna do about the Turks?" RFK continued to press the president not to abandon the earlier proposal. "What is the rush about this?"—Bobby added peevishly—except for deciding on the timing of an air strike? JFK tersely approved the letter, in which he clearly had very limited confidence, before promptly resuming the discussion of the Turkish missile withdrawal. He was determined to leave the diplomatic door wide open despite the fact that several military options were still on the table.

General Taylor, however, injected a significant dissent, reporting that the JCS had met that afternoon and recommended that "the big [bombing] strike" should begin no later than Monday morning, the twenty-ninth, "unless there is irrefutable evidence in the meantime that offensive weapons are being dismantled and rendered inoperable"—followed by "the invasion plan, seven days later." "Well," RFK teased, with perhaps a hint of self-mockery, "I'm surprised!" and laughter briefly punctured the unrelenting pressure in the Cabinet Room.

Alarming news arrived at around 6:00 P.M. that a U-2 had been shot down over Cuba by a Soviet surface-to-air missile—and the pilot killed. The president, as a result, became even more determined to respond favorably to Khrushchev's missile trade proposal. JFK recognized that Turkey and NATO would inevitably conclude "that this is on the cheap for them, they'll say the United States is pulling out in order to try to make a deal on Cuba. I mean, no matter whether we say it's to protect Turkey or not, that's the way they're gonna think about it." Nonetheless, the president clearly believed that diplomatic and political embarrassment and losses in the midterm elections were preferable to risking a nuclear world war.

Ironically, but not surprisingly, the president sent the attorney general to propose a secret Cuba-Turkey deal to Ambassador Dobrynin. JFK knew that Bobby's personal views would never trump his personal loyalty. Indeed, even after returning from the meeting with Dobrynin and joining the late evening ExComm meeting, RFK continued to resist the trade. "Can't we wait? Isn't it possible to get through tomorrow" without getting into "the Turkey business?" The attorney general, always fearful about appearing weak, predicted that "if they [the Soviets] find us playin' around and figuring on Turkey, and accept we're willing to make some deal; if I were they, I'd push on that, and then I'd push on [the Jupiters in] Italy." Instead, he urged again trying to get Khrushchev back to his October 26 offer by remaining "hard and tough on this."

But even the hawkish attorney general, undoubtedly mindful of the secret understanding reached by the small group in the Oval Office earlier that evening as well as his own just concluded discussion with Dobrynin, acknowledged that if U Thant failed to negotiate a deal for the concurrent suspension of the blockade and the delivery of weapons to Cuba, "and the whole thing looks like it's collapsing and we're gonna have to go in there [Cuba]," then we go to the NATO allies with the Turkish proposal despite our preference to keep the issue "completely in the Western Hemisphere."

In the final moments of the third "Black Saturday" meeting, sometime after 9:00 P.M., McNamara exhorted Bobby Kennedy that the time for talking was over: "In other words," the administration needs "to really escalate this." RFK's final words on the ExComm tapes were characteristically blunt and uncompromising. "I'd like to take Cuba back," he remarked wistfully; "That would be nice."

Ambassador Dobrynin delivered a letter from Khrushchev to Robert Kennedy two days later. The message explicitly identified the terms of the agreement reached on that fateful weekend: Soviet withdrawal, in Khrushchev's words, of "those weapons you describe as offensive"; on-site verification by U.N. inspectors; a U.S. pledge not to invade Cuba; plus, a secret American commitment to remove the Jupiter missiles from Turkey. After consulting with the president, RFK returned the letter, and in line with the confidential strategy adopted in the Oval Office on the evening of October 27, refused to formalize in writing the secret understanding about the Turkish missiles.

RFK admitted, according to Dobrynin, that he could not "risk getting involved in the transmission of this sort of letter, since who knows where and when such letters can surface or be somehow published—not now, but in the future—and any changes in the course of events are possible. The appearance of such a document could cause irreparable harm to my political career in the future. This is why we request that you take this letter back."[9]

Determined to avoid creating a paper trail of his "informal" arrangement with Dobrynin about the Turkish missiles, Robert Kennedy went so far a few days later as to falsify his memo to Dean Rusk about the meeting by actually crossing out a reference to this top secret understanding.[10] In a very real sense, this deliberate falsification of the historical record was the first step in writing *Thirteen Days*.

Finally, three weeks later, after tough negotiations at the U.N. over issues such as whether the Soviet IL-28 bombers in Cuba were "offensive" weapons (Khrushchev finally agreed to remove them), the president prepared to announce the lifting of the naval quarantine around Cuba. Hours before the scheduled November 20 statement to the nation, RFK urged his brother to resist giving any public assurances that the U.S. would not invade Cuba. With the quarantine removed, he argued, the noninvasion promise was the only remaining lever for putting pressure on Khrushchev. The president seemed uneasy: "Now how do we prevent this from looking too much like we're welching on it as well?"[11] "We didn't say we're gonna give formal assurances," RFK countered. "I don't think that we owe anything as far as Khrushchev is concerned; nor does he expect it at the moment." He did concede, however, "maybe we wanna throw this in as a piece of cake."

But JFK continued to wonder whether a U.S. noninvasion promise would also strengthen Khrushchev's political position in the Kremlin and perhaps make it easier for him to eventually withdraw his conventional forces from Cuba as well. In the end, as RFK had urged, the president toughened his stance: since on-site inspection and verification had not been implemented (as a result of Castro's refusal to permit U.N. personnel to enter Cuba), JFK declared that the preconditions for the U.S. noninvasion pledge had not been met.

The ExComm tape recordings explicitly contradict the claims that Robert Kennedy had become "a chastened man" or had "matured from a kneejerk hawk to a wise and restrained diplomat" over the course of the Cuban missile crisis.

4   The Mythmaking of Robert McNamara

Before we attack [Cuba], you've gotta be damned sure [the
Soviets] understand it's coming. In other words, you need to
really escalate this.

—Robert McNamara, October 27, 1962

ROBERT STRANGE MCNAMARA, only forty-four years old in 1961
when he became JFK's secretary of defense, was almost immediately touted as one of the stars of the new president's so-called best and
brightest. His brainpower, all-consuming work ethic, and eagerness to utilize
scientific management in government quickly earned him a reputation as the
administration's top whiz kid. But above all, his commitment to civilian direction of the military and his willingness to question both military judgment
and expenditures led President Kennedy to regard him, as Robert Kennedy
later wrote, "as the most valuable public servant in his Administration and in
the government."[1]

As a result, McNamara's later vilification as the architect of the escalation
of the Vietnam war is all the more striking. He treated Vietnam, as one historian put it, as "an applied social science experiment," and by 1966 had become
a virtual straw man for what the antiwar movement called "McNamara's
war."[2] He left the defense department in 1968, profoundly disillusioned by the
policy he had helped to create, and he spent the rest of his long life trying to
explain how the U.S. had misjudged the situation in Vietnam and expressing
regret for his own hubris. His memoir, *In Retrospect: The Tragedy and Lessons
of Vietnam,* was published in 1995; he also became a leading spokesman for the
reduction and elimination of nuclear weapons.

The high point of McNamara's quest for redemption, however, came in

2003 with the release of director Errol Morris's *The Fog of War: Eleven Lessons from the Life of Robert S. McNamara*. The film won an Academy Award for Best Documentary Feature. The overwhelming majority of the film, of course, dealt with the war in Vietnam, but some important segments explored McNamara's role in the Cuban missile crisis. Most commentators ignored those sections; but one analyst, Fred Kaplan, recognized that McNamara's effort to "paint himself as no less dovish than [President] Kennedy in dealing with the Russians" was "a self-serving travesty"—a judgment incontrovertibly confirmed by the ExComm tapes.[3]

In fact, McNamara's effort to revise his role in the ExComm meetings had already begun only a year after the crisis. In the fall of 1963, the defense secretary told JFK about his recent conversation with Admiral Hyman Rickover, in which the latter claimed that Admiral George Anderson, chief of naval operations in October 1962, had been "absolutely insubordinate" and tried to subvert the president's orders. "He wanted to sink a ship," Kennedy replied, and McNamara confirmed, "That's right." However, as documented later in this chapter, McNamara had actually supported Robert Kennedy's hard-line stance on enforcing the blockade; nonetheless, he referred to "the instructions that *you and I* were giving relating to the quarantine and the limiting of action in relation to stopping the Russian ships" (emphasis added).[4]

Four decades later, McNamara professed in *The Fog of War* that the Russians and the Cubans knew about Operation Mongoose, and they also "knew what in a sense I really didn't know: we had attempted to assassinate Castro under Eisenhower and under Kennedy and later under Johnson."[5] What does "in a sense" even mean in that context? The administration's covert activities in Cuba were explicitly mentioned at several ExComm meetings (particularly on the morning of October 26), and it is obvious that the secretary of defense was *not* out of the loop. In fact, McNamara's top deputy, Roswell Gilpatric, represented the defense department on the committee which discussed plans to overthrow and/or assassinate Castro—the Special Group (Augmented), chaired by Robert Kennedy. And Edward Lansdale, who was primarily in charge of clandestine operations against Cuba, was assistant secretary of defense for special operations under McNamara.

McNamara also endorsed the myth that JFK had adopted Bobby Kennedy's brilliant strategy of accepting Khrushchev's Friday offer (to remove the missiles in exchange for a U.S. promise not to invade Cuba) and ignoring his public letter of Saturday (proposing a trade of Soviet missiles in Cuba for U.S.

missiles in Turkey). Indeed, McNamara's characterization of the second letter is both bizarre and baffling: "Then before we could respond [to the Friday letter], we had a second message dictated by a bunch of hard-liners [the erroneous interpretation first proposed during the October 27 ExComm meetings]. And it said, in effect, 'If you attack, we're prepared to confront you with masses of military power.'" He does not mention that the second letter proposed a missile trade—which the president accepted despite the essentially unanimous and strident opposition of his advisers, including McNamara. (Evidence released since the fall of the Soviet Union has also confirmed that Khrushchev himself was responsible for both letters. The chairman was responding to what he interpreted as "feelers from the Kennedy camp" that a trade might be negotiable and "dictated his new letter in the presence of the rest of the Presidium." The fact that the letter was made public, and included an admission that Khrushchev had indeed deployed nuclear missiles in Cuba, "confirmed that he was seeking a settlement.")[6]

McNamara further claims that "it was luck that prevented nuclear war," despite the fact that "Kennedy was rational; Khrushchev was rational; Castro was rational." The assertion about Castro is certainly debatable in light of Soviet ambassador to Cuba Aleksandr Alekseev's recollections about Castro's demeanor when he cabled Moscow, demanding a nuclear strike against the U.S. in the event of an attack on Cuba. Khrushchev, fortunately, rejected what he construed as the Cuban leader's nuclear first-strike proposal because it could spark a thermonuclear world war.[7] Morris, unfortunately, let these inaccuracies pass without comment.

❧

Understandably, the defense secretary, like many others at these nerve-racking meetings, was erratic and inconsistent. His frequently belligerent instincts, in addition, were also tempered by a clear reluctance to cross the president or the attorney general. It is, up to a point, accurate to say that McNamara's initial response to the discovery of Soviet nuclear missiles in Cuba, at the first (October 16) ExComm meeting, was consistent with his assertion in the *Fog of War* that "I was trying to help him [JFK] keep us out of war." He initially argued that any military action against the missile sites had to be carried out before the missiles became operational (the warheads had yet to be located) because "if they're launched there is almost certain to be chaos in part of the East Coast or the area in a radius of 600 to 1,000 miles from Cuba." He stressed as well that the southeastern U.S. might still be vulnerable to conventional or nuclear attack by Castro's air force flying low to avoid radar: "It would be a very heavy price to pay in U.S. lives for the damage we did to Cuba."

The defense secretary, nonetheless, also maintained that even though diplomatic negotiations with the U.S.S.R. should be explored, the U.S. must be prepared for an all-out attack on Cuba—contending that air strikes should be carried out, not only on the missile sites but also on the airfields, aircraft, and potential nuclear warhead storage sites. The air strikes would last several days and would result in hundreds or even thousands of Cuban casualties; he did not mention Soviet casualties. McNamara did not stop there: the bombing would be only a prelude to a full air and sea invasion about seven days after the start of the air campaign. Finally, he called for military mobilization and a possible presidential declaration of national emergency.

At the evening meeting on October 16, however, McNamara suddenly announced that he did not think that the missiles in Cuba significantly altered the world balance of power, and distanced himself from the JCS recommendation to bomb the missile sites as well as Soviet bombers, fighter planes, and warhead storage facilities. He endorsed the immediate preparation of a specific bombing strike plan, but at the same time, with strikingly uncharacteristic self-doubt, urged his colleagues to consider the consequences of military action: "I don't know quite what kind of a world we live in after we've struck Cuba and we've started it. . . . After we've launched 50 to 100 sorties, what kind of a world do we live in? How do we stop at that point? I don't know the answer to this," he admitted grimly.

The defense secretary stressed, "I don't believe it's primarily a military problem. It's primarily a domestic political problem," and urged his colleagues to consider: "What do we expect Castro will be doing after you attack these missiles? Does he survive as a political leader? Is he overthrown? Is he stronger, weaker? How will he react? How will the Soviets react? How can Khrushchev afford to accept this action without some kind of rebuttal? . . . Where? How do we react in relation to it?"

The next day, October 17, Robert Kennedy later wrote, McNamara "became the blockade's strongest advocate."[8] The evidence on the tapes is far more convoluted and contradictory. On October 18, in fact, McNamara abandoned the caution he had recommended on the evening of October 16 and boldly endorsed the JCS demand for an all-out air and land attack on Cuba: "In other words," he announced, "we consider nothing short of a full invasion as practicable military action." President Kennedy was taken aback by the defense secretary's about-face and asked: "Why do you change? Why has this information changed the recommendation?" McNamara declared that there were too many targets, including many not yet located, to be realistically destroyed by air strikes. As a result, there was a heightened chance of the loss of Guantánamo and/or attacks on the civilian population on the eastern coast of the U.S. from the new missile bases or the Soviet nuclear bombers. "I think we would find it hard to justify" these casualties, McNamara explained, "in relation to the very limited accomplishment of our limited number of [air] strikes."

He continued, notwithstanding, to maintain that "it's not a military prob-lem that we're facing; it's a political problem; it's a problem of holding the alliance together; it's a problem of properly conditioning Khrushchev for our future moves." These new circumstances, including "the problem of dealing with our domestic public," rather than a meaningful change in the military balance of power, he reasoned, justified an invasion of Cuba.

President Kennedy responded with uncharacteristic harshness to McNa-mara's striking reversal. Most of the allies, Kennedy declared forcefully, regarded Cuba "as a fixation of the United States and not a serious military threat. . . . because they think that we're slightly demented on this subject. . . . they will argue that taken at its worst the presence of these missiles really doesn't change" the nuclear balance of power. Indeed, only minutes later, the president floated the trial balloon that would eventually redefine the crisis— "If we said to Khrushchev . . . 'if you're willing to pull them out, we'll take ours out of Turkey'"—an idea McNamara would first support and then pas-sionately oppose.

Later in the meeting, McNamara became somewhat more circumspect (as he often did when his views conflicted with those of the president or the attor-ney general), emphasizing that at least several hundred Soviet citizens would surely be killed by the air strikes. "We're using napalm, 750 pound bombs. This is an extensive strike we're talking about. . . . I think the price is going to be high. It may still be worth paying to eliminate the missiles. . . . The very least it will be," he added, likely in response to the hint made earlier by the president, "will be to remove the missiles in Italy and Turkey."

The defense secretary reiterated that the missiles would not be withdrawn from Cuba without concessions—"Now the minimum price are missiles out of Turkey and Italy"—but he doubted that the Soviets would settle for that after their forces had been killed in Cuba. If the alliance remained intact, and the missiles were removed from Cuba, Turkey, and Italy, McNamara speculated, "that's the best possible solution. There are many worse solutions. .... I really think that we've got to think these problems through more than we have. At the moment I lean to the blockade because I think it reduces the very serious risk of large-scale military action from which this country cannot benefit."

RFK, in particular, disparaged the blockade option because it did not force the Soviets to stop construction of the existing missile sites. "Oh, no, no," McNamara countered. "What we say is, 'We are going to blockade you. This is a danger to us.' We insist that we talk this out and the danger be removed [from Cuba]." General Taylor brusquely asked the defense chief to explain his objection to air strikes against the missiles and bombers. "My real objection to it," McNamara replied bluntly, "is that it kills several hundred Russians."

The defense chief emphasized that the intelligence already in hand was sufficient for developing a "well thought-out course of action" on the only two alternatives being discussed: a slow move to military action (a political statement followed or accompanied by a blockade), or a rapid move to military action (a brief warning to Khrushchev followed by an air attack). Early in the discussion, the defense secretary had passionately endorsed invading Cuba, but by the end of the meeting, undoubtedly responding to JFK's determined resistance, he did not even list invasion as an option. McNamara's latest about-face must have been troubling and puzzling to many of his ExComm colleagues.

By Saturday, October 20, after the president's return from the Midwest, McNamara endorsed the "blockade route" as a first step toward the removal of the missiles; he also recommended negotiations for "the withdrawal of United States strategic missiles from Turkey and Italy" and even suggested a possible "agreement to limit our use of Guantánamo to a specified limited time." Finally, he stated that a surprise strike was "contrary to our tradition" and that the eight hundred sortie air strikes proposed by the JCS would kill thousands of Russians and Cubans: "In such an event, the United States would lose control of the situation which could escalate to general war."

This was the high point of McNamara's relatively brief and erratic dovish phase. Beginning the next morning, his support for the blockade began to erode and he drifted steadily into the hawkish camp, finally becoming one of its toughest spokesmen on Black Saturday, October 27.

By Monday, October 22, as the draft of the president's speech to the nation was being finalized, several advisers urged JFK to also move forward with plans for a full invasion. Kennedy countered that it was neither strategically nor politically helpful to "have it hanging over us that we're preparing [an] invasion." McNamara objected, reminding the commander in chief that "you ordered us to be prepared for any eventuality," and urged announcing instead "that we're prepared to quarantine [the] movement of weapons by whatever means, period."

The following day, after the president's speech had made the crisis public, McNamara raised a particularly thorny question: whether to pursue and board a Soviet ship that had turned and headed away from Cuba. "It's both a legal question and a practical question," he observed. "The legal foundation of such an act is confused. As a practical matter, I don't believe we should undertake such an operation." "Not right now," the president affirmed, and McNamara added, "Not immediately. That's right. So my instruction to the navy was, 'Don't do it.'" "That's right," the president quickly agreed, "'cause they'd be grabbing stuff that might be heading home."

Robert Kennedy, however, countered that it would be very advantageous to seize a vessel believed to be carrying missiles, in order to examine and get pictures of the Soviets' latest weapons—but not during the first forty-eight hours. McNamara then abruptly reversed the position he had taken just moments before, calling RFK's idea "an excellent suggestion, but not to apply the first day," and endorsed stopping a ship: "even if it turns around and proceeds indefinitely away from Cuba, we would nonetheless stop it and search it because it very probably would have offensive weapons on board."

The president short-circuited the discussion and decided to defer this decision until the blockade went into effect. He added, however, "Now what do we do tomorrow morning . . . ? We're all clear about how we..." he paused for several seconds, "...handle it?" Some strained laughter broke out just before JFK's last few words, which were spoken in a wry, tongue-in-cheek tone revealing his awareness that no one in Washington or Moscow could predict or control the outcome of this potentially deadly confrontation at sea.

And as the president learned the next day (Wednesday, October 24), the inherent danger in that naval confrontation had been substantially exacerbated by the presence of several Soviet submarines near Cuba. McNamara, nonetheless, made the startling announcement that he had set up a new procedure just yesterday and had already sent a message informing the Soviets.

The defense secretary asserted confidently, "We have depth charges that have such a small charge that they can be dropped and they can actually hit the submarine without damaging the submarine." "They're practice depth charges," General Taylor explained. "We propose," McNamara continued, "when our forces come upon an unidentified submarine we will ask it to come to the surface for inspection by transmitting the following signals, using a depth charge of this type and also using certain sonar signals which they may not be able to accept and interpret. Therefore, it's the depth charge that is the warning notice and the instruction to surface."

Robert Kennedy, who *may* have read a transcript or listened to the tape of this meeting in drafting *Thirteen Days*, claimed that the president was profoundly unsettled by McNamara's cold certainty that these antisubmarine weapons could be used harmlessly, and with such precision, that the U.S.S.R. would not be provoked into military retaliation. RFK later vividly recalled that President Kennedy covered his mouth with his hand and clenched and unclenched his fist as "we stared at each other across the table."[9]

General Taylor reminded the defense chief that the sonar signal would be tried first, followed by the depth charge, and McNamara repeated that "The sonar signal very probably will not accomplish its purpose." The president's skepticism was immediately apparent, and he asked, "If he [the submarine] doesn't surface or if he takes some action to assist the merchant ship, are we just gonna attack him anyway?" Taylor interjected, "We're going to attack him because—" but the president cut him off sharply: "I think we ought to wait on that today, 'cause we don't wanna have the first thing we attack is a Soviet submarine. I'd much rather have a merchant ship."

McNamara firmly disagreed: "I think it would be extremely dangerous, Mr. President, to try to defer attack on this submarine in the situation we're in. We could easily lose an American ship by that means. The range of our sonar in relation to the range of his torpedo, and the inaccuracy, as you well know, of antisubmarine warfare is such that I don't have any great confidence that we can push him away from our ships and make the intercept securely."

The president must have been struck by the contradiction between McNamara's acknowledgment of the imprecision of submarine warfare and his confidence about using practice depth charges to harmlessly force a Soviet submarine to surface. The defense secretary warned that it would be especially dangerous to limit the discretion of the naval commander on the scene: "I looked into this in great detail last night," he pointedly told the president, "because of your interest in the question." The plan was to use antisubmarine helicopters, equipped with "weapons and devices that can damage the submarine. And the plan therefore is to put pressure on the submarine, move it out of the area by that pressure, by the pressure of potential destruction, and then make the intercept. But," the usually self-assured defense chief admitted, "this is only a plan and there are many, many uncertainties." "Okay," JFK yielded, despite his obvious doubts, "let's proceed."

In fact, the president's doubts were justified, and his only major decision during the crisis to accept this type of risky advice was nearly catastrophic. One of four Soviet submarines submerged in Cuban waters was encircled by the U.S. Navy and came under hours of attack from "signaling depth charges" (practice depth charges) that exploded right next to the vessel. The grenade-like explosions felt like "sledgehammers on a metal barrel"; the temperature in the submarine rose to over 122 degrees; and some crewmen lost consciousness. The irate captain, unable to surface for communication with the Soviet defense ministry but determined to make the Americans pay a heavy price, ordered the arming of a nuclear-tipped torpedo. Fortunately, he reconsidered and instead surfaced at night in an area illuminated by searchlights from U.S. Navy ships. In a slightly different version of events, discussed at the October 2002 Havana conference, the captain actually gave the order to fire because he believed that World War III had already begun—but was finally persuaded to wait by another officer.[10]

Robert Kennedy then raised a question which clearly embarrassed the usually self-confident and thoroughly prepared McNamara: "I presume that somebody on the destroyer speaks Russian." McNamara replied quietly, "We've asked about that Bobby and I don't have any answers." "May we get this, as a matter of procedure, at the quickest possible point," the president instructed firmly, "that you can get a Russian-speaking person on every one of these ships?" "Yes, Mr. President," a subdued McNamara responded.

By the conclusion of the meeting the president finally made his position clear to everyone in the room: a confrontation at sea was to be averted if at all possible. "It seems to me," he stated categorically, "we want to give that ship a chance to turn around. You don't wanna have word goin' out from Moscow, 'Turn around,' and suddenly we sink their ship."

By the following morning (October 25), however, McNamara urged the president to toughen the blockade: "I believe," he stressed, "we should establish a pattern of boarding as a quarantine technique and do it immediately.

. . . I think you should instruct them [the navy] to be prepared to intercept tomorrow during daylight." And when RFK added, "And no matter where it might be"—a reference to ships that had turned around and were hundreds of miles away from Cuba—McNamara this time expressed unconditional agreement.

The defense secretary also urged JFK to add petroleum, oil, and lubricants (POL) as well as aviation gas to the list of embargoed items and to set up a pattern of low-level surveillance flights, which because they were unarmed, would throw the Soviets and the Cubans off guard. The U.S. could then quickly convert these flight patterns into surprise air attacks on the missile sites, the Soviet bombers, the airfields, the surface-to-air missile sites, and the warhead storage facilities. McNamara admitted, in sharp contrast to his previous endorsement of the blockade, that he had never believed these weapons would be removed from Cuba "without the application of substantial force. . . . economic force and military force."

He also expressed alarm at the prospect of a protracted and inconclusive status quo in Cuba as the missile sites were rushed to completion. The defense secretary recommended letting an East German passenger ship (carrying 1,500 civilians) through but if necessary stopping and boarding "a Soviet tanker with a deck cargo" (presumably of missiles). It was essential to "appear to be forceful" by increasing aerial surveillance over Cuba during the day and using flares to check on work done at night. "These two actions I think in themselves will convince both our public and the world that we are maintaining an adequate . . . a forceful position." McNamara also assured the president, "We have a lot of harassing actions ["Exactly," RFK interjected eagerly] we could carry out, and incidents we can provoke if we'd wish to."

The following morning (Friday, October 26), McNamara continued to push for toughening the U.S. stance. He announced that the Soviets were rapidly assembling the IL-28 nuclear-capable bombers photographed in Cuba and strongly recommended adding bomber fuel to the items embargoed by the blockade. President Kennedy, clearly discomfited, replied that he would rather add POL because it was directly related to the missiles rather than the bombers: "the missiles are the more dramatic offensive weapons. There's gonna be such bombers everyplace." McNamara suggested including both bomber fuel and related petroleum products, but JFK persisted, "I would rather tie as much as we could to the missiles." "Can't we do them both?" McNamara urged again; the president finally agreed to announcing that the

U.S. was restricting the delivery of fuel that contributed to the construction of the missile sites as well as aviation fuel for the bombers; but, he reemphasized, "I think the missiles are the dramatic one. Bombers—hell, or they might say, 'we can destroy all your bombers everyplace.'"

McNamara pressed as well for announcing "that it is our policy to continue surveillance—day and night." He proposed sending in eight to ten aircraft that day, followed by four that night using about ten flares to illuminate each target. The flares would be thrown out of the planes at about 5,000 feet and become operational at around 2,000 feet, allowing the pilots "to determine the extent to which development of the offensive weapon systems is continuing." Dean Rusk had earlier expressed concern that the flares could be mistaken for explosions by the Cubans or the Russians, but the defense chief suggested they could be warned in advance. After further discussion, the president sided with Rusk and decided to defer night surveillance. The limited information that might be obtained was simply not worth the risk of unintentionally prompting the Russians or the Cubans to believe that a military attack had begun.

A later intelligence briefing revealed that construction of the missile sites was accelerating and that Castro had ordered antiaircraft fire against U.S. reconnaissance planes over Cuba. The president once again began to consider military action along the lines that had first been debated at the early ExComm sessions. His overriding concern, especially after receiving Khrushchev's letter proposing to remove the missiles in exchange for an American promise not to invade Cuba, was to reach a settlement, but if that failed, then to eliminate the missiles in Cuba before they could be fired.

As the ExComm reconvened on the morning of Saturday, October 27, McNamara acknowledged that the tanker approaching the quarantine line was unlikely to be carrying prohibited materials; nonetheless, he stressed the need to take some action: "I think we ought to stop it, anyhow, and use force if necessary." He also renewed the pressure to "keep the heat on" by initiating night surveillance using flares, but the president again opted for a delay.

Reports soon arrived of Khrushchev's public announcement that he would remove Soviet missiles from Cuba if the U.S. removed its Jupiter missiles from Turkey. The realization gradually spread through the room that this was indeed a new proposal. In fact, President Kennedy had been probing the option of a Turkey-Cuba deal with the ExComm for more than a week; it quickly became apparent that the opposition to such a deal was stronger than ever. Nonetheless, the president immediately made his position plain: "We're gonna be in an insupportable position on this matter if this becomes his [Khrushchev's] proposal. . . . to any man at the United Nations or any other rational man, it will look like a very fair trade." JFK admonished his advisers: "Let's not kid ourselves" into thinking that we can simply dismiss this offer.

McNamara, RFK, Rusk, Bundy, John McCone, George Ball, Paul Nitze, Douglas Dillon, Llewellyn Thompson, Maxwell Taylor, and Ted Sorensen tenaciously and unanimously exhorted the president to reject any deal involving U.S. missiles in Turkey.[11] McNamara asserted that the U.S. should instead be pushing demands for halting construction on the bases, followed by the removal of the missiles. "How can we negotiate," the defense secretary demanded angrily, "with somebody who changes his deal before we even get a chance to reply and announces publicly the deal before we receive it? . . . So my point is we oughta really keep the pressure on them . . . [and] just turn it down publicly."

President Kennedy nevertheless underscored that a public offer could not be disregarded and bluntly acknowledged that Khrushchev had been diplomatically astute: "They've got a very good prod and this one is gonna be very tough, I think, for us." It would be very difficult for the U.S. "to move with world support" against Cuba. "This is a pretty good play of his."

The defense chief, however, unflinchingly declared that since reports had just been received that U.S. reconnaissance aircraft had been fired on, "A limited strike is out. So the military plan now is basically invasion. We should start the strike, call up the reserves. We need the air units for the invasion in any case." He recommended five hundred sorties on the SAM sites and the airfields, followed by "an invasion in about seven days."

As the pressure mounted to reject Khrushchev's second letter, JFK made his position unmistakable: "Today it sounds great to reject it, but it's not going to after we do something!" A short time later, as resistance continued, he added: "It seems to me that we oughta be reasonable. . . . We're gonna have to take our weapons out of Turkey" if we want to limit and contain the crisis.

McNamara would have none of it and continued to insist that a more immediate issue was what to do now that U.S. planes had been fired on—and a decision would have to made within twenty-four hours. "Either we decide not to send them in at all or we decide to send them in with proper cover. If we send them in with proper cover and they're attacked, we must attack back, either the SAMs and/or MiG aircraft that come against them or the ground fire that comes up. . . . My main point is," McNamara continued, "I don't think at this particular point we should show a weakness to Khrushchev" on either continuing air surveillance or on using force on the blockade. The president, although recognizing that McNamara might be right, turned again to his preferred course of action: "Now let's get on to the Turkish thing. . . . we oughta . . . begin a negotiation with the Turks now."

Startling news soon arrived that a U-2 had been shot down by a SAM missile over Cuba—and the pilot, Major Rudolf Anderson, killed. The shock in the room is palpable on the tape. "How do we interpret this?" the president asked. McNamara admitted, "I don't know how to interpret it." The defense chief nonetheless declared emphatically, "if we're gonna carry out surveillance each day, we must be prepared to fire each day." "We can't very well send a U-2 over there," President Kennedy acknowledged, "and have a guy killed again tomorrow."

"I think that we oughta announce," the president finally instructed, "that action's being taken to protect our aircraft." "Exactly," McNamara asserted; "Then we oughta go in at dawn and take out that SAM site. And we oughta . . . be prepared to take out more SAM sites and knock out the aircraft." The president agreed only to announce that the U-2 had been shot down and that subsequent flights would be protected, but he also added a striking coda: "Then we'll go back to what we're gonna do about the Turks and NATO." Nervously tapping on the table, he again insisted on immediately consulting with the Turks: "We need to explain to them what's happening over here. Otherwise, we're gonna be carrying a hell of a bag."

President Kennedy soon left the room, and McNamara took the opportunity to press his resistance to a Turkish deal. "We must be in a position to attack quickly. We've been fired on today! . . . So we must be prepared to attack Cuba. . . . with an all-out attack, . . . and I personally believe that this is almost certain to lead to an invasion." And, he added ominously, "If the Soviet Union attacks the Turkish missiles, . . . we must respond." He stopped short of suggesting that this tit-for-tat scenario for military escalation could easily end in global nuclear war.

McNamara complained that even if the trade offer was accepted, Khrushchev might delay or try to alter it; then "nothing happens and we're losing airplanes." "Lemme go back a second," the usually business-like defense secretary burst out, his stress and frustration erupting: "When I read that message of last night this morning, I thought, my God! I'd never base a transaction on that contract. Hell, that's no offer! There's not a damn thing in it that's an offer! You read that message carefully—he didn't propose to take the missiles out. There isn't a single word in it that proposes to take the missiles out. It's twelve pages of fluff."

John McCone, however, echoing an earlier JFK remark, pointed out that "his message this morning wasn't that way—his public message." McNamara repeated that he was referring to the Friday message: "The last-night message was twelve pages of fluff. That's no contract. You couldn't sign that and say we know what we signed." Then he exploded again: "And before," he clapped his hands for emphasis, "we got the damned thing read, the whole deal changed, completely changed!"

Near the conclusion of the late evening meeting on October 27, after RFK had met with Ambassador Dobrynin and made the secret Cuba-Turkey trade offer, McNamara again exhorted the president, "This time we would make it perfectly clear if they attack our aircraft, we're going in after some of their MiGs," regardless of the consequences. As the discussion finally wound down, an obviously exhausted McNamara asked Robert Kennedy, "Got any doubts?" "No," the attorney general responded, "I think we're doin' the only thing we can do." "I think the one thing, Bobby," McNamara added, "we must surely do is before we attack them, you've gotta be damned sure they [the U.S.S.R.] understand it's coming. In other words, you need to really escalate this." "Yeah," RFK murmured. "And then we need to have two things ready," McNamara added, "a government for Cuba, because we're gonna need one after we go in with five hundred aircraft. And secondly, some plans for how to respond to the Soviet Union in Europe, 'cause sure as hell they're gonna do something there."

The final resolution of the crisis, which of course included the secret Cuba-Turkey missile trade opposed by McNamara and virtually the entire ExComm, will be thoroughly discussed in Chapter 9, on the Trollope ploy myth. However, Robert McNamara's personal myth, that "I was trying to help [President Kennedy] keep us out of war," can no longer be taken seriously after listening to the ExComm tape recordings.

5 The Forgotten Voice of Dean Rusk

> There's no such thing, I think, as unilateral action by the United
> States.
>
> —Dean Rusk, October 16, 1962

I N DECEMBER 1960, President-elect Kennedy announced the appointment of career diplomat Dean Rusk as secretary of state. JFK had considered several much better-known possibilities, such as Senate Foreign Relations Committee chairman J. William Fulbright, but ultimately settled on Rusk because he really intended, in determining policy, to be his own secretary of state. Indeed, one Washington insider concluded at the time that Rusk was simply "the lowest common denominator."[1] The relationship between the president and the nation's top diplomat always remained cordial and proper, but never approached the familiarity enjoyed by Sorensen, Bundy, or McNamara.

Almost from the start, stories circulated in Washington that the president was dissatisfied with Rusk, particularly after the secretary's reportedly contradictory advice in the run-up to the Bay of Pigs disaster. But it was eventually Rusk's alleged conduct during the Cuban missile crisis that sealed his reputation as a conventional bureaucrat who lacked fresh ideas and "would sit quietly by, with his Buddha-like face and half-smile, often leaving it to Bundy or to the President himself to assert the diplomatic interest."[2] Looking back, it now seems obvious that Rusk, like Adlai Stevenson, was a poor fit for the tough, alpha-male, best-and-brightest image that typified media and public perceptions of the youthful new administration.

Robert Kennedy's hostility to Rusk was a topic of Washington gossip long before the publication of *Thirteen Days*—particularly as the likely source of persistent rumors that Rusk would be dumped after JFK's reelection in 1964. But it was in that slender volume, and in his private papers, that RFK really zeroed in on the still incumbent secretary of state. Bobby declared that Rusk had initially been in favor of air strikes at the ExComm meetings, but after that he was generally silent or missing: "he had other duties during this period of time and frequently could not attend our meetings."

RFK even went so far as to claim that because Rusk was absent so often, he lost the opportunity, as the senior cabinet officer, to chair the meetings; as a direct result, the participants spoke as equals and "the conversations were completely uninhibited and unrestricted. . . . a tremendously advantageous procedure that does not frequently occur within the executive branch of the government, where rank is often so important."[3] In fact, the president himself was implicitly recognized as the senior authority at the meetings, and he clearly encouraged open discussion. Nonetheless, in Bobby Kennedy's view, Rusk's most significant contribution to the ExComm was the fortuitous result of his frequent absence from the meetings. This accusation has become part of the accepted lore of the missile crisis. Only months after the publication of *Thirteen Days*, for example, former secretary of state Dean Acheson sneered, "One wonders what those 'other duties and responsibilities' were, to have been half so important as those they displaced."[4]

What indeed could have been half as important as dealing with the very real possibility of nuclear war! There is, however, one major problem with this claim about Rusk's frequent absence from the White House meetings: *it is flatly untrue!* There were twenty ExComm meetings convened by the president between October 16 and October 29. Dean Rusk attended nineteen; the only one he failed to attend was on the evening of October 18 when he was required to host a dinner at the State Department for Soviet foreign minister Andrei Gromyko, who had met with the president earlier in the day. (Rusk also missed part of the morning meeting on October 23 because he was at OAS headquarters in Washington on one of the most difficult diplomatic assignments of that week: negotiating a unanimous vote in favor of the blockade.)

The vast majority of the nineteen ExComm meetings Rusk participated in were recorded, and his presence and contributions are indisputable. (The notes from the unrecorded meetings are equally authoritative about Rusk's participation.) The notion that Rusk's frequent absence somehow enabled the meetings to become open and spontaneous is, at best, disingenuous nonsense.

As this chapter will demonstrate, Rusk was himself a major contributor to that "uninhibited and unrestricted" atmosphere.

The ExComm participants, RFK also declared, were "men of the highest intelligence, industrious, courageous, and dedicated to their country's well-being. It is no reflection on them that none was consistent in his opinion from the very beginning to the very end. That kind of open, unfettered mind was essential." But he also suggested that there was a dark side—weakness—displayed during the crisis, alleging that "some, because of the pressure of events, even appeared to lose their judgment and stability."[5] Three years before making this generic charge in *Thirteen Days*, however, Bobby Kennedy, in an oral history interview, had specifically identified Rusk as having "had a complete breakdown mentally and physically" during the Cuban missile crisis.[6]

Rusk's three children (particularly the two who were teenagers living in Washington with their parents in 1962) recall that their father was calm but somber and preoccupied during the crisis and that afterwards he immediately returned to his normal routine at the State Department; there was never a hint of any kind of physical or mental breakdown.[7] If such a collapse had indeed occurred—and nothing of that kind remains secret very long in the sieve that is Washington, D.C.—it is inconceivable that JFK and later LBJ would have retained Rusk as secretary of state for eight years (the second-longest term in U.S. history).[8] In short, there is not a shred of evidence from the tapes or any other official, public, or private source to substantiate this rather nasty piece of character assassination.

Finally, Bobby Kennedy rebuked Rusk for failing to do his job as the nation's highest-ranking diplomat by articulating and defending the diplomatic perspective at the ExComm meetings. RFK even claimed to have asked Rusk why he had resisted carrying out this key responsibility; the secretary of state allegedly replied that he had wanted to prevent the group from "moving too far or too fast." "He said he had been playing the role of the 'dumb dodo' for this reason. I thought it was a strange way of putting it."[9] The alleged "dumb dodo" remark is ubiquitous on the Internet and almost invariably cited as if it were Rusk's personal assessment of his own role in the ExComm meetings—rather than RFK's completely unsubstantiated allegation. Rusk's children, however, do not recall ever hearing their father use the term "dodo" or "dumb dodo."

In the context of the well-known friction between Rusk and RFK, it seems implausible that the secretary of state would have made such a demeaning statement about himself to someone he neither liked nor trusted—particularly since the charge is completely fictitious. In fact, Rusk *constantly* injected the diplomatic perspective into the meetings, doggedly stressing that unilateral action was impossible for a nation that had treaty commitments to more than forty allies. If anything, his colleagues often felt that he spoke too often and too long about the diplomatic viewpoint. As McGeorge Bundy later recalled, "None of us could suppose that he [Rusk] was insensitive to the interests of our allies, and none could think him eager to make unwise concessions to Soviet pressure."[10]

In the early 1980s, the former members of the ExComm were informed by the Kennedy Library that the tapes from the first day of the secret meetings would soon be declassified. I happened to be in the office of the library's director, Dan Fenn, when the usually imperturbable Dean Rusk called to vent his anger at having been recorded without his knowledge. Now, ironically, it is those tapes that allow historians to differentiate Rusk's actual contribution from Robert Kennedy's incomplete, misleading, and biased account.

～

Rusk spoke up for the first time on the morning of October 16 after viewing the photos of the Soviet missile deployment in Cuba and listening to the initial reactions of the president and his ExComm colleagues. "There's no such thing," he pointed out, "I think, as unilateral action by the United States." Any confrontation with the U.S.S.R. over Cuba would inevitably impact all of America's forty-plus allies around the world. "So I think we have to think very hard" about surprise air strikes or an invasion. But he also recommended a diplomatic alternative, a direct contact with Castro through the U.N. to warn that the U.S.S.R. "was preparing Cuba for destruction or betrayal" by floating hints about giving up its base in Cuba if the U.S. abandoned West Berlin. In fact, the Kennedy administration treated Cuba as little more than "an afterthought" and made no effort to deal directly with Castro. The Canadian ambassador to the U.S. informed Rusk that Cuba "was prepared at any time to negotiate its differences with the USA." But the secretary of state dismissed the offer on the grounds that Castro was "'a total instrument of Moscow.'"[11]

Rusk's proposal for diplomatic contact was certainly not the result of concern for Castro's survival: he also urged increased aerial surveillance of Cuba, a reinforcement of U.S. personnel at the Guantánamo naval base, and a more vigorous commitment to the U.S.-backed guerrilla forces working to "create maximum confusion on the island. We won't be too squeamish at this point about the overt/covert character of what is being done." (One of the most ironic elements in the missile crisis was the presence of the American naval installation at Guantánamo Bay, on the southeastern tip of Cuba, guaranteed by a 1934 treaty. Castro had been warned, after diplomatic relations were broken early in 1961, not to interfere with the operation of the base.)

The secretary of state, notwithstanding, kept a constant eye on the need for diplomatic communication to prevent a potentially fatal misunderstanding and stressed the need to alert "our allies and Mr. Khrushchev that there is an utterly serious crisis in the making here . . . because Mr. Khrushchev may not himself really understand that or believe that at this point. . . . We have an obligation to do what has to be done, but to do it in a way that gives everybody a chance to pull away from it before it gets too hard." If the Russians "shoot those missiles," Rusk stressed—before, during, or after American air strikes—"we're in a general nuclear war."

The president raised the issue of Soviet motives in Cuba and speculated that Khrushchev's maneuver might be a reaction to the fact of overall American nuclear superiority. Rusk took the argument one step further, suggesting that the deployment in Cuba might reflect Khrushchev's emotional resentment about American missiles in Turkey and Italy: he "may feel that it's important for us to learn about living under medium-range missiles and he's doing that to sort of balance that political, psychological flank." No one, however, raised the possibility that the missiles might be, at least in Khrushchev's mind, defensive—an effort to protect Cuba against a second Kennedy administration-sponsored invasion.

Rusk was conscientiously acting out his role as the nation's senior diplomat, repeatedly urging his colleagues to consider the impact of the Cuban crisis on international relations and even expressing sympathy for NATO's anxiety about being exposed to "all these great dangers without the slightest consultation, or warning, or preparation." And, he cautioned, "we could find ourselves isolated and the alliance crumbling." He also kept the Berlin issue at the center of the discussion, asserting grimly, "I'm beginning really to wonder whether Mr. Khrushchev is entirely rational about Berlin." He expressed doubt that the Soviets would actually use nuclear weapons in Cuba against the United States, but conceded bleakly, "we could be just utterly wrong." The secretary later returned to the State Department for further discussions which lasted until almost midnight.

Forty-eight hours later, on Thursday, October 18, after intelligence updates indicated that the work on the sites was proceeding rapidly, Rusk explained that the situation appeared to be more serious than he had originally thought; this new information, he announced, "changes my thinking on the matter." The Soviet buildup was not "just an incidental base for a few of these things" but "a formidable military problem," and failure to act "would undermine our alliances all over the world, very promptly." The secretary of state read from the president's explicit September 4 warning to the Soviets that "the gravest issues would arise" if offensive nuclear weapons were shipped to Cuba, and virtually challenged JFK to live up to his words. "If we do nothing," the Soviets "would consider this a major back-down" and would conclude "that they've got it made as far as intimidating the United States is concerned."

But Rusk also continued to urge prudence as well as preparedness; military action against Cuba, he counseled, "involves very high risks indeed" of Soviet reprisals around the world—in Berlin, in Korea, or even "against the United States itself." If the administration challenged the Soviet decision to embark "upon this fantastically dangerous course," he warned, "no one can surely foresee the outcome." He predicted that the American people would back military action if they believed that everything possible had been done to avoid it. The secretary therefore recommended further "consultation with Khrushchev." He thought it unlikely that the Soviets would back down, but the effort "might have in it the seeds of prevention of a great conflict." He also suggested the possibility of a declaration of national emergency or even a declaration of war on Cuba. But when the president hinted at the possibility of a Cuba-Turkey missile exchange, Rusk objected that such a move "would be quite serious." He then summed up the administration's dilemma: Khrushchev might feel obligated to respond militarily but could be deterred because he knew the U.S. would respond in kind. "Or maybe he's a little crazy," Rusk hypothesized, "and we can't trust him."

In the later discussion about whether a surprise attack on Cuba was consistent with American values and traditions, Rusk found himself in rare agreement with Bobby Kennedy, who had suddenly expressed belated reservations about attacking a small country without warning. The secretary of state, at ease with biblical imagery, assured the president that warning the Soviets would be preferable to "carrying the mark of Cain on your brow for the rest of your lives." But, he insisted, since the president would be taking political risks by giving an advance notification, Khrushchev would be expected, "in order to keep the fig leaf on for the President," to cease work on the bases and withdraw Soviet missile technicians.

Rusk also urged the president to repeat the warning he had issued in September when later that day he met with Soviet foreign minister Andrei Gromyko: "See if he will lie about it," he proposed coyly, clearly hoping to catch his Russian counterpart in a brazen deception. Robert Kennedy expressed concern that Gromyko might argue that the Soviet missiles in Cuba were no more offensive than the U.S. missiles in Turkey—"Then what do you do?" In fact, several members of the Kennedy administration had warned in private about a dangerous American "double standard" toward missiles in Turkey versus missiles in Cuba. Rusk firmly rejected the comparison, insisting that the Jupiter decision was made in the context of the NATO alliance "as a result of Stalin's policies. It makes all the difference in the world."[12] He also speculated that "They must know now that we know. They're working around the clock down there."

When RFK subsequently ridiculed the notion that a blockade could bring down Castro, Rusk countered that a blockade accompanied by limited air strikes "would be a pretty good sized wallop [and] . . . a minimum in any event, wouldn't it?" Rusk's position, therefore, during the first days of the ExComm meetings was clearly far more complex and nuanced than RFK's simplistic claim that he simply supported air strikes on the missile sites. That evening, as the ExComm met secretly in the White House living quarters, the secretary of state hosted the dinner for his Soviet counterpart, Andrei Gromyko. One can only imagine the contrast between the contrived words of the diplomatic toasts and the private thoughts of the guests at that awkward event.

Several key meetings were held at the State Department and in the Oval Room in the White House living quarters between Friday afternoon, October 19, and Sunday afternoon, October 21. The most important result of those (unrecorded) meetings was the president's final decision to respond, at least initially, to the Soviet missile deployment in Cuba with a blockade. By the time the full ExComm reconvened in the Cabinet Room, on the morning of Monday, October 22, attention had shifted to writing the president's letter to Khrushchev and refining his speech to the nation later that evening.

Secretary Rusk, again emphasizing the diplomatic track, proposed a possible United Nations role in supervising the removal of nuclear missiles from any country that was not a nuclear power, which in effect meant Cuba, Turkey, and Italy. The president seemed interested and added, "Why don't we go all the way? That gives us an excuse to get 'em out of Turkey and Italy? . . . We're much better off if they're removed. . . . I think we oughta be looking to the day when they're removed from Cuba, Italy, and Turkey." JFK had considered several recommendations early in 1961 for substituting submarine-launched Polaris missiles for the Jupiters in Turkey. But the Turks had "objected vigorously," and the Vienna summit and the resulting tensions over Berlin essentially settled the issue. "Kennedy at least theoretically had an opportunity to cancel the deployment, since construction had not yet begun when he entered office. He seriously considered doing so and yet deliberately decided to go ahead." The Jupiters were deployed to preserve American credibility despite widespread feelings in both the Eisenhower and Kennedy administrations that they were completely unreliable.[13]

JFK also raised the possibility of including warships from OAS nations on the quarantine patrol line, but Rusk pointed out rather caustically, "Our armed forces think only Americans can fight!" The secretary also backed the president's determination to make absolutely clear to the JCS that American personnel in Turkey were not to fire the Jupiter missiles at the Soviet Union, even if attacked, without a direct presidential order, because they might erroneously conclude that "a nuclear war is already on."

That afternoon the Joint Chiefs joined the ExComm meeting, and Rusk clearly had their presence in mind when he cautioned that "if any of our colleagues think that this is, in any sense, a weak action, I think we can be quite sure that in a number of hours we'll have a flaming crisis on our hands. This is gonna go very far, and possibly very fast."

The president was still concerned that critics might ask why the administration had decided not to attack the missiles. RFK advised sticking to "the Pearl Harbor thing," but Rusk suggested emphasizing the diplomatic obligation to consult with the OAS and the U.N. before taking any action. The secretary of state also urged the president to point out publicly that the missiles in Cuba represented "a special threat" to the United States and the forty-one allies all over the world who were dependent on American "nuclear support." He insisted that a deployment "of this magnitude is not something that we can brush aside simply because the Soviets have some other missiles that could also reach the United States." The missiles in Cuba "would double the known missile strength the Soviet Union has to reach this country." In fact, American intelligence had significantly overestimated the number of ICBMs in the U.S.S.R. The Cuban deployment was even more numerically significant than Rusk knew at the time.[14]

President Kennedy, always mindful of Soviet pressure in Berlin, wanted to be prepared to undercut any effort by the U.S.S.R. to characterize the Cuban quarantine as an aggressive action; unlike the Soviet Berlin blockade in 1948, it affected only offensive weapons and did not stop food or medicine or threaten war. "But the central point here is," Rusk asserted firmly, "that we're in Berlin by right as well as by the acknowledgment and agreement of the Soviet Union. They're bringing these things into Cuba contrary to the Rio Pact. There's just all the difference in the world between these two situations." The president was impressed by this argument and seemed confident that the administration could make a convincing case in the court of world public opinion that the limited blockade of Cuba was not comparable to the Berlin blockade.

With only a few hours remaining until his 7:00 P.M. speech, the president, joined by Rusk, McNamara, Thompson, and McCone, met with the leaders of Congress to inform them (not consult them) about the blockade decision. Rusk emphasized that the buildup in Cuba was "a major and radical move in Soviet policy and Soviet action." The U.S.S.R., he pointed out, had never placed missiles outside of their own territory, not even in the satellite states of Eastern Europe. (American officials did not know at the time that the Soviet Union had deployed nuclear missiles, very briefly and secretly, in East Germany in 1959.) He also noted that Soviet policy had become tougher over the past year, and labeled the Cuban gamble the most "reckless and hazardous" Soviet move since the Berlin blockade of 1948–49.

Soviet policy makers, he reasoned, had decided that the "peaceful-coexistence theme was not getting them very far," and the missiles in Cuba suggested the clear ascendancy of "the hard-line boys" in the Kremlin. Perhaps anticipating congressional accusations that the president's decision was too little and too late, Rusk stressed that the blockade was only a first step, a diplomatic pause to allow "the people on the other side to have another thought before we get into an utterly crashing crisis, because the prospects that are ahead of us at this moment are very serious." Since Khrushchev had surely underestimated the American response, he continued, "a brief pause here is very important in order to give the Soviets a chance to pull back from the brink here," before this becomes "a very grave matter indeed." Rusk was the *only* ExComm participant, other than the president, to persistently refer to the possibility that the crisis in Cuba could rapidly escalate to nuclear war.

At 6:00 P.M., an hour before President Kennedy addressed the nation, Secretary Rusk met with Soviet ambassador Dobrynin and handed him an advance copy of the president's speech and a cover letter from JFK to Khrushchev. He warned Dobrynin that the U.S.S.R. had made a serious miscalculation and later recalled that the ambassador seemed to age "ten years in front of my eyes." Dobrynin reportedly looked sick as he left the State Department.

Rusk briefed the diplomatic corps later that evening. "I would not be candid and I would not be fair with you," he admitted, "if I did not say that we are in as grave a crisis as mankind has been in." In the early morning hours, after another exhausting day, Rusk and Harlan Cleveland, assistant secretary of state for international organization affairs, prepared to go home to get a few hours of sleep. Cleveland dropped his boss off at his home, wished him a good night, and casually remarked, "I'll see you in the morning." Rusk replied, "I hope so." Cleveland later recalled that he had been so busy that "the full enormity" of the situation "hadn't hit me until that moment." These somber words, coming from the usually reticent and unflappable Rusk, struck Cleveland as the emotional "equivalent of screaming."[15]

The following morning, October 23, with the crisis finally public, the president and his advisers discussed how to orchestrate support for the blockade at home and especially in Europe by displaying selected U-2 photographs at the U.N. debate and contacting influential journalists and key congressional Republicans. They also reviewed contingency plans, if the blockade should fail, for bombing the missiles sites and the SAM sites (if a U-2 was shot down) and for invading Cuba.

Late in the meeting, however, Dean Rusk abruptly returned from the emergency session of the Organization of American States. The secretary, uncharacteristically ebullient, announced, "we'll have the resolution, with a large majority, by shortly after three." Several ExComm members exclaimed, "Oh, gee," "Wonderful," "Oh, God," and "Oh, terrific, terrific." Rusk mentioned that he had told several OAS delegates that the resolution was vital since there could be naval contact that afternoon. McNamara observed that the quarantine could therefore begin at dawn tomorrow. "Yeah, but don't tell them that," Rusk joked, since he had pressured the OAS with the specter of contact within hours. "No," McNamara replied against a background of laughter. The quarantine actually went into effect at 10:00 A.M. on the following morning.

The secretary, becoming somewhat more subdued, admonished his enthusiastic colleagues, "Don't smile too soon here, boys"; but a relieved Alexis

Johnson exclaimed that if the OAS voted before the Security Council meeting later that day, "Oh, that's gonna be a big help. Mmm. Pshewwwww. Our diplomacy is working." Rusk nonetheless reflected soberly: "Well, my God! . . . I think it was very significant that we were here this morning. We've passed the one contingency: an immediate, sudden, irrational [nuclear] strike [by the U.S.S.R.]." Rusk later recalled waking up that morning and saying to himself, "'Well, I'm still here. This is very interesting.'" The immediate response of the Soviet Union to the president's speech had not been a nuclear first strike.[16] Everyone understood his relief that they had all lived to see another day. Alexis Johnson exulted, "Oh gee, that's great. Oh, that's great news. That's terrific. We really caught them with their contingencies down." Rusk's optimism was soon confirmed when the OAS unanimously endorsed the quarantine proclamation.

Even Robert Kennedy, talking privately with his brother just hours after the OAS vote, declared, "you got all the South American countries and Central American countries to vote unanimously [for the resolution] when they kicked us in the ass for two years." Now, RFK reasoned, if shots had to be fired across the bow or a ship had to be disabled and boarded, "It's not just the United States doing it." It is important to note that he gives all the credit for this diplomatic coup to "you," that is, the president. In *Thirteen Days*, Bobby Kennedy also praised the OAS for its "unique sense of unity" and noted that several nations "contributed men, supplies, and ships during the several weeks that followed."[17] In neither case did he mention the pivotal role of Dean Rusk.

The ExComm reconvened later on the evening of October 23 as the president prepared to sign the quarantine proclamation. McNamara, however, raised a particularly tricky question: whether to pursue and board a Soviet ship which had turned and headed away from Cuba. "I don't believe," he advised, "we should undertake such an operation." The president promptly agreed, but RFK countered forcefully that the ships turning around were very likely the ones carrying prohibited weapons; they should be boarded, he urged, in order to photograph and investigate Soviet military hardware.

Rusk protested that the diplomatic disadvantages of boarding a ship that had reversed course far outweighed the value of any potential military intelligence. The diplomatic problem, he rather patronizingly lectured the attorney general, is "that from the Soviet point of view they're gonna be as sensitive as a boil because it's whether they think we're really trying to capture and seize and analyze and examine their missiles and their warheads and things. Now the purpose [of the blockade] is to keep 'em out of Cuba. This adds a very important element into it, you see" and would contravene the announced, legal purpose of the blockade. As RFK likely bristled, the president chose to defer any decision until after the blockade had actually gone into effect. This disagreement, which resurfaced the next day, was likely a factor in RFK's hostility to Rusk. No one else differed with Bobby Kennedy so openly, directly, or often at the ExComm meetings.

The secretary of state's attempt to avoid unnecessary provocations was undoubtedly based on the latest intelligence reports—which were not encouraging. "We've had no indications," he told the president, "of any Soviet instructions . . . in any way to pull away. . . . Just the converse." JFK decided to wait for at least twenty-four hours after the quarantine went into effect before making a decision. "I think," he concluded bleakly, "we're gonna have all our troubles [starting] tomorrow morning."

The president and his advisers gathered in the Cabinet Room the next morning (Wednesday, October 24) at virtually the moment that the quarantine proclamation, signed fifteen hours earlier, became legally operational. Rusk revealed that the most recent intelligence intercept had indicated that Cuban forces had been instructed not to fire at surveillance aircraft except in self-defense; he also suggested that in spite of the Kremlin's threats to resist U.S. efforts to stop Soviet ships, Khrushchev's "public line seems designed to leave him with some option to back off if he chooses." Nonetheless, he advised, it seemed probable that the Soviets would risk an incident at sea on the assumption that heightened tensions would increase international pressure on the U.S. to end the quarantine. In short, they had not yet decided whether to seek a diplomatic compromise or "whether to risk escalation."

News soon arrived from the Office of Naval Intelligence "that all six Soviet ships currently identified in Cuban waters . . . have either stopped or reversed course." President Kennedy, obviously skeptical, cut in to ask, "Why don't we find out whether they're talking about the ships leaving Cuba or the ones coming in?" Rusk quipped, "Makes some difference," and some edgy laughter can be heard at the table. The secretary also revisited a point he had disputed with the attorney general at the previous evening's meeting: he acknowledged that circumstances might change later but insisted that the administration had "to be quite clear what the object of this present exercise is: it is to stop these weapons from going to Cuba. It is not to capture them for ourselves at this stage. It is not to do anything other than keep 'em from going to Cuba."

Bobby Kennedy, curiously silent about the very issue he had contested with Rusk the previous day, then asked whether the new information about the ships reversing course was being supplied to the navy. Rusk, in a rare moment of agreement with RFK, affirmed, "Yeah, we better be sure the Navy knows that they're not supposed to pursue these ships."

That evening the president and his advisers met for the second time in two days with the congressional leadership. Rusk first reviewed the international diplomatic scene. He observed that despite remarks as "bitter and as violent as ever," the Soviets seemed "to go to some pains to keep the finger on the Cuban-U.S. aspects of the matter rather than the U.S.S.R.-U.S. aspects of the matter." He also noted that the state-controlled press in the Soviet Union, perhaps trying to avoid "war scares there," had apparently not revealed the presence of the Cuban missiles to their own people. "We do think," he cautioned, "although the situation is highly critical and dangerous, that it is not frozen in any inevitable way at this point."

Senator Richard Russell, one of the blockade's harshest congressional critics, acknowledged the importance of the OAS resolution: "Mr. President," Although I have been "at times highly critical of the State Department, I would like to take this opportunity to heartily congratulate the Secretary of State on what I regard as a magnificent triumph in the Organization of American States on yesterday—and rather lost sight of in all of the momentous march of events. But I thought it was a tremendous job. . . . I never would have believed it could've been done."

Rusk thanked Russell (the senior senator from his home state of Georgia) and assured the congressional leaders that the State Department would continue to watch Soviet reactions very closely "to see what is likely to happen," but he admitted, "I don't think I can give a definitive view today as to what the real attitude of the Soviet Union is on this matter. Our best judgment," he added rather colorfully, "is that they are scratching their brains very hard at the present time, deciding just exactly how they want to play this, what they want to do about it."

In Moscow, after the implementation of the quarantine, Khrushchev, unbeknownst to anyone in Washington, had begun to prepare for a calculated retreat from the nuclear abyss. "Moscow would have to find another way to protect Fidel Castro" by offering to remove the missiles in exchange for an American pledge not to invade Cuba and by ultimately allowing U.N. inspection of the missile sites. After the Presidium had approved this new initiative, Khrushchev announced, "'Comrades, let's go to the Bolshoi Theater this evening. Our own people as well as foreign eyes will notice, and perhaps it will calm them down.'" He later acknowledged, however, "We were trying to disguise our own anxiety, which was intense."[18]

Twenty-four hours after the quarantine had gone into effect, the ExComm met again. After a lively discussion, most participants agreed that it was unwise, as a first step in enforcing the quarantine, to stop and board a tanker. "From my point of view," Rusk reasoned, "a tanker is not the best example," since petroleum, oil, and lubricants (POL) were not on the contraband list and there was no suspicious cargo visible on deck, and "there's not much room for them beneath deck." JFK agreed that this strategy would give the administration more time, and Rusk added that it would also avoid provoking an incident at sea during the current diplomatic negotiations at the U.N.

On the other hand, the fact that several ships appeared to have turned around raised hopes that the Soviet leader was rethinking his official hard-line stance. Rusk advised being very careful about giving the general impression that most ships had turned back because if the navy grabbed one, "it will put the bee on us for being—" "Warmongers," the president muttered, finishing Rusk's sentence. JFK also ruminated that it was politically risky to make too much of the ships that had evidently reversed direction: "I don't want a sense of euphoria passing around," he counseled. "That message of Khrushchev is much tougher than that." He added, "We first wanna get the test case to be a better one than a tanker."

McNamara nonetheless revived "the idea you had, Bobby, that you go out there and if it turns around, you board it anyhow." RFK again endorsed the proposal, but Rusk, for the third time, reiterated the diplomatic objections: if "it has radioed Moscow that it has turned around and it's still boarded, that's bad. Isn't our purpose to turn it around without shooting, if we can?" Even the normally combative assistant defense secretary, Paul Nitze, agreed with Rusk: "I think Dean is right"; if the ships indeed turn around, "that's fine," but those that reach the blockade must be inspected.

"Is there a political advantage," the president asked, "in stretching this thing out? That's really the question. Are we gonna get anything out of the U.N. or Khrushchev?" Rusk tried to clarify U Thant's U.N. proposal: a simultaneous moratorium on the introduction of missiles to Cuba and a suspension of the blockade. JFK was convinced that "We're not gonna get anyplace with this thing" but reluctantly agreed to give the U.N. some more time so that "it doesn't make us look quite as negative." He seemed eager to fix the blame for the probable failure of the U.N. peace plan on U Thant: "I'd rather stick the cat on his back. . . . We can't take the quarantine off until he offers a substitute and he hasn't offered a substitute." And, he added, the U.N. plan did nothing about the removal of the missiles already in Cuba.

The secretary of state shifted the focus of the meeting to another diplomatic initiative, which he called "a very interesting possibility"—a Brazilian proposal to declare Latin America a nuclear-free zone. The president seemed cool to the idea, asking for clarification on whether they meant "nuclear-free" or "missile-free" and pointing out that the U.S. had proof of missiles in Cuba but no verification of nuclear warheads. "I just wanted to mention this possibility," Rusk explained, "because this could create an enormous pressure in the [U.N. General] Assembly and around the world, and I think on the Soviet Union, on the presence of these weapons in Cuba." President Kennedy, evidently not very interested, changed the subject.

Paul Nitze intervened to urge the president to ignore the distinctions between ships and fully enforce "the principle of a blockade . . . I think that would be the easiest in the end." But Rusk urged caution, "because in the circumstances, it's already escalated very, very fast." The president finally decided: "We don't want to precipitate an incident" and set off military escalation. "So let's think a little more about it."

The ongoing and unresolved concerns about how to handle and enforce the blockade carried over into the October 25 evening meeting. McNamara recommended letting a passenger ship through rather than risk the political fallout from possible civilian casualties. The defense chief offered an alternative: intercepting "a Soviet tanker with a deck cargo," which should arrive by midday tomorrow. "And I would *strongly* recommend we do just that." The president seemed receptive, but Bobby Kennedy insisted that the real issue was the continuing buildup in Cuba. Instead, he reopened the issue of bombing the missile sites after all. That was the only way, he argued, to demonstrate continued American toughness with Cuba.

No one openly endorsed reviving the bombing option. Rusk's reaction was restrained but unmistakably critical. "When you really step back and look at it for a second . . . the quarantine is now fully effective." Several voices can be heard affirming, "That's right" or "That's correct." RFK promptly backed off, essentially conceding Rusk's point. "If you wanted to really wait," he admitted, the effectiveness of the blockade provided an excuse, "without losing face." Moments later RFK even added, "It's a hell of a thing, really, when you think of it, that fifteen ships have turned back. And I don't think we really have any apologies to make." "Mr. President," Rusk admitted somewhat diffidently, "since I recommended a blockade, I haven't been very helpful about applying it in particular instances." But he repeated that seizing either a tanker or a passenger ship as "our first case" was risky and dangerous. "If the Navy fired on, disabled or sank" a tanker or a passenger ship, he warned, "I think we're just in a hell of a shape."

The president finally cut through the increasingly circular discussion. He ruled out stopping the passenger ship and decided in addition to give Khrushchev two more days before stopping a tanker, because U Thant's U.N. initiative held out at least a small "chance of easing this." But JFK also edged closer to RFK's much tougher stance: "I think if the work continues, we either have to do this air business" or add POL to the quarantine, "because we got to begin to bring counter pressure because otherwise the work's going on and we're not really doin' anything else." RFK agreed, obviously heartened by the president's renewed determination.

By the time the ExComm convened on the following morning (Friday, October 26), a CIA report had confirmed that construction of the MRBM and IRBM sites was "proceeding without interruption."[19] Since those sites would not be affected by the quarantine in any case, additional military steps—including air attacks—remained a very real possibility. McNamara, Bundy, McCone, and General Taylor urged the president to ratchet up the quarantine. Rusk, on the other hand, counseled a twenty-four-hour delay in order to give the U Thant talks some additional time at the U.N.

The bombing option, however, revived the previous evening by RFK, picked up the support of the soft-spoken treasury secretary, Douglas Dillon; he recommended downplaying the seizure of a Soviet ship and, if construction continued, redirecting the confrontation toward Cuba "by preparing for air action to hit these bases," thus putting pressure on the U.N. "to get inspectors in there to stop this thing."

McNamara again proposed using flares to illuminate the missile bases for nighttime surveillance. Rusk urged delaying nighttime flights "until we've had a crack at the U Thant discussions." He also expressed concern that the flares might be provocative because they had been used in previous combat situations as preparation for night bombing raids: "we're not sure what the interpretation of the other side would be." McNamara insisted that the Cubans could be warned in advance about the flares; but after further discussion, JFK backed Rusk and delayed approving night surveillance flights with flares.

The secretary of state refocused the discussion on the negotiations set to resume later that morning in New York for a U.N.-sponsored moratorium on the delivery of weapons to Cuba and a concurrent suspension of the quarantine. In one of his most forceful monologues, Rusk insisted that there must be no further delivery of offensive weapons to Cuba and that the Soviets must halt the construction of missile sites and render all missiles and warheads already on Cuban soil inoperable. The only way to assure that these conditions were met, Rusk warned, and "we have to insist upon that very hard," would be to require that U.N. inspectors from neutral nations take over the sites; but, he predicted ominously, Cuba and the U.S.S.R. would strenuously resist outside inspection and "what will happen is that the Soviets will go down . . . the path of talking indefinitely, while the missile sites come into full operation. . . . And then we are nowhere."

An effective inspection effort, Rusk stressed, would require at least three hundred personnel "drawn from countries that have a capacity, a technical capacity, to know what they're looking at and . . . what measures have to be taken to insure inoperability." He listed as examples Sweden, Switzerland, and Austria, or perhaps Brazil and Canada. "We can't have Burmese or Cambodians going in there" only to be "led down the garden path" by Soviet missile experts. In addition, he contended that the quarantine must remain in place until the U.N. could set up an effective alternative, "But we would have to keep our force in the immediate background to move promptly if the UN arrangements are not trustworthy." Any final agreement, he stipulated, "must include no further arms shipments, no continued buildup and a defanging of the sites that are already there."

Rusk also reintroduced another potential diplomatic strategy for increasing political pressure on the U.S.S.R.: declaring Latin America a nuclear-free zone. The idea had gained little traction a day earlier, but the secretary further elaborated on his reasoning: if the United States could get a large percentage of the U.N. to support a nuclear-free Latin America, "you may give the other side an occasion for pulling back, because they've been supporting nuclear-free zones for years. And they may find in this a face-saving formula."

Lastly, Rusk suggested contact with Castro through the Brazilian ambassador in Havana. He speculated that if Cuba regarded the missiles as a defense against an invasion, the OAS could announce that if the missiles were removed it would refuse to sanction an invasion; and "the U.S. would not risk upsetting hemispheric solidarity by invading a Cuba so clearly committed to a peaceful course." The secretary bluntly admitted that this concluding offer "was the seduction, as far as Castro is concerned." A few moments earlier, President Kennedy had concluded, "If that's one of the prices that has to be paid to get these out of there, then we commit ourselves not to invade Cuba." Rusk firmly restated the point: if the Cubans agree to "get rid of these offensive weapons then, I assume, that it is not our purpose to invade Cuba." Nitze, Bundy, Dillon, McCone, and RFK disagreed, mainly because the Soviet-Cuban connection would remain intact and Castro might export weapons to other nations in the hemisphere. Rusk conceded that the offer to Castro "does not give assurances against any kind of rascality."

Secretary Rusk nonetheless predicted that "a major back-down" by the Soviets was extremely unlikely; and when he asked, "Have we seen a missile on a launcher?" a chorus of voices responded firmly, "Right next to it!" (The ExComm did not know that Khrushchev, as revealed by declassified Soviet documents, had ordered the nuclear warheads to be stored miles away from the missiles and the launchers.) Rusk advised the president to resist pressure to relax the quarantine until arms shipments and the buildup of missile sites and bomber facilities had ceased and the weapons had been rendered inoperable. Nonetheless, when General Taylor proposed increasing the pressure by starting night photography of Havana, Rusk cautioned again that it was still essential "to explore the political thing . . . before we put on the night photography." JFK agreed.

President Kennedy, as the meeting concluded, cited Dillon's earlier endorsement of RFK's rekindling of the bombing option, and proposed "a presentation tomorrow by the Defense Department on air action again. . . . In some ways that's more advantageous than it was even a week ago." He was becoming less confident that the Soviet Union had actually "blinked" by diverting ships carrying offensive weapons away from Cuba and seemed to be leaning toward breaking the logjam over U.N. negotiations—perhaps by bombing the missile sites after all. The ExComm hard-liners, as a consequence of the evolving diplomatic stalemate, appeared poised to potentially gain the upper hand.

Just after 6:00 P.M., a lengthy, emotional, and personal message from Khrushchev began arriving at the State Department. The "knot" of nuclear war could be untied, the chairman proposed, if the Soviet Union ceased sending armaments to Cuba and the United States pledged not to invade: "Then the necessity for the presence of our military specialists in Cuba would disappear." Khrushchev's language was elliptical, especially on verification, but his meaning seemed clear: the missiles would be removed if the United States agreed not to invade Cuba.[20]

Shortly after the ExComm convened early the following morning (Saturday, October 27), reports arrived of a new Khrushchev proposal—announced publicly over Moscow Radio—that the U.S.S.R. would remove its missiles from Cuba if the U.S. removed its missiles from Turkey. The initial confusion in the room eventually gave way to the realization, as Rusk put it, that "This appears to be something quite new." It was also a turning point for the secretary of state—who joined the hard-liners on the missile trade issue and became far more confrontational and uncompromising during the three meetings on Black Saturday.

Within minutes, in sharp exchanges with Bundy, McNamara, Nitze, and Ball, the president insisted that Khrushchev's public proposal could not be ignored or rejected. Kennedy seemed especially irritated with Rusk: "I've talked about it now for a week. Have we got any conversations in Turkey with the Turks?" The secretary of state, clearly discomfited, admitted, "We've not actually talked with the Turks."

When Ted Sorensen affirmed that "practically everyone here would favor the private [Friday] proposal," Rusk acknowledged, "We may not be offered a choice." But the secretary promptly repeated his opposition to a trade, arguing that NATO–Warsaw Pact arms represented a separate problem: "They've got hundreds of missiles looking down the throat of every NATO country. . . . The Cuba thing is a Western Hemisphere problem, an intrusion into the Western Hemisphere. . . . I think that we must insist . . . that U Thant not fall for this."

When the full text of Khrushchev's message arrived, Rusk tried to decipher the new, apparently tougher Soviet position: "I suppose the boys in Moscow decided this [earlier proposal] was too much of a setback for 'em." He also speculated that the personal and emotional Friday night letter must have been sent out "without clearance," and a consensus quickly developed that "The Politburo intended this one"—thus originating one of the most persistent misconceptions and myths associated with the missile crisis. Rusk also predicted that Turkey would publicly reject the withdrawal of the Jupiter missiles.

Later that afternoon, at the meeting that began around 4:00 P.M., Rusk candidly expressed hope for "a revolt in NATO" against removing the Jupiters from Turkey, and urged giving U Thant some more time "to work on the original [Friday] track if possible." He also expressed doubt about whether the Turkish scheme in Khrushchev's latest letter was intended as "a real sticking point up to the point of shooting with them" or merely "an attempt at the last minute to try to get something more after they had indicated last night they will settle for something less."

Rusk also proposed new language for JFK's message to Khrushchev in order to deal with the latest Moscow offer: "As I was preparing this letter," he read, "I learned of your broadcast message today. That message raises problems affecting many countries and complicated issues not related to Cuba or the Western Hemisphere. The United States would be glad to discuss these matters with you and other governments concerned. The immediate crisis is in Cuba and it is there that very prompt action is necessary. With that behind us, we can make progress on other and wider issues."

President Kennedy recognized at once that Rusk's proposed language did *not* reflect his own persistent stance in favor of a possible Turkey-Cuba missile trade—his advisers appeared to be trying a rather transparent end run around his position. JFK's pique about these stalling tactics had begun to intensify: "Well, isn't that really rejecting their proposal of this morning?" he quickly countered. "I wouldn't think so," Rusk replied. JFK responded firmly. "If we go reject it, I think we ought to have all of NATO rejecting it." Rusk nonetheless persisted, "Mr. President, if NATO seems solid on this [rejecting the Cuba-Turkey linkage], this has a chance of shaking Khrushchev off this point."

The secretary proposed, as a possible alternative to the trade, that "the missiles in Cuba and the missiles in Turkey be turned over to the U.N. for destruction." The president ignored the idea and reiterated, "I think the real problem is what we do with the Turks first." Rusk then suggested "shaking Khrushchev off this position of this morning" by calling up additional military units, declaring a state of national emergency, and initiating some mobilization both at home and in NATO. He also stressed that Ambassador Stevenson and U Thant might still work out an agreement at the U.N. without bringing Turkey into the discussion and reminded the president that the Turks had already rejected (in 1961) substituting Polaris missiles for the Jupiters; "the Turkish reaction was, 'Well, the missiles are here and as long as they're here, you're here.'" The secretary of state clearly intended to keep an awareness of the diplomatic perspective of America's allies front and center at the meetings.

The shocking news that a U-2 had been shot down over Cuba, and the pilot killed, dramatically increased the tension and anxiety in the Cabinet Room. The ExComm nonetheless remained resolutely opposed to the trade. Rusk again reminded JFK, "Well, last night he was prepared to trade them for a promise not to invade." "That's right," the president pointed out yet again; "now he's got something completely new."

After the ExComm had dispersed at nearly 8:00 P.M., Ball, Bundy, Gilpatric, RFK, McNamara, Rusk, Sorensen, and Thompson met with President Kennedy, at his invitation, in the Oval Office. The president revealed that he was about to send RFK to meet with Dobrynin and solicited advice on what his brother should tell the ambassador. Dean Rusk, clearly recognizing JFK's determination, then edged away from his earlier opposition to the trade and suggested that RFK should advise Dobrynin that although a public quid pro quo for the missiles in Turkey was unacceptable, the president was prepared to remove them once the Cuban crisis was resolved. The idea was quickly adopted and the participants pledged to secrecy.

Later that evening, and without the knowledge of the entire ExComm, JFK also worked secretly with his secretary of state, apparently at the latter's initiative, to cobble together a fall-back plan in the event the Kremlin rejected the offer. Rusk phoned former deputy U.N. secretary general Andrew Cordier and arranged for him to assist in implementing an emergency back-channel strategy by which U Thant would announce a "neutral" United Nations plan through which the U.S. and the U.S.S.R. would mutually agree to remove their missiles from both Turkey and Cuba. The secretary general would make the public request only after receiving private word from Rusk that negotiations had stalled or failed. JFK was prepared to gamble that if the United States publicly accepted this allegedly neutral plan, despite the domestic political risks, it would be very difficult for the Soviets to reject it. Khrushchev's unexpected decision, the following morning, to accept the noninvasion pledge in return for removing the missiles from Cuba (and a secret American commitment to dismantle the Jupiters in Turkey) made the Cordier gambit moot. Rusk did not reveal this closely held contingency plan for over twenty-five years.[21]

At the late evening ExComm meeting, cognizant of the RFK-Dobrynin meeting and the secret trade offer that had just been made, Rusk speculated that Khrushchev has "got to worry a great deal about how far he wants to push this thing" and urged the president, by tomorrow, "to take certain steps to build up the pressure. We have enforced surveillance. We shoot at anybody who gets in our way. We see whether U Thant produces any result tonight or during the morning. We intercept that Soviet ship." These steps, the secretary asserted, would "keep the monkey on Cuba's back . . . [and] the accidental fact that some Russian technicians may be around at the time we have to shoot, since they've already fired the first shot, is something that is regrettable, but . . . we're enforcing this with respect to Cuba, not the Soviet Union." The point of this pressure was to get Khrushchev "back to a pact [the Friday offer] that we can live with." Our preference, the secretary of state concluded, even though half the people in the room (including Rusk himself) knew that a missile trade deal had already been proposed to the U.S.S.R., is to "go ahead with this Cuban business" without reference to any NATO issues.

～

This account of Secretary of State Dean Rusk's role in the ExComm meetings should convince any open-minded historian or reader to reject the self-serving myths and half-truths in *Thirteen Days* (and in the related writings of Arthur Schlesinger Jr.).

Dean Rusk did not miss most of the ExComm meetings because of other responsibilities; was not silent, passive, indecisive, or reluctant to recommend tough decisions; did not play the role of "dumb dodo" by failing to articulate the diplomatic perspective; did not fortuitously allow the discussions to become "completely uninhibited and unrestricted" by virtue of his absence; and did not have a physical or mental breakdown during the crisis.

Rusk was actually an outspoken and influential participant in the discussions and was more often—at least until his hostility to the Turkish trade on October 27—a voice for caution and diplomacy than anyone other than the president.[22] Indeed, he came closest to personifying the dovish role that RFK shrewdly assigned to himself in *Thirteen Days*. That fact, plus Rusk's willingness to openly and repeatedly oppose Robert Kennedy's demands for potentially dangerous and provocative actions, likely helps to explain the attorney general's efforts to diminish and discredit the secretary of state's often pivotal role in the ExComm discussions.

In his personal memoir, published in 1990, Rusk noted that during the first week of the crisis, because of concerns over leaks and premature disclosures before the president's speech made the crisis public, "I kept to my schedule and had Under Secretary of State George Ball sit in for me at many meetings." Unfortunately, readers have often interpreted this remark as confirmation of RFK's claim that Rusk did not attend most ExComm meetings. In fact, the former secretary of state was referring to State Department working groups— *not* the ExComm meetings, which Rusk (and Ball) consistently attended.[23]

Rusk's older son, David, recently recalled, "For years up to the time that Pop finally agreed to collaborate with [younger son] Rich[ard] on *As I Saw It*, he had explained that he would prefer to just leave it to professional historians, working from a perspective of several decades, to reach their judgments about his time in office. He was particularly skeptical of 'instant histories' by 'insiders'—real or self-proclaimed."[24]

The time has come, in short, to accept the conclusive evidence on the ExComm tapes and stop viewing the Dean Rusk of the missile crisis through the lens of his later role in the escalation of the Vietnam war.

A grim but focused President Kennedy just seconds before addressing the nation and revealing the discovery of Soviet nuclear missiles in Cuba.

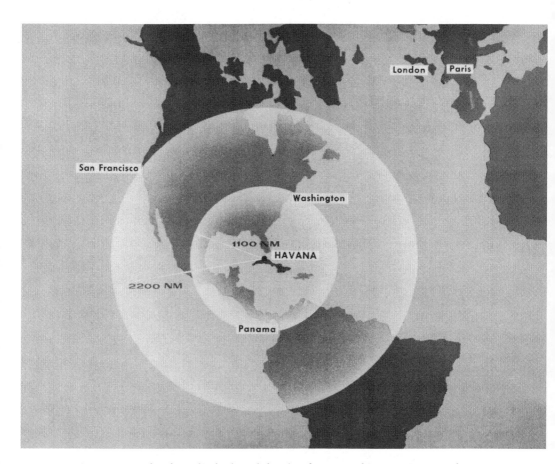

Department of Defense display board showing the range of Soviet MRBMs and IRBMs in Cuba.

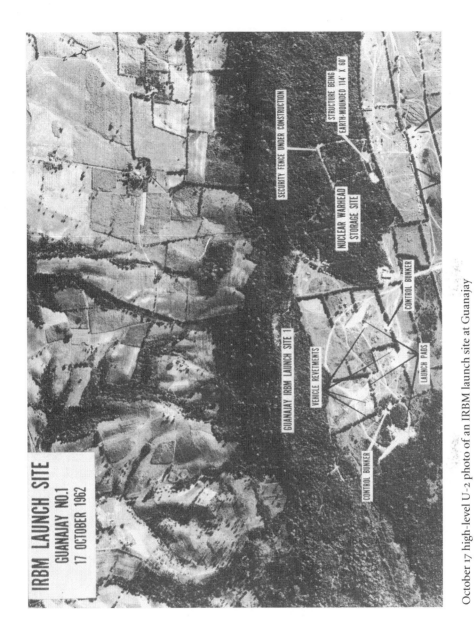

Labels within image:

IRBM LAUNCH SITE
GUANAJAY NO.1
17 OCTOBER 1962

SECURITY FENCE UNDER CONSTRUCTION

STRUCTURE BEING
EARTH-MOUNDED 114' X 60'

NUCLEAR WARHEAD
STORAGE SITE

GUANAJAY IRBM LAUNCH SITE 1

VEHICLE REVETMENTS

CONTROL BUNKER

LAUNCH PADS

CONTROL BUNKER

October 17 high-level U-2 photo of an IRBM launch site at Guanajay

October 25 low-level surveillance photo of an MRBM launch site at San Cristobal

JFK and Ambassador Llewellyn Thompson (foreground) meet with Soviet Foreign Minister Andrei Gromyko (right) and Ambassador Anatoly Dobrynin in the Oval Office on October 18

President Kennedy signs the quarantine proclamation in the Oval Office on October 23

The October 29 ExComm meeting (the only meeting photographed), view 1: Facing the president's side of the table (Presidential Seal on the wall behind JFK). *On JFK's left:* Robert McNamara, Roswell Gilpatric (pen in hand), Maxwell Taylor (not in uniform), Paul Nitze (right end of table). *On JFK's right:* Dean Rusk, George Ball (writing), John McCone's white hair just visible on the left end of the table in front of the fireplace.

The October 29 ExComm meeting, view 2: Facing the bookcases on the side opposite the President. *From left to right:* Robert Kennedy (standing), Donald Wilson (partially obscured), Theodore Sorensen, McGeorge Bundy, Douglas Dillon, Lyndon Johnson, Llewellyn Thompson, U. Alexis Johnson.

6 The Erratic Expertise of Llewellyn Thompson

You [President Kennedy] shouldn't give any indication that we're ready to talk about the Turkish thing. . . . it's a further sign of weakness.

—Llewellyn "Tommy" Thompson, October 27, 1962

T HE FORMER AMERICAN AMBASSADOR to the Soviet Union, Llewellyn Thompson (ambassador-at-large during the missile crisis) is all but absent from Robert Kennedy's *Thirteen Days*, the template for the conventional wisdom on the ExComm meetings. And yet, despite failing to detail the ambassador's views and input, RFK declared that President Kennedy felt that Thompson's advice, predictions, and recommendations about the Russians were "uncannily accurate . . . and surpassed by none." Even Thompson's superior, Secretary of State Dean Rusk, acknowledged the ambassador's status as the ExComm's "prime expert on the Soviet Union."[1]

Arthur Schlesinger Jr., who as we have seen insisted that RFK was "a dove from the start," also called Thompson one of the attorney general's most "steadfast allies."[2] Thompson's dovish reputation, however, reached its apogee in Robert McNamara's reminiscences in Errol Morris's *The Fog of War*. McNamara, in discussing the first of the "eleven lessons" from his life, declares that the capacity to "empathize with your enemy" is indispensable for political leadership in the nuclear age.

As his chief example, McNamara cites the good fortune that "at the elbow of President Kennedy was Tommy Thompson, the former U.S. ambassador to Moscow," who with his wife, Jane, "had literally lived with Khrushchev and his wife upon occasion." McNamara singles out Thompson for urging JFK to reject the "hard" Saturday message from Moscow's hawks and to respond instead to the "soft" Friday message from Khrushchev himself:

> The president said to Tommy, "We can't do that, that'll get us nowhere." Tommy said, "Mr. President, you're wrong." Now that takes a lot of guts. Kennedy insisted that "We're not going to get these missiles out of Cuba, probably anyway, by negotiation," and the ambassador replied, "I don't agree Mr. President. I think there's still a chance." Kennedy replied, "That he'll back down?" Thompson explained that "The important thing for Khrushchev, it seems to me, is to be able to say, 'I saved Cuba. I stopped an invasion.'" In Thompson's mind was this thought: Khrushchev's gotten himself in a hell of a fix. He would then think to himself, "My God, if I can get out of this with a deal that I can say to the Russian people: Kennedy was going to destroy Castro and I prevented it." Thompson, knowing Khrushchev as he did, thought Khrushchev will accept that. And Thompson was right. That's what I call empathy. We must try to put ourselves inside their skin and look at us through their eyes, just to understand the thoughts that lie behind their decisions and their actions. Khrushchev's advisers were saying, "There can be no deal unless you somewhat reduce the pressure on us, when you ask us to reduce the pressure on you."[3]

In McNamara's view, it was Thompson (rather than RFK) who preserved the peace by persuading President Kennedy to adopt a shrewd and subtle strategy (essentially the Trollope ploy) based on the ambassador's empathy and personal knowledge of Khrushchev—and it worked.

As we will see, however, as compelling and dramatic as this story is, it is also false and misleading. Kennedy actually rejected Thompson's advice that the U.S. could pressure Khrushchev to withdraw the missiles from Cuba without also agreeing to remove the Jupiter missiles from Turkey. JFK's full remarks, in context, go well beyond McNamara's incomplete rendering cited above:

> Now we're not gonna be able to effect that. It seems to me that we oughta be reasonable. We're not gonna get these weapons out of Cuba, probably, anyway, but I mean, by negotiation. We're gonna have to take our weapons out of Turkey. I don't think there's any doubt he's not gonna [agree to remove the Cuban missiles first] . . . now that he made that [trade offer] public. Tommy, he's not gonna take 'em out of Cuba if we don't [take the Jupiters out of Turkey as well].

If any one person preserved the peace by virtue of the ability to "empathize with your enemy," it was the president himself, who insisted that world opinion would support the trade and that preserving the unity of NATO was not a rational justification for risking a nuclear world war. Thompson, as revealed by the clash over the missile trade, was often one of RFK's most steadfastly hawkish allies. In fact, the ambassador's role throughout the ExComm discussions repeatedly conflicts with the claims made by Robert Kennedy and McNamara.

~

Thompson did not attend the October 16 meetings; his absence, however, was noted by both the president and McGeorge Bundy, who speculated about his "first sense of how he sees this." The ambassador joined the (unrecorded) discussions at the State Department on the following day, and his initial explanation was that Khrushchev had engineered the confrontation over missiles in Cuba to gain leverage on Berlin—just what the president himself believed.

At the morning meeting on October 18, he advised against air strikes "because you'd have killed a lot of Russians" and instead endorsed the blockade. But at the same time, he predicted that the U.S.S.R. would be unlikely to run a blockade if it were backed up by a formal declaration of war. He also tried to educate the president on the Russian view of the world: "The Russians have a curious faculty of wanting a legal basis despite all of the outrageous things they've done."

As to the weapons already in Cuba, he advised the president to "Demand they're dismantled," but if air surveillance proved they were armed, then there would be no choice but to take them out. The ambassador also suggested that Khrushchev would use "a lot of threatening language" about nuclear war but was more likely to react to air strikes in Cuba with a quid pro quo attack on a U.S. base in Turkey "and then say, 'Now I want to talk.'" Khrushchev's entire purpose, he now insisted, rather than to put pressure on Berlin as he had stressed the previous day, was to "build up to talks with you in which we try to negotiate out the bases" in Cuba and Turkey.

Thompson accurately predicted that Khrushchev would essentially say, "'What are you getting so excited about? The Cubans asked us for the missiles to deal with these émigré bases. . . . These are simply to deal with the threat to Cuba.'" But the ambassador stressed that "naturally, we take exception to that." Nonetheless, he admonished the president, "You want to make it, if you do any of these steps, make it as easy as possible for him to back down." If he replies, "'This is so serious, I'm prepared to talk to you about it.' We could scarcely refuse then—that's if you have a world war being threatened."

However, he also concluded that "since Castro's gone this far in conniving" in the installation of the missiles, "it seems to me that in the end that Castro has to go"—clearly an endorsement of either an invasion or an escalation of covert operations to eliminate Castro. Finally, he warned that "I don't think he [Khrushchev] could ever just back down."

When the president solicited advice on whether the blockade proclamation should include a declaration of war on Cuba, Thompson, as he had suggested earlier, strongly backed such a declaration; he contended that it could be justified as a necessary step to eliminate a threat to the U.S., which is "a little different from saying that we're going to war to destroy [Cuba]." But the president vigorously disagreed because a declaration of war would appear unnecessarily aggressive to the Soviets and could provoke retaliation in Berlin that might spiral out of control.

Thompson later qualified his support for declaring war on Cuba, suggesting that Khrushchev might observe the blockade without a declaration of war simply because of the logistical difficulties in sustaining military action around Cuba (which was almost seven thousand miles from the U.S.S.R.); on the other hand, he might also risk "the big action in Berlin, which is this gamble which he's shown for four years he's reluctant to take." The ambassador also pointed out that Khrushchev had personally initiated this aggressive posture in Berlin—"I mean he's taken credit for it, time and time again"—and recalled that after the American U-2 was shot down over the U.S.S.R. in 1960, the Soviet military "who normally never talked to me, came over and tried to calm me down" because "they were concerned that Khrushchev was being impetuous and running risks."

Thompson was also initially receptive to the president's first intimation about making a deal on the Jupiter missiles, since the U.S. could simply substitute submarine-launched Polaris missiles to protect Turkey. Thompson even suggested formally inviting Khrushchev to come to the U.S. to discuss a trade. Otherwise, "it seems to me you're playing Russian roulette, you're really flipping a coin as to whether you end up with world war or not."

By the following Monday, October 22, the blockade decision had been finalized and the president, citing Thompson's first remarks from the previous week, concluded that the Soviet-Cuban gambit was "a probing action" to test whether Khrushchev could get away with grabbing Berlin. The ambassador agreed, returning to his initial explanation and recalling that Khrushchev "made it quite clear in my last talk with him that he was squirming" under the pressure not to back down over Berlin.

During the early evening meeting with the leaders of Congress, in which the president was forced to defend the blockade decision against harsh criticism from Senators Richard Russell and William Fulbright, JFK cited Thompson's strong conviction that the Soviet Union would regard an "attack on these SAM sites and missile bases with the killing of four or five thousand Russians as a greater provocation than the stopping of their ships."

The president also asked Thompson, who "has had a lot of conversations with Khrushchev . . . to say something about his evaluation of his purposes." The ambassador recalled that at their farewell talk last July, Khrushchev had indicated that "time's running out" on the Berlin problem—"he felt that he'd gone too far out on a limb to go back"—and Thompson again categorically declared that the timing and purpose of the Cuban buildup was to provoke "a showdown on Berlin. In my view that's the main thing that he has in mind." He did not mention his previous and equally firm conclusion that Khrushchev was trying to force a deal for the removal of the U.S. missiles in Turkey.

Thompson reported the following day (October 23) that the ambassadorial group would meet later that afternoon to consider how to respond to possible Soviet actions against Berlin, such as more rigorous inspection of U.S. truck convoys entering the city. JFK replied that outnumbered U.S. forces were not in a favorable position to resist such a demand, which he clearly did not regard as very serious. The ambassador suggested stopping the truck convoys rather than permitting Soviet inspections; but the president insisted that it would be difficult to start them again after they had been halted. It was far better simply not to make an issue about truck inspections.

Two days later (Thursday, October 25), after the president had received Khrushchev's letter denouncing the blockade as "an act of aggression," Thompson suggested that the Soviet leader's harsh language "indicated preparation for resistance by force, that is, forcing us to take forcible action." After lengthy discussions of how to enforce the blockade, the president decided to let an East German passenger ship through without inspection, and turned to the ambassador, asking directly, "What do you think, Tommy?" "Oh, I think you've really considered it right," Thompson replied, but he added, "I'm a little troubled by Khrushchev's strong letter of yesterday" and wanted to be sure that we "show him that we're not backing away because of a threat. On the other hand, he is backing away [by turning some ships around] and that tips the balance."

Thompson also cited a talk he had with the Yugoslav ambassador "without my bringing it up." He had said to Thompson: "'I just want to tell you one thing. I don't agree with your analysts in your papers, that Khrushchev thinks you're afraid to act or are weak.'" The diplomat cited several private conversations with Khrushchev and confided that "he said he doesn't think this." Thompson also predicted that "The Soviets will find it far easier to remove these weapons or to move them to port for a removal than they would to accept [United Nations] inspections, I think. Putting Soviet technicians under U.N. people, I think they would resist." (The U.S.S.R. would in fact agree to U.N. inspections as part of the final agreement negotiated by RFK and Ambassador Dobrynin. But Castro was to render the issue moot by barring the inspectors because international inspection violated Cuba's national sovereignty.)

Thompson's advice had been undeniably contradictory and changeable. But his greatest reversal would come on the most crucial day of the crisis, Saturday, October 27. During the first week, he had reacted positively to the president's hints about cutting a deal that would require withdrawing the Jupiter missiles from Turkey. He had even floated the notion of proposing such a trade and suggested inviting Khrushchev to Washington for negotiations instead of waiting for the chairman's planned November visit to the U.N. in New York. "'This won't wait for your trip in November,'" the ambassador had chuckled; "'come on over.'"

But when news arrived on the morning of Saturday, October 27, confirming Khrushchev's Moscow Radio proposal of precisely such a deal, Thompson threw all his influence, experience, and expertise behind derailing any Cuba-Turkey missile swap. Indeed, he reacted almost as if he had never heard of or supported the idea before; and despite his own earlier statements that Khrushchev did not think that the president was weak or afraid to act, he now asserted that the chairman was probing for a soft spot and would interpret any discussion of a swap as proof of weak presidential leadership. He urged Kennedy to instruct Ambassador Stevenson at the U.N. to "immediately say we will not discuss the Turkish bases." JFK brushed aside Thompson's recommendation; "rather than saying that, until we get time to think about it," he instructed that Ambassador Stevenson try to get clarification of this new and "entirely different" Soviet proposal: "You're going to find a lot of people thinking this is rather a reasonable position."

Thompson countered that Khrushchev might have mistakenly concluded that Austrian foreign minister Bruno Kreisky's October 25 speech proposing a Cuba-Turkey missile trade "was inspired by us." But the president refused to accept this argument: "They've got a very good prod and this one is gonna be very tough, I think, for us. It's gonna be tough in England, I'm sure, as well as other places on the continent." U.S. military action in Cuba, he insisted, would give the U.S.S.R "not a blank check but a pretty good check to take action in Berlin on the grounds that we are wholly unreasonable. Most people will think this is a rather even trade and we ought to take advantage of it." It would be very difficult, as a result, for the U.S. to move against Cuba with international support. And, of course, once military hostilities began, it could quickly become almost impossible to stop escalation short of a nuclear exchange.

Thompson refused to back down and repeated that Khrushchev's Friday evening letter "made this proposal that the whole problem's raised by our threat to Cuba and we're prepared to remove that threat [with a noninvasion pledge]. This point [about Turkey in the second letter] undercuts that effort entirely." "For one or two reasons," Thompson explained, "they've changed their minds on this. One was that they may have picked up this Kreisky thing and thought they could get more. The other was Khrushchev may have been overruled. In either case, we've gotta change that, which means we have to take a tough line" and stop this "wobbling."

Later (when JFK was out of the room), Thompson was even more bluntly critical of what he called the president's interest in "changing our whole policy for a public relations aspect"—unless, he warned, a definite decision has already been made "that we're going in" to Cuba. He even went so far as to recommend violating diplomatic confidentiality by releasing Khrushchev's private Friday evening letter. After all, he argued, after JFK had returned to his seat, Khrushchev had announced his trade proposal publicly "before you got it, and I'd do the same thing. Then you've got to fasten the world focus back on Cuba and Latin America and the fact that we're prepared not to invade [if the missiles are removed]. And this makes it, I think, much tougher for him to go ahead." President Kennedy passed over Thompson's suggestion without comment.

The ambassador, whose experience in the Soviet Union had singular influence on the ExComm, was clearly becoming more and more disturbed by the president's position: "Mr. President, if we go on the basis of a trade, which I gather is somewhat in your mind, we end up, it seems to me, with the Soviets still in Cuba with planes and technicians and so on. Even though the missiles are out, that would surely be unacceptable and put you in a worse position." President Kennedy replied forcefully that the U.S. would be forced into hundreds of air strikes and an invasion "all because we wouldn't take [useless] missiles out of Turkey." Thompson reiterated that it was still in our interest to get Khrushchev to return to the Friday proposal. But the president observed skeptically, "now this other public one, it seems to me, has become their public position, isn't it?"

"This is maybe just pressure on us," Thompson speculated. "The important thing for Khrushchev, it seems to me, is to be able to say, 'I saved Cuba. I stopped an invasion.' And he can get away with this if he wants to, and he's had a go at this Turkish thing, and that we'll discuss later." The president carefully distanced himself from Thompson's opposition to linking Turkey and Cuba: "That is a substantive question because it really depends on whether we believe that we can get a deal on just the Cuban [issue] or whether we have to agree to his position of tying it [Turkey to Cuba]. Now Tommy doesn't think we do. I think that having made it public, how can he take these missiles out of Cuba if we just do nothing about Turkey?" Thompson stubbornly repeated that Khrushchev might still accept the Friday missile removal/noninvasion deal since he could still say that the U.S. threat to Cuba had started the crisis and he had removed that threat.

Finally, evidently recognizing the president's determination on the Turkish deal, Thompson endorsed alerting the Turkish and Italian prime ministers that if surveillance planes were fired on again, the U.S. could be compelled to use force in Cuba which in turn could result in Soviet attacks on the Jupiter missiles: "We are therefore considering whether or not it would be in your interest for us to remove these . . . and we may be having to take this up in NATO." "We oughta send that to the Turks," JFK agreed emphatically, "'cause it's their neck. And, of course, they're liable to say, 'Well, we can take it.' So we've gotta have it look to the general interest as well as theirs. . . . Now they're not gonna want to do it, but we may just decide we have to do it in our interest." Of course, the president acknowledged, it would be far better politically to have NATO publicly endorse taking the Jupiters out.

Thompson, however, well into the grueling, nearly four-hour late afternoon meeting, remained deeply skeptical about the trade, emphasizing his concern that even if the Soviets removed the missiles, "they'll leave their technicians in Cuba, their bombing planes in Cuba, and we're in a hell of a mess. . . . any suggestion that we're going to accept this," short of "an irrevocable decision that we're going to take these out by bombing [Cuba], is very dangerous. . . . I can't believe it's necessary, when you know the night before he was willing to take this other line." Khrushchev might now be thinking, he surmised, "'These boys are beginning to give way. Let's push harder.' I think they'll change their minds," he predicted, "when we take any forceful action, stopping their ship, or taking out a SAM site that ends up killing the Russians—somewhere."

"You can see that we have two conflicting things here," Thompson continued; "one is to prepare for an attack on Cuba, and the other is to get a peaceful solution along the lines which he proposed [on Friday]. And the purposes are conflicting. If you want to get him to accept this thing that he put in his letter last night, then you shouldn't give any indication that we're ready to talk about the Turkish thing. . . . to mention this . . . is bad for the perspective of Khrushchev. I think it's a further sign of weakness."

The president, acknowledging the all but unanimous resistance from his advisers, asked for further clarification: "Let's see what the difference is, then we can think about that. What is the difference?" "I think we clearly have a choice here," Thompson boldly reaffirmed, "that either we go on the line that we've decided to attack Cuba and therefore are set to prepare the ground for that or we try to get Khrushchev back on a peaceful solution, in which case we shouldn't give any indication that we're going to accept anything on Turkey because the Turkish proposal is, I should think, clearly unacceptable." The ambassador shrewdly appealed to the president's political instincts, predicting that the release of Khrushchev's private October 26 message would diminish any need to discuss Turkey. "It seems to me the public will be pretty solid on that, and that we ought to keep the heat on him and get him back on a line which he obviously was on the night before."

JFK moved to conciliate the opponents of a Turkish deal by agreeing that "we oughta go the first route which you suggest by sending him a letter that tries to get him back [to the Friday offer]." But at the same time, he reiterated his lack of confidence in that strategy by insisting on moving forward immediately on the missile trade option: "Then it seems to me we oughta have a discussion with NATO about these Turkish missiles." But Thompson warned yet again that the offer was a trap: "That's why I think it's very dangerous to indicate any tentative play on this thing. He's really got us there."

Llewellyn Thompson was one of only eight ExComm members invited by the president to the brief meeting in the Oval Office later that Saturday evening. President Kennedy clearly could not understand why the ExComm was ready to risk a nuclear world war in order to keep some otherwise useless and outdated missiles in Turkey. In the end, JFK imposed his decision on his advisers and sent Robert Kennedy to make the secret missile trade offer to Ambassador Dobrynin. Thompson, like the others in the room, pledged to keep that decision confidential. The ambassador died in 1972, long before this covert agreement became public.

The ExComm tapes fundamentally contradict both RFK's claim that Thompson's "advice on the Russians and predictions as to what they would do were uncannily accurate" and McNamara's contention that it was the ambassador's empathy for the Soviet perspective that made it possible for President Kennedy to achieve a negotiated settlement.

7 The Selective Memory of McGeorge Bundy

You [President Kennedy] will, in fact, get into the invasion before you're through—either way.

—McGeorge Bundy, October 18, 1962

MCGEORGE BUNDY, President Kennedy's special assistant for national security affairs, is hardly mentioned in *Thirteen Days*. Bundy's role in the meetings received far less attention than that of RFK's favorite, Robert McNamara, and even less than that of his recurring adversary, Dean Rusk. Bobby Kennedy was unimpressed by Bundy's performance—accusing him privately of "strange flipflops. First he was for a strike, then a blockade, then for doing nothing because it would upset the situation in Berlin, and then, finally, he led the group which was in favor of a strike—and a strike without prior notification, along the lines of Pearl Harbor." RFK even hinted that the national security adviser had been irresolute or weak-willed.[1] This suggestion is particularly striking since Bundy was, at the time, almost invariably characterized in the press as brilliant, self-assured, arrogant, and aggressive. Arthur Schlesinger Jr.'s assessment was typical: "Bundy possessed dazzling clarity and speed of mind as well as great distinction of manner and unlimited self-confidence."[2]

In an obvious effort to adjust the historical scales in his own favor, Bundy devoted 72 pages of his 617-page memoir to the Cuban missile crisis. He portrays himself as a rational, thoughtful, even-handed pragmatist—neither a hawk nor a dove; but this view does not square with the evidence on the tapes, especially *after* the first forty-eight hours of the ExComm meetings. And not surprisingly, Bundy does not mention his frequent clashes with the president or his own fierce resistance to the missile trade on Saturday, October 27. Instead, he merely acknowledges, in classic understatement, that "The discussion all day Saturday was intense."[3]

It was Bundy who received the news about the U-2 photos on the evening of October 15 and famously decided to let President Kennedy, who had returned in the early morning hours from political campaigning, get a good night of sleep before viewing the pictures the next morning.[4] He also, after getting a list of names from the president, organized the first ExComm meeting a few hours later.

~

The president's national security assistant initially said very little on that first morning of meetings until Rusk raised the possibility that Khrushchev had installed missiles in Cuba to balance the U.S. deployment in Turkey. At that point, Bundy asked how many Jupiter missiles were in Turkey; McNamara, unsure of the specifics, answered hesitantly, "About fifteen, I believe to be the figure," and Bundy tentatively concurred, "I think that's right." He also argued that Khrushchev's distinction between offensive and defensive weapons was "all mixed up" and contemptuously dismissed the Soviet leader's argument that the nuclear missiles in Cuba were purely defensive and no threat to the United States.

Bundy seemed sympathetic to Rusk's concerns that the NATO allies might oppose military action in Cuba on the grounds that "if they can live with Soviet MRBMs, why can't we?" They would not be supportive, he warned, if the U.S. risked losing Berlin or sparking an all-out war between the superpowers merely to avoid a threat Europe had faced for years. "The prospect of that pattern," Bundy noted grimly, "is not an appetizing one." He argued that there would be a "substantial political advantage in limiting any air strikes, in surgical terms, to the thing that is in fact the cause of action"—the missile sites alone—and also urged the president not to abandon the possibility of political negotiations.

At the October 16 evening meeting, the president, perhaps still hoping against hope that the crisis might be based on a technical misunderstanding, asked CIA deputy director Marshall Carter if there was any question in his mind that these weapons were actually offensive ballistic missiles. The general's response was confident but somber: "There's no question in our minds, sir. And they are genuine. They are not a camouflage or a covert attempt to fool us." Bundy, however, refused to drop the president's point and urged General Carter to consider that it could be "really catastrophic" to make "a bad guess" about the explosive power and range of these Soviet missiles: "We mustn't do that. How do we really know what these missiles are and what their range is? . . . That's really my question. How do we know what a given Soviet missile will do?" Carter responded with additional technical data about identical missiles in the Soviet Union, but Bundy was unconvinced: "I know that we've had these things in charts for years. But I don't know how we know." Finally, after McNamara and Rusk came to Carter's defense, Bundy reluctantly backed off: "I would apparently agree," he murmured rather diffidently, "given the weight of it."

McNamara recommended an announcement that the U.S. would attack if Cuba initiated any offensive action against the United States. "Attack who?" Bundy inquired. "The Soviet Union," McNamara responded matter-of-factly. Bundy, clearly startled, reminded the commander in chief that Khrushchev had "been very, very explicit with us, in communications to us, about how dangerous this is." "That's right," JFK replied, expediently overlooking American covert operations in Cuba: "He's initiated the danger, really, hasn't he? He's the one playing God, not us."

Bundy nonetheless questioned whether the missiles were actually as important as they seemed: "quite aside from what we've said and we're very hard-locked on to it, I know: what is the strategic impact on the position of the United States of MRBMs in Cuba? How gravely does this change," he rapped the table for emphasis, "the strategic balance?" The defense secretary made clear that he did not agree with the JCS that the missiles in Cuba had altered the strategic balance, and even General Taylor admitted that their importance might be psychological and political as well as military. "Oh," Bundy remarked with a rather cynical laugh, "I asked the question with an awareness" of the political realities.

Bundy nevertheless reminded his colleagues that an attack on Cuba could quickly escalate to all-out war: "The political advantages are very strong, it seems to me, of the small strike. It corresponds to 'the punishment fits the crime' in political terms. We are doing only what we warned repeatedly and publicly we would have to do. You know, we are not generalizing the attack." "One thing that I would still cling to," Bundy avowed, "is that he's [Khrushchev] not likely to give Fidel Castro nuclear warheads. I don't believe that has happened or is likely to happen."

"Why does he put these in there, though?" JFK pondered, and Bundy explained that the warheads were Soviet controlled: "That's right. But what is the advantage of that?" JFK persisted. "It's just as if we suddenly began to put a major number of MRBMs in Turkey. Now that'd be goddamn dangerous, I would think." Bundy boldly pointed out, "Well we did it, Mr. President," and JFK replied rather lamely, "Yeah, that was five years ago. But that was during a different period then."

JFK may have been trying, very awkwardly, to hang the Turkish missile albatross around the neck of the Eisenhower administration by "forgetting" that he himself had chosen to proceed with the deployment and had never ordered the removal of the missiles. (At a Kennedy Library conference in 1988, Bundy responded to a question about whether JFK had taken steps to pull the Jupiter missiles out of Turkey by raising his arms toward the heavens and exclaiming in essence: "Jack, you never ordered the removal of the Turkish missiles. You merely expressed an opinion about their lack of strategic value. A presidential opinion is not a presidential order.") Later in the ExComm deliberations, Douglas Dillon, who had served in the Eisenhower administration, admitted, "we didn't know what else to do with them, and we really made the Turks and Italians take them." JFK urged Sorensen to jot down that remark for the book they would later write—again evading his own role in the Jupiters' deployment.[5]

Even if the missiles were Russian, General Carter observed, it might be useful to consider them "entirely Cuban" if the U.S. should decide to invade. "Ah, well," Bundy observed irreverently, clearly relishing the use of power, "what we say for political purposes and what we think are not identical here." In fact, when Khrushchev was informed about JFK's forthcoming speech on October 22, he did consider "another possibility": "in case of attack," the U.S.S.R. could announce that "'all of the equipment belonged to the Cubans and the Cubans would announce that they will respond.' He assured his [Kremlin] colleagues that he did not envision letting Castro threaten the use of the medium-range ballistic missiles against a U.S. invasion, but as a way of deterring the United States the Cubans could declare that they would 'use the tactical ones.'"[6]

Bundy also, quite casually, raised a sensitive issue. "We have a list of the sabotage options, Mr. President. . . . it's not a very loud noise to raise at a meeting of this sort, but I think it would need your approval. I take it you are in favor of sabotage." Of course, Bundy did not know that the meeting was being taped. Nonetheless, the circuitous language in his reference to JFK's support for sabotage suggests an almost instinctive inclination to offer the president some degree of "plausible deniability." JFK rejected mining international waters, which could antagonize neutral or friendly nations, but did not object to what Bundy described as "deniable internal Cuban activities."

"I can't understand their [the U.S.S.R.'s] viewpoint," JFK admitted; "I don't think there's any record of the Soviets ever making this direct a challenge ever, really, since the Berlin blockade." He seemed especially intrigued by Ambassador Dobrynin's insistence that the U.S.S.R. would not put offensive nuclear weapons in Cuba: "Now either he's lying, or he doesn't know." Bundy replied skeptically, "I wouldn't bet a cookie that Dobrynin doesn't know a bean about this." JFK, nervously and audibly slapping his knee, was clearly intrigued: "You think he does know." (JFK frequently slapped his knee, or sometimes tapped his teeth, in stressful situations.) But RFK, who had personally spoken with the ambassador, concluded firmly, "He didn't know . . . in my judgment."[7]

As the meeting began to break up, Bundy proposed a scheme for dropping paratroopers into Cuba after air strikes to determine which sites had actually been destroyed—thus hopefully confirming the success of taking out only "the thing that gives the trouble [the missiles] and not the thing that doesn't give the trouble." But McNamara dismissed the idea as too risky and Bundy acknowledged, "it's probably a bad idea." He did insist, however, that plans should be worked out to evaluate both "the chances of success" as well as "the pluses and minuses of nonsuccess" of any military action.

General Carter, however, was very uneasy about the air strikes: "This comin' in there on Pearl Harbor [with a surprise attack] just frightens the hell out of me as to what goes beyond." Bundy, obviously puzzled, asked, "What goes beyond what?" and Carter replied, "What happens beyond that? You go in there with a surprise attack; you put out all the missiles. This isn't the end; this is the beginning, I think." It was the first time that comparing surprise air strikes in Cuba to the Japanese attack on Pearl Harbor would unsettle the ExComm deliberations. Of course, in December 1941 the possibility of nuclear escalation did not yet exist.

Two days later, on Thursday, October 18, new U-2 photography had turned up evidence of intermediate-range ballistic missile (IRBM) launchers in Cuba. The intermediate missiles had a range of over two thousand miles, about twice that of the MRBMs, and carried far deadlier warheads. Soviet

IL-28 bombers, capable of delivering nuclear payloads, were also discovered. The ExComm reconvened with a renewed momentum for immediate military action; Bundy too became steadily more aggressive.

General Taylor pointed out that the latest photographs, especially those identifying IRBMs, proved that the Soviets "are moving very fast to make those weapons operational." Despite his earlier doubts about invading Cuba, he concluded that it might already be too late to eliminate the entire missile threat without an invasion: "We can't take this threat out by actions from the air." "You mean," Bundy interposed, "that for the long pull you're gonna have to take the island." "Yes, you can't destroy a hole in the ground," Taylor continued. Only diplomatic action or physical occupation of the sites "can prevent this kind of threat from building up." The JCS chairman did not think that a blockade alone was enough; it had to be implemented concurrently with other military actions. Bundy, in response, counseled the president, "simultaneously, it seems to me, you declare that a state of war exists and you call the Congress."

CIA director John McCone warned against getting locked into open-ended negotiations with the Soviets while the work on the sites proceeded. "The only offer we would make," JFK responded, "it would seem to me, that would have any sense, . . . giving him some out, would be our Turkey missiles." Bundy affirmed that such an offer would also be valid as an adjunct to surprise air strikes. Despite "all the wicked things that have led to this," he advised that a message should be "in Khrushchev's hands" at the moment the air strikes begin, stating "that we understand this base problem and that we do expect to dismantle our Turkish base. That has one small advantage," Bundy added, "which is that if he strikes back, we have at least given him a peaceful offer. I don't think we can keep that Turkish base." But when Rusk objected to a direct Cuba-Turkey missile exchange, Bundy quickly backed off, explaining that a missile swap was only "one way" of minimizing the danger since "this is a political not a military problem."

McNamara reminded his colleagues about the substantial risks from unannounced air strikes: at least several hundred Soviet citizens would be killed. "Killed?" Bundy asked. "Absolutely!" McNamara emphasized. The plan was for a comprehensive air attack. "Well, I hope it is!" Bundy announced eagerly—in sharp contrast to the doubts he had expressed just two days earlier about carrying out extensive bombing of Cuba. He also argued that the failure to act militarily in Cuba would lead to a "very rapid" deterioration of

NATO, especially if the Russians retaliated by attempting to seize West Berlin. "If we could trade off Berlin, and not have it our fault," Bundy quipped—but he was the only person to laugh.

Bundy also joined the essentially unanimous chorus of support for simultaneously announcing both a blockade *and* a declaration of war, insisting that a blockade alone was illegal and "an act of aggression against everybody else." He uncompromisingly lectured the president: "your whole posture" must reflect the fact that Khrushchev has done "unacceptable things from the point of view of the security of the hemisphere." The national security adviser dismissed concerns about "the freedom of Cuba" and confidently predicted that with or without a declaration of war, "You will, in fact, get into the invasion before you're through—either way."

The president did not comment directly, but did concede that announcing plans for air strikes against the missile sites was still an option: "It isn't Pearl Harbor in that sense. We've told everybody. Then we go ahead Saturday and we take 'em out and announce that they've been taken out, and any more that are put in, we're gonna take those out." "And the [Soviet] air force [in Cuba]," Bundy stipulated, and the president repeated, "And the air force. And [we say] that we don't want any war." JFK also emphasized that the air strikes would take place on Saturday, because "Sunday has historic disadvantages," a mordant reference to Sunday, December 7, 1941—the watershed date of their lives.

Bundy predicted that Khrushchev would respond to a bombing announcement by calling for a summit meeting and urged the president not to accept unless the Soviets agreed to an immediate halt to construction of the missile sites. The real issue, he emphasized, was the "level of readiness" of the missiles. But JFK replied that it didn't make "a hell of a difference" how many sites were ready if the Soviets really intended "to fire nuclear missiles at us." "If they were rational, Mr. President," Bundy retorted.

The meeting gradually broke up, and after the president left the room some fragmentary conversations continued for several minutes. Bundy acknowledged that "The great advantage" of a blockade without air strikes "is you don't kill any Russians." But Deputy Under Secretary of State Alexis Johnson declared that a unilateral blockade without a declaration of war "is about the worst [choice] of all," and Bundy pronounced, rather surprisingly since RFK was still in the room, "You must declare, I think the President did not fully grasp that."

General Taylor demanded that the "collapse of Castro" should remain a top priority, and Bundy predicted that Castro would not "sit still for a blockade and that's to our advantage. I'm convinced myself that Castro has to go. . . . I just think his demon is self-destruction and we have to help him to that." In that case, McNamara cautioned, "the price is going to be larger. . . . At the moment I lean to the blockade" because the risks are far less than those of surprise air attacks. "Russian roulette and broken alliances," Bundy remarked pensively, and McNamara agreed.

Later, on the evening of October 18, Bundy swung around yet again, surprising his colleagues by arguing against *any* military action because it could spark a confrontation in Berlin. Instead, he urged the president "merely to take note of the existence of these missiles and to wait until the crunch comes in Berlin." But by the next morning, Bundy had changed his position yet again and told JFK that after a sleepless night he had concluded that the quarantine was "dangerous and uncertain" because it did not deal with the missiles sites already under construction in Cuba and could lead to a Soviet blockade of Berlin. "'Well, I'm having some of those same worries,'" Bundy recalled President Kennedy saying: "'Have another look at that [the air strike option] and keep it alive.'" Bundy also recalled that "advocates of the air strike wanted to strike everything that could fly in Cuba, and that wasn't exactly what the President had in mind."[8] Bundy, however, had already been on both sides of that question.

On Monday, October 22, with President Kennedy's speech to the nation only hours away, the ExComm was preoccupied with finalizing the wording of the message to Khrushchev which would be handed to Ambassador Dobrynin when the president went on the air. "I think we oughta be looking to the day," JFK mused, reviving the theme he had raised a few days earlier, "when they're [the nuclear missiles] removed from Cuba, Italy and Turkey." Bundy suggested that a "neutral-nation proposal for immediate inspection instead of sanitization [surgical air strikes]" might be acceptable. "Don't forget," he counseled, apparently backing away from his recent advocacy of surprise air attacks, "you can't have everything in one bite."

Bundy also urged the president to reassure the European allies that the American response in Cuba was primarily aimed at protecting Berlin and reinforcing European security. "Those are good points," JFK affirmed. "I don't think we've thought enough about 'em in our communications to these heads of state." He urged that all background briefings for ambassadors and diplomats should stress America's credibility on Berlin and the preservation of the strategic balance. The NATO allies must be made to feel that they had been fully informed and consulted, Kennedy reasoned, so that they didn't react to the blockade as a symptom of America's Cuba fixation.

The president remained concerned, however, that critics might ask why the administration had decided not to attack the missile sites. Bundy recommended avoiding any reference to "the difficulty of hitting these targets" since air strikes might still be necessary in a few days. "It is a fact that even with the air strike," JFK conceded, "we couldn't perhaps get all the missiles that are in sight." "Entirely true, Mr. President," Bundy snapped rather patronizingly; "But I don't think the next few days is the time to talk about it." President Kennedy reacted with atypical irritation: "Well, I know, but I want everybody to understand it, Mac, if you don't mind. The fact of the matter is there are missiles on the island which are not in sight!"

A few minutes later, the president suggested that no matter what the U.S. did in Cuba, the Soviets were "getting ready to move on Berlin anyway." He insisted that the naval quarantine was not a threat, because it affected only offensive weapons and did not stop food or medicine or threaten war. "Even today," he added, "the Soviets inspect our, at least stop our [truck] convoys going into Berlin." "People get out, don't they?" he asked. Bundy, rather disdainfully, replied, "No, sir, the people do not get out and this troop inspection is a complicated one. They have ample means of surveillance, but inspection is not the word we want to use." Gilpatric confirmed that U.S. forces sometimes did get out of the trucks and let the Soviets "look in through the tailgates to the trucks." JFK seized on this apparent vindication in his spat with Bundy: "They do let them. Yeah."

General Taylor, however, raised a public relations issue: "Mr. President, I should call attention to the fact we're starting moves [troop movements] now which are very overt, and will be seen and reported on and commented on." "Precautionary, every one of them!" Bundy muttered irritably. Taylor persisted, "And you'll be faced with the question, 'Are you preparing to invade?'" "We don't want to look as if we got scared off from anything," Bundy counseled; but JFK pointedly observed that it was neither strategically nor politically helpful to "have it hanging over us" that we're preparing an invasion. He asked instead for a report on how troop movements had been publicized or censored during "the first days" of the Korean War.

On the morning following the president's televised speech, Tuesday, October 23, McNamara complained that during his press briefing the previous evening he had been pushed repeatedly for details on the administration's future moves. "It is of great importance," Bundy contended, "unless we get a clear-cut decision around this table to change"—and he rapped the table for emphasis—that "we stay right with the President's speech," leaving open any and all diplomatic and military options. But when JFK asked if "my letter to Khrushchev" had been released to the public, Bundy interjected with palpable annoyance, "No sir! We told Khrushchev that we would not do so!"

Bundy did insist, however, that the U-2 photos were "becoming of great importance in the international debate" and mentioned that Ambassador Adlai Stevenson had called to say that photographic proof could be critical at the U.N. debate. The president seemed genuinely surprised: "There is a question about whether these things really exist?" Bundy, citing skepticism in the European press, especially in Britain and France, mentioned a statement by the president of Mexico that "'if the evidence was conclusive, the attitude of Mexico towards Castro and Cuba would change.' And I think we ought to get the conclusive evidence and I think this is the way to do it." President Kennedy agreed to Stevenson's request.

The ExComm met again on the morning of October 24 at almost the exact hour that the naval quarantine around Cuba had gone into effect. CIA director John McCone soon made a dramatic announcement: "Mr. President, I have a note just handed me . . . it says that all six Soviet ships currently identified in Cuban waters—I don't know what that means—have either stopped or reversed course." Kennedy cut in to ask McCone to get additional details: "Why don't we find out whether they're talking about the ships leaving Cuba or the ones coming in?" "I'll find out," McCone promised, and left the meeting. Rusk quipped that the distinction made a real difference; Bundy murmured, "It sure does," and some edgy laughter can be heard at the table.

McCone soon returned and confirmed that six Russian ships heading to Cuba had indeed stopped or reversed direction well before reaching the naval quarantine line. JFK interposed firmly: "If this report is accurate, then we're not gonna do anything about these ships close in to Cuba." Bundy appeared to agree: "The ships further in, we would not wish to stop, would we?"

Later that afternoon, Bundy recommended that the administration "get in touch with the Soviets and get their view on the generation of this crisis and why we've reacted." He also asked the president for clearance to release photos proving that the Soviets had camouflaged some of the missile sites. "The Russians have been very resistant to let us say what is a fact," Bundy declared contemptuously. They "did camouflage these things by their standard practice, very carefully. They proceeded by night, our agents' reports now indicate—our refugee reports. They have never been good at overhead camouflage," he shouted; "It's just [how] doctrinally backwards they are! [The awkward phrase "doctrinally backwards" was almost certainly a reference to Russian military doctrine or methodology.] If we can break this out of intelligence and use it to back our aim, it would help" with our European allies. JFK approved making the camouflage photos available to the press.

The next day, October 25, much of the morning ExComm discussion centered on how to enforce the quarantine. RFK observed that sooner or later a ship would have to be intercepted, but Bundy expressed the hope that U Thant might convince the U.S.S.R. to avoid challenging the quarantine: "It's not likely, but it's conceivable." "In that case," JFK agreed, it was better to delay initiating a naval confrontation. Bundy cautioned, however, "There's nothing, Mr. President—I've just checked the language in your speech—which requires you to stop any ship, simply, 'If found to contain cargoes of offensive weapons, it will be turned back.'" JFK murmured "Yeah," as Bundy concluded, "The way in which we find this [contraband] is our business." JFK expressed the hope that since some ships had turned back Khrushchev might be rethinking his hard-line public stance, and by waiting to intercept a ship the U.S. could avoid appearing to be warmongers. "Well, we're caught with one crowd or the other," Bundy observed cynically. Nonetheless, he insisted that ships reaching the blockade line must be inspected. "Otherwise they're deciding," he warned authoritatively, "what meets our proclamation."

"Well we can't take the quarantine off," the president pointed out, until U Thant "offers a substitute and he hasn't offered a substitute." Bundy boldly suggested addressing that issue right off the bat in the statement to the U.N.: "Why don't we say that in sentence one? There's no pain in that. That's an absolutely fundamental proposition with us. The quarantine is there to prevent the introduction of offensive weapons" and could be lifted only if three conditions were met: a halt in the delivery of offensive weapons to Cuba, cessation of construction of the missile sites, and reliable inspection and verification. The greatest danger, Bundy warned, was that "the status quo doesn't come to have a momentum of its own" if the negotiations at the U.N. dragged on indefinitely.

In that case, Bundy underscored firmly, "there is a real case to be made, which has perhaps not been presented as strongly this morning as it could be, for doing it [enforcing the quarantine by stopping all ships] and getting it done," so that the United States retained the initiative in determining the effectiveness of the quarantine. He boldly admonished the commander in chief, "It is important for you to know, Mr. President, that there is a good, substantial argument and a lot of people in the argument on the other side, all of whom will fall in with whatever decision you make." "Why don't you just go ahead," Paul Nitze argued in support of Bundy, and enforce the quarantine "against everybody, not selecting ships or the types of ships. But just go ahead and do that." "That's correct," Bundy affirmed. The president, notwithstanding, finally concluded, "This is not the appropriate time to blow up a ship." "Right," a subdued Bundy replied.

At the October 25 afternoon meeting, McNamara, with the president's agreement, argued that an East German passenger ship carrying 1,500 civilians and approaching the quarantine line should not be stopped. But JFK expressed concern that the U.S. could not unilaterally and indefinitely observe U Thant's request to avoid an incident at sea if Khrushchev refused to keep his ships away from the quarantine. Bundy pointed out, rather smugly, that U Thant's message applied only to Soviet vessels and the ship in question was East German. He also renewed his argument from the morning meeting, emphasizing the danger to American credibility in simply revealing to "the [Soviet] bloc that you're not stopping [any ships]."

JFK and his advisers were becoming increasingly concerned that the crisis had reached a dangerous impasse since the missiles already in Cuba would not be affected by the quarantine—making additional political or military steps seem all but inevitable. Indeed, an early morning CIA report had confirmed that construction of the MRBM and IRBM sites was "proceeding without interruption."[9] The administration did not try to conceal the massive movement of troops and supplies heading to southern Florida, and the press was reporting that an invasion of Cuba was imminent.

This heightened tension was immediately evident at the morning meeting on Friday, October 26. "Mr. President," Bundy advised, "my suggestion is that we should reconstitute Mongoose [the covert project directed by RFK to sabotage the Cuban economy and destabilize Castro] as a subcommittee of this committee" to deal with planning to create a new civil government for Cuba in the event of an invasion. McCone agreed, specifically reminding the president, "it's a matter you called me about last night." The president was likely assuming that all military options discussed since October 16 remained on the table if the blockade failed to compel the withdrawal of the missiles from Cuba.

Bundy stressed that "These are very important matters" and suggested making "part of the discussion at the Mongoose meeting this afternoon . . . the paramilitary, the civil government, the correlated activities to the main show that we need to reorganize." JFK pointed out that someone at State, CIA, and Defense should be in charge of these plans. "Post-Castro Cuba," Bundy reminded his colleagues, "is the most complex landscape."

The discussion then returned to the status of the quarantine, and McNamara revealed that navy personnel were, at that very moment, on board the *Marucla*, a Lebanese freighter, but he assured the president that "It won't be held long." The Greek crew cooperated fully with the inspection, which lasted nearly three hours, and the *Marucla* was permitted to proceed toward Cuba. No one had expected that stopping a Soviet-chartered ship would be so uneventful.

Several issues were then briefly discussed, including adding POL to the quarantine list, starting nighttime surveillance using flares, and dropping leaflets over Cuba warning of the danger to the Cuban people created by the missiles. Bundy, however, urged JFK not to be distracted by secondary issues: "Mr. President," he declared vigorously, "I believe myself that all of these things need to be measured in terms of the very simple, basic, structural purpose of this whole enterprise: to get these missiles out. Now Castro is a problem. If we can bring Castro down in the process, dandy. If we can turn him on other people, dandy. But if we can get the missiles out..." The president agreed that "we ought to concentrate on the missiles right now."

Bundy was particularly harsh in condemning the U.N. proposal for a simultaneous suspension of the blockade and a standstill in the construction of the missile sites, endorsed earlier in the meeting by U.N. ambassador Adlai Stevenson. "It's the inoperab[ility of the missiles] that's obvious," Bundy demanded, "and if we adopt a course at the U.N. which presumes that they [the missiles] might stay there, we've had it. He [Stevenson] must get that clearly in his head." "Then we have a double choice, Mr. President," unless we choose to "do nothing [the position he had endorsed on October 18]. One is to expand the blockade and the other is to remove the missiles by force."

JFK was becoming less confident that the Soviet Union had actually "blinked" by diverting ships carrying offensive weapons away from Cuba. He seemed to be leaning toward breaking the logjam over U.N. negotiations by turning up the heat on the Soviet Union—perhaps by bombing the missile sites after all. Later that afternoon, after reviewing the latest photos, the president privately asked for John McCone's recommendation: the CIA director unhesitatingly endorsed "moving quickly on an air strike."

Operation Mongoose discussions resumed later that day in the Pentagon, with emphasis on setting up a civil government in Cuba after an invasion had presumably toppled Castro. JFK finally decided that the U.N. plan was unacceptable. The U.S. would lift the quarantine only if the U.S.S.R. suspended arms shipments, ceased construction of the missile bases, and immobilized the missiles, with independent verification, within forty-eight hours.

Shortly after 6:00 P.M. on Friday evening, a new message from Khrushchev began arriving at the State Department. The letter was emotional and personal. The copy delivered to the American embassy had included Khrushchev's handwritten notations, and many assumed that it was a direct appeal from Khrushchev to Kennedy. The Soviet leader argued that the weapons in Cuba were defensive, but he no longer denied their presence. Nuclear war could be avoided, he proposed, if the Soviet Union ceased sending arms to Cuba and the United States pledged not to invade.[10]

The ExComm reconvened early on Saturday morning, October 27, and was promptly confounded by news that Khrushchev had made another offer, broadcast on Moscow Radio, proposing to remove the missiles in Cuba if the U.S. removed its missiles from Turkey. "In case this is an accurate statement," the president asked, "where are we with our conversations with the Turks about the withdrawal of these?" The question provoked immediate skepticism and resistance from Nitze, Ball, and Rusk. Bundy insisted that if Khrushchev had changed his terms and backed away from last night's letter, the president should not soften his resolve. When JFK insisted, with obvious irritation, that Khrushchev might have altered his position overnight, Bundy brashly asserted that "I" would stick to the terms in the Friday letter. President Kennedy replied firmly that rejecting the trade would be insupportable in terms of world opinion because "to any man at the United Nations or any other rational man, it will look like a very fair trade."

Once the trade proposal had been confirmed, JFK pressed Rusk on whether discussions had started with the Turks since, he repeated impatiently, he had been discussing this possibility for a week. Bundy contended again that the administration should stick to the Friday proposal, but the president continued to maintain that the Saturday proposal was the latest Soviet position—and it had been made public. "If we accept the notion of the trade at this stage," Bundy warned, "our position will come apart very fast." The president's dissatisfaction bubbled over again: "Well, I'd just like to know how much we've done about it, because, as I say, we talked about it." Bundy replied rather condescendingly, "We decided not to, Mr. President. . . . If we had talked to the Turks," he lectured, "it would already be clear that we were trying to sell our allies for our interests. That would be the view in all of NATO. Now it's irrational and it's crazy, but it's a terribly powerful fact." The president reiterated, "you're going to find a lot of people thinking this is rather a reasonable position." "That's true," Bundy reluctantly admitted.

With the president briefly out of the room, Paul Nitze demanded, "Say we're not gonna do that." "Yeah, I agree," Bundy replied; "That has to be said . . . And then direct attention back . . . to the fact that the Cuban matter remains urgent. The buildup is continuing." The U.S. should instead be pushing demands for halting construction on the bases, followed by the inoperability and removal of the missiles. "This should be knocked down publicly," Bundy stipulated, by separating out the Turkish issue and focusing attention on Cuba: "Privately we say to Khrushchev: 'Look, your public statement is a very dangerous one because it makes impossible immediate discussion of your private proposals and requires us to proceed urgently with the things that we have in mind. You'd better get straightened out! . . . We don't have very much time.'"

After the president rejoined the meeting, Bundy continued to defend the right of the Turkish government to say that NATO military arrangements have nothing to do with Cuba. "It seems to me," he declared firmly, "it's important that they should. If anyone pulls them in it will be us and they can't be expected to do that." Instead, Bundy urged the president to say that "the current threat to peace is not in Turkey—it is in Cuba. There's no pain in saying that even if you're going to make a trade later on." The immediate threat is in Cuba, he repeated, rapping the table for emphasis, "and that is what has got to stop." But, the president reaffirmed, "They've got a God[damn] . . . they've got a very good proposal, which is the reason they've made it public."

Bundy explained that an informal consensus had emerged while the president had been out of the room. "We have concluded that the Friday evening message was written personally by Khrushchev, but the Saturday morning public message resulted from his own hard-nosed people overruling him; this public one . . . they didn't like what he said to you last night." "Nor would I," Bundy added, "if I were a Soviet hardnose."

President Kennedy nevertheless underscored again that the public offer could not be disregarded and bluntly acknowledged that Khrushchev had been politically astute: "the fact that work is going on is the one defensible public position we've got. They've got a very good prod and this one is gonna be very tough, I think, for us." U.S. action in Cuba, he insisted, would give the U.S.S.R wide latitude to seize Berlin because "we are wholly unreasonable. Most people will think this is a rather even trade and we ought to take advantage of it." It would be, as a result, very difficult for the U.S. to gain world support for action against Cuba. "This is a pretty good play of his."

"I myself," Bundy pronounced self-confidently, "would send back word . . . that last night's stuff was pretty good. This is impossible at this stage of the game and that time is getting very short. . . . But I think it's very important to get them to get the message that if they want to stop something further in Cuba they have to do better than this public statement."

Soon after, the president spoke to Ambassador Stevenson in New York. After hanging up, JFK exclaimed with an acerbic chuckle, "What about our putting something in about Berlin [in the U.N. negotiations]? . . . I mean just to try to put some sand in his gears for a few minutes." "In what way?" Bundy inquired, sounding confused. The president, evidently thinking of the comparable Russian demand for noninvasion guarantees for Cuba, responded in an unusually sarcastic tone of voice, "Well, satisfactory guarantees for Berlin!"

President Kennedy, as the late afternoon Black Saturday meeting got under way, quickly renewed his argument that Khrushchev's missile trade proposal had to be taken seriously. Bundy nonetheless reported that he had talked to Ambassador Charles Bohlen in Paris who felt that "the knockdown of the Turkey-Cuba" link had been well received in France. Of course, no such "knockdown" had been authorized by the president. Also, despite JFK's determined arguments in favor of discussing the Turkish option with NATO, Bundy revealed that he had instructed the U.S. ambassador to NATO to tell the alliance's representatives that the U.S. opposed involving Turkey in a Cuban settlement. Remarkably, JFK did not comment on Bundy's brushes with outright insubordination.

George Ball also objected to including Turkey as "a quid pro quo" and Bundy chimed in, "That's my worry about it." "No! With negotiations!" JFK replied impatiently. Bundy then cut the president off with a stinging dissent: "There are two different audiences here, Mr. President, there really are. And I think if we sound as if we wanted to make this trade to our NATO people and to all the people who are tied to us by alliance, we are in real trouble." The national security adviser unflinchingly admonished the commander in chief: "I think that we'll all join in doing this if this is the decision. But I think we should tell you that that's the universal assessment of everyone in the government that's connected with these alliance problems," that if the United States appeared to be trading the defense of Turkey for the elimination of the threat from Cuba, "we just have to face a radical decline in the effectiveness" of NATO.

President Kennedy, addressing Bundy as "Mac," nonetheless repeated firmly, "this trade has appeal. Now, if we reject it out of hand, and then have to take military action against Cuba, then we'll also face a decline" in NATO and a loss of support around the world. He conceded that it was worth trying "to word it so that we don't harm NATO. But the thing that I think everybody would agree to is that while these matters, which are complicated, are discussed, there should be a cessation of work. Then I think we can hold general support for that. If they won't agree to that, the Soviet Union, then we retain some initiative. That's my response." The president had decided that the door had to be left open to negotiations on removing the Jupiter missiles from Turkey, notwithstanding Bundy's almost certainly exaggerated claim of "universal" opposition within the administration.

After the president left the room to take a call from NATO supreme commander General Lauris Norstad, Bundy asserted that "Turkey and Cuba is not workable for us except in the context of our doing a violent thing. And if we've done a violent thing," the usually self-assured national security adviser admitted, "we none of us know where to go. The one chance of avoiding that is to impress Khrushchev and get him back where he was last night." When the president returned, Bundy promptly and forcefully declared, "The justification for this message [trying to get Khrushchev back to the Friday proposal] is that we expect it to be turned down, expect to be acting [militarily] tomorrow or the next day. That's what it's for and it's not good unless that's what happens." Several voices can be heard affirming, "That's right." Bundy did not address what might happen if the U.S. attacked Cuba and simultaneously rejected Khrushchev's public missile trade offer.

But JFK would not budge on the need to call an immediate meeting of the NATO Council to discuss the Turkish missile issue; Bundy finally agreed: "I don't think there's any pain in the meeting. Why don't we get the meeting called? . . . It's one thing to stand them down, Mr. President, in political terms as a favor to the Turks [presumably making a Soviet attack on Turkey less likely], while we hit Cuba. It's quite another thing to trade them out, I think."

Recognizing JFK's determination, however, Bundy proposed an alternative: "Let's speculate with this, Mr. President. If you have that conviction and you are yourself sure this is the best way out, then I would say that an immediate personal telegram of acceptance [of Khrushchev's Cuba-Turkey swap] was the best thing to do." JFK objected, however, on political grounds: "What I think we'd have to do is get the Turks to agree. . . . [rather than] accepting it over their opposition and over NATO opposition. . . . I'd rather go the total blockade route," he explained, "which is a lesser step than this military action. What I'd like to do is have the Turks and NATO equally feel that this is the wiser move."

Bundy reiterated that "the disadvantage of having a NATO meeting and going to the Turks tonight and tomorrow is that you don't give this [Friday] track a fair run." He proposed instead telling NATO, if the president persisted, "'To free our hands in Cuba, we must get these missiles out of Turkey,' is what we say." And when McNamara asserted, "We're not trading Turkish missiles for Cuban missiles," Bundy affirmed, "No. No." "It will be seen as a trade by a great many people, Mr. President," he admonished. "There's no doubt about that. We've looked that one in the eye." The president agreed that Turkey and NATO would conclude that the U.S. was protecting its own interests first by making a deal on Turkey and that nothing the administration said would change their opinion. That result was diplomatically unfortunate but infinitely preferable to initiating a global nuclear war over the Turkish missiles.

JFK urged getting the proposal ready for an emergency NATO meeting on Sunday morning, but Bundy still dissented, "No, I would not do it tomorrow, Mr. President, myself." President Kennedy simply disregarded Bundy's objection: "I think we oughta get moving on it. The fact is, time's running out."

~

McGeorge Bundy's actual role in the ExComm meetings demonstrates conclusively that Bobby Kennedy's assessment in *Thirteen Days* ("He was for a strike, then a blockade, then for doing nothing because it would upset the situation in Berlin, and then, finally, he led the group which was in favor of a strike—and a strike without prior notification, along the lines of Pearl Harbor") is inaccurate, incomplete, and misleading. Above all, *Thirteen Days* conceals the fact that Bundy was, on Black Saturday, one of RFK's most outspoken allies in resisting a Turkey-Cuba missile trade.

The ExComm tapes also raise some very serious questions about Bundy's own published recollections of those sessions. He not only obfuscates his own resistance to the missile trade proposal but also evades his frequent and querulous disputes with the president. Bundy often seemed to forget that *he* was not the president, and his self-centered and repeated admonitions about what "I" or "I myself" would do clearly strained JFK's patience. He was, rather than the thoughtful, even-handed pragmatist who was neither a hawk nor a dove, the only person at the meetings who repeatedly provoked JFK's temper and irritation.

Of course, to his credit, Bundy was arguably doing his job as national security adviser. He understood correctly that JFK did not wish to be surrounded by yes-men. However, his later claim that he sometimes "chose the role of 'devil's advocate' to focus the dialogue in meetings" simply fails to convincingly account for the compelling evidence on the tapes.[11]

Bundy, rather ironically, also endorsed the Trollope ploy myth in his published memoir. "What Robert Kennedy did was to insist successfully on the value of a clear *acceptance* of Khrushchev's first proposal." He declared that "No one believed we could or should accept Khrushchev's new [Saturday] offer as it stood. . . . Kennedy's understanding of the political power of Khrushchev's second letter made him pessimistic about the prospect of success in returning to the first. Yet in the end *he not only chose that course but recognized the importance of giving it clear priority over any effort to persuade the Turks of the advantage of getting missiles in their country off the board*" (emphasis added).[12] This assertion is blatantly and indisputably contradicted by the verbatim evidence on the ExComm tapes.

Furthermore, Bundy recalls that Dean Rusk "had been listening all day to the President's unwillingness to let," what Bundy himself concedes was "an intransigent position on these unwanted weapons stand between his country and the safe removal of the Soviet missiles from Cuba." He also claims that "Rusk shared this sentiment. . . . To Dean Rusk it was and is clear that measured against the dangers we faced on October 27, this assurance [to remove the Jupiters] was worth many times any possible cost." In fact, until Rusk's breakthrough proposal at the small Oval Office meeting that evening, the secretary of state had resisted the trade throughout the day as forthrightly as Bundy himself.[13]

8   The Determined Diplomacy
of Adlai Stevenson

That's what they [the Soviets] said these weapons were for: to
defend the territorial integrity of Cuba.
—Adlai Stevenson, October 26, 1962

UNITED NATIONS AMBASSADOR Adlai Stevenson's role in the
missile crisis has been dominated by two episodes: his televised
October 25 "until hell freezes over" exchange with Soviet ambassador Valerian
Zorin at the U.N. and the later charge by two journalists, with close ties to the
Kennedys, that he had advocated appeasement, "a Munich," at the ExComm
meeting on October 26.[1] Stevenson had enjoyed a surge of popularity in polls
after the U.N. debate. But only a few weeks later, he found himself embarrassed and on the defensive about the appeasement accusation, and considered resigning. Eventually, the president (who denied any connection to the
article) made public a letter supporting Stevenson, and the press eventually
lost interest in the story. The missile crisis controversy was especially bitter
for Stevenson because he had already been publicly embarrassed in April 1961,
when he unknowingly showed doctored CIA photographs at the U.N. as part
of the administration's attempt to cover up the U.S. role in the Bay of Pigs
fiasco.

The relationship between Stevenson and the Kennedys had never been
more than formal and proper at best. Bobby Kennedy had worked in Stevenson's 1956 presidential campaign but eventually became convinced that the
former Illinois governor was weak and indecisive and voted for Eisenhower.
JFK always felt that Stevenson's aloofness had led to his own narrow defeat for

the Democratic vice presidential nomination that same year. And the Kennedys never forgot or forgave Stevenson's quixotic attempt at the 1960 Democratic National Convention to win a third consecutive presidential nomination—essentially eliminating any chance that Stevenson would be chosen as JFK's secretary of state. Finally, Stevenson's hesitancy to accept the U.N. ambassadorship only increased the Kennedys' perception that he was too irresolute to wield real power.

~

On Monday, October 16, just after the first ExComm meeting, the unusually tense president hosted a previously scheduled luncheon for the Crown Prince of Libya, also attended by Stevenson; later, he showed the ambassador the U-2 photos. The next morning, Stevenson sent a note to the president arguing that the Soviet missiles in Cuba would inevitably be regarded around the world as a quid pro quo for U.S. missiles in Turkey. He urged the president to remain open to negotiations on "*the existence of nuclear missile bases anywhere . . . before we start anything*" (emphasis in original). The ambassador also declared that "we can't negotiate with a gun at our head" and accused the Soviets of upsetting "the precarious balance in the world in arrogant disregard of your warnings—by threats against Berlin and now from Cuba—and that we have no choice except to restore that balance, i.e., blackmail and intimidation *never*, negotiation and sanity *always*" (emphasis in original).[2] It was the first hint of the missile trade strategy that would eventually shape the outcome of the crisis, and the president tentatively floated the idea at the ExComm meeting the very next morning.

Stevenson also attended an (unrecorded) meeting on October 20—at which the president finalized his decision to start with a blockade. The ambassador suggested "that at an appropriate time we would have to acknowledge that we were willing to take strategic missiles out of Turkey and Italy if this issue were raised by the Russians." In addition, he urged the evacuation of the Guantánamo naval base. President Kennedy sharply rejected Stevenson's recommendation because it "would convey to the world that we had been frightened into abandoning our position." As matters would eventually play out, Stevenson's stance later made the president's support for a trade of the Turkish and Italian missiles—without yielding anything on Guantánamo—seem somewhat more palatable to the ExComm hawks. (McNamara, earlier in the meeting, had also suggested a possible "agreement to limit our use of Guantánamo to a specified limited time"; see Chapter 4.)

Stevenson arranged to have some U-2 photos available for the upcoming U.N. Security Council debate and used the photos with consummate skill on Thursday, October 25, to humiliate Soviet U.N. ambassador Zorin (who had been kept in the dark by his own government). He later conferred with Secretary General U Thant on the U.N. proposal to simultaneously suspend both arms shipments to Cuba and the blockade so that negotiations could begin on resolving the crisis. The U.N. ambassador, basking in the enthusiastic public response to the televised U.N. debate, flew to Washington for the Friday morning ExComm meeting.

Dean Rusk praised Stevenson's performance at the U.N.: "He put Zorin in the position where Zorin made himself ridiculous. And this kind of attitude throughout the U.N. is very helpful." (Even RFK, hardly a Stevenson loyalist, later gave the ambassador's U.N. success substantial coverage in his *Thirteen Days*.[3]) President Kennedy, however, soon initiated one of the most acrimonious exchanges of the ExComm meetings when he turned to Stevenson and asked, "Governor, do you want to talk a little and give us your thoughts?" (Stevenson had served as governor of Illinois from 1949 to 1953—his only elective office.) The U.N. ambassador surely sensed that the ExComm was stacked against him: Bundy, Dillon, McCloy, and McCone were Republicans and he was dubious about the backing of the Kennedys as well; the antagonism in the Cabinet room toward Stevenson was almost palpable.

The ambassador nonetheless endorsed U Thant's plan for a concurrent standstill on the delivery of missiles to Cuba and the lifting of the quarantine. "Would the work on the sites be ceased?" the president asked skeptically. "Work on the sites, of course," Stevenson replied. Does this "insure that they are inoperable!" Bundy demanded. The question of assuring the inoperability of the sites already in Cuba, Stevenson explained, would be left for subsequent negotiations. The reaction to the ambassador's remarks was extremely harsh. Rusk, Nitze, Bundy, McNamara, and McCone insisted that the dismantling of the existing sites had to be the top priority *before* suspending the quarantine.

Stevenson continued hesitantly, "I'm trying to make clear to you that this was a standstill. There would be no more construction, no more quarantine, no more arms shipments. Now when you say, 'make them inoperable,' that's not a standstill. . . . But I don't think that there should be any misunderstanding about what was intended here, which was a standstill and only a standstill." The besieged U.N. ambassador further explained that the Soviets would dismantle the bases and withdraw these weapons from the hemisphere, but "what they will want in return is, I anticipate, a new guarantee of the territorial integrity of Cuba. Indeed," he argued audaciously, "that's what they said these weapons were for: to defend the territorial integrity of Cuba" against an American invasion—an argument that had been conspicuously missing from the ExComm discussions. Stevenson then dropped the other shoe: "It is possible that the price that might be asked of us . . . might include dismantling bases of ours, such as Italy and Turkey, that we have talked about." ExComm superhawk, Paul Nitze, later recalled, "I was outraged by his [Stevenson's] attempt at total appeasement."[4]

John McCloy, Stevenson's "assistant" at the U.N., had been silent during the ambassador's presentation. A special adviser to JFK on disarmament, McCloy had been brought back from Europe to "assist" Stevenson at the United Nations and had flown to D.C. with the ambassador for the ExComm meeting. The administration had publicly explained McCloy's assignment to the U.N. as an effort to add a bipartisan Republican voice to the negotiations. In fact, McCloy was sent to New York because of White House concern that Stevenson was not tough enough to deal with the Soviets.

McCloy ripped into Stevenson's failure to deal immediately with the weapons pointed "right now . . . at our hearts." The president intervened to say that the quarantine itself would not remove the weapons already in Cuba in any case: "So you've only got two ways of removing the weapons." One way, JFK emphasized, coming strikingly close to Stevenson's position on the Jupiter missiles, "is to negotiate them out, or in other words, trade them out. And the other is to go in and take them out. I don't see any other way you're going to get the weapons out."

McCloy nonetheless continued emotionally: "Look, this is the security of the United States! I believe the strategic situation has greatly changed with the presence of these weapons in Cuba." "The only thing that I'm saying," Kennedy repeated, "is that we're not gonna get them out with the quarantine. . . . We're either gonna trade 'em out or we're gonna have to go in and get 'em out—ourselves. I don't know of any other way to do it."

Stevenson soon asked to be excused to take a call from an aide at the United Nations. "OK, sure thing," JFK replied. "Why don't you go in my office." The phone conversation was recorded, and Stevenson grumbled about being pressured to add the inoperability of the missiles to the standstill proposal. He must have experienced mixed emotions as he talked in the Oval Office—possibly at the president's desk. It would have been very difficult for the twice-defeated presidential candidate to sit alone in the office he clearly felt that *he* deserved to occupy.[5]

The president observed with unusual bluntness, "Governor Stevenson has this proposal for dealing with the missiles, which nobody's very much interested in. [Stevenson was still on the phone in the Oval Office.] But the point is that the blockade is not going to accomplish the job either, so we've got to have some other alternatives to accomplish what Governor Stevenson suggests may or may not be accomplished by negotiations."

The U.N. moratorium plan, JFK finally decided, was not acceptable to the United States unless the U.S.S.R. suspended arms shipments, ceased construction of the missile bases, and immobilized the missiles within forty-eight hours; the United States would then, after compliance had been independently verified, lift the quarantine. The secretary general was very gloomy about such a deal; the Soviets, and particularly the Cubans, he predicted, would never allow outside inspectors into Cuba.

In the end, over the next thirty-six hours, the president accepted (secretly) Khrushchev's Saturday, October 27, proposal to mutually remove U.S. missiles from Turkey and Soviet missiles from Cuba. At the same time, the administration invented a cover story that Khrushchev had abandoned his missile trade plan and instead accepted U.S. agreement to his Friday, October 26, proposal to remove the missiles in exchange for an American promise not to invade Cuba.

The president, in essence, chose the path that Ambassador Stevenson had first suggested on October 17. But the midterm congressional elections were only weeks away, and planning for the 1964 presidential campaign was moving forward as well. If, as seemed likely, the conservative Arizona senator Barry Goldwater won the Republican presidential nomination, nothing could have been more damaging to the president's reelection prospects than the charge that he had been "soft on communism." The leak to Bartlett and Alsop, suggesting that Stevenson had advocated "a Munich," successfully diverted attention from the president and squared perfectly with the emerging cover story that later became known as the Trollope ploy.

9　The Trollope Ploy Myth

> I suggested, and was supported by Ted Sorensen and others,
> that we ignore the latest Khrushchev letter and respond to his
> earlier letter's proposal.
>
> —Robert Kennedy, *Thirteen Days*, 1969

SEVERAL MONTHS AFTER the 2003 publication of my narrative history of the Cuban missile crisis ExComm meetings, I received a call from a television production company preparing a program about letters written by American presidents. They asked if I might be interested in discussing John F. Kennedy's missile crisis letters to Nikita Khrushchev. I explained that these letters were not really personal since they had been composed by the president and a group of advisers rather than by JFK himself. I suggested instead that we might discuss one of the most famous incidents relating to the Kennedy-Khrushchev correspondence: on the evening of October 26, the Soviet leader sent a letter offering to remove the missiles from Cuba if the U.S. pledged not to invade the island nation. But early on October 27, Khrushchev suddenly changed his offer—publicly—by demanding instead that the U.S. also withdraw its Jupiter missiles from Turkey in exchange for the removal of the missiles in Cuba.

According to the conventional story, Robert Kennedy suggested accepting the proposal in Khrushchev's first letter and ignoring the second message. This allegedly brilliant diplomatic strategy came to be called the "Trollope ploy"—a reference to a plot device by nineteenth-century British novelist Anthony Trollope, in which a woman interprets a casual romantic gesture as a marriage proposal. RFK's idea has been hailed for decades as the ingenious and cunning diplomatic breakthrough that led to resolving the crisis.

The producer of the program expressed interest in including a "revisionist" perspective; we later did some thirty minutes of filming in which I carefully explained that RFK's inspired strategy makes a great story but that the ExComm tapes prove that it never actually happened. President Kennedy's determination to avoid nuclear war made him unwilling to take such a high-risk gamble on a mere diplomatic sleight of hand. When the program was broadcast, however, the editors used about five seconds of the interview—during which I merely spoke the words "the Trollope ploy"—and then cut to actor Martin Sheen, who had played RFK in a 1974 dramatization of the missile crisis. Sheen recapitulated the standard account and praised RFK's brilliance in preventing the U.S. and the U.S.S.R. from sliding into a nuclear war. The filmmakers obviously decided that the conventional explanation was less complicated and more dramatic—especially coming from an actor and celebrity.

This kind of slipshod "history" is neither surprising nor uncommon on television; yet even among historians and ExComm participants the Trollope ploy remains an all but immovable fixture in the legend and lore of the missile crisis. In 2003, Robert McNamara continued to peddle this mythology in Errol Morris's Academy Award-winning film about his public career (see Chapter 4). And as recently as 2008, Ted Sorensen, at the time the last major survivor of the ExComm meetings, also refused to abandon this time-honored fable (see Chapter 1).

The prologue to Sorensen's five-hundred-plus-page personal memoir began with his role in the Cuban missile crisis, which he rightly regarded as the most unforgettable and consequential event of his public career. His account is all too familiar: RFK urged the president "to ignore the second letter . . . conveying a much stiffer tone" and to accept the proposal in the first, more "hopeful" letter.[1]

Sorensen justifiably recalled that he "felt the weight of the world on my shoulders" as he began, at the direction of JFK and with the aid of RFK, to draft the letter to Khrushchev. "It was a giant gamble on our part. . . . [But] we succeeded . . . [and] the world stepped back from the very brink of destruction and has never come that close again. I am proud that my letter helped contribute to that conclusion."[2]

But is that what really happened? Sorensen frankly acknowledged "the hazards of memory, inevitably influenced by selectivity and hindsight."[3] Today, however, historians can finally get it right by turning to the ultimate primary historical source: the verbatim recordings of the ExComm meetings.

The tale of this inspired maneuver for responding to Khrushchev's two conflicting letters began with Stewart Alsop and Charles Bartlett, writing in the *Saturday Evening Post* a few weeks after the crisis and exploiting leaks possibly from the Kennedy brothers themselves. Their article, which also accused Ambassador Stevenson of advocating "a Munich" (see Chapter 8), launched the notion that Robert Kennedy "had dreamed up the 'Trollope Ploy' to save the day." Several years later, anticipating a run for president in a nation bitterly divided by the Vietnam war, RFK was eager to take credit for hitting upon the path to peace in 1962: "I suggested" accepting Khrushchev's Friday proposal "that the Soviet missiles and offensive weapons would be removed from Cuba under UN inspection and verification, if, on its side, the United States would agree with the rest of the Western Hemisphere not to invade Cuba."[4]

Arthur Schlesinger Jr., writing several years after the crisis, also claimed that RFK "came up with a thought of breathtaking simplicity and ingenuity: why not ignore the second Khrushchev message and reply to the first?" Ted Sorensen had initially suggested in 1965 that JFK himself had "decided to treat the latest [October 27] letter as propaganda and to concentrate on the Friday night [October 26] letter" and had delegated RFK and Sorensen to come up with the right wording. However, when Sorensen completed the manuscript of *Thirteen Days*, published in 1969 after RFK's assassination, he did not challenge Bobby Kennedy's claim to have first suggested this breakthrough strategy.[5]

Several historians have insisted that "the idea was hardly Robert Kennedy's alone ... [and] entered the discussion gradually and was embraced by several members" and that the Trollope ploy "is a little too elegant to explain the muddle and confusion of the debate on Saturday, October 27." There has, nonetheless, been a long-standing consensus among most historians and journalists—and in film dramatizations of the crisis—that the Trollope ploy was "a brilliant way to handle it," "an ingenious ploy," "an extraordinary diplomatic move," and that RFK met with the Soviet ambassador on the evening of October 27 "to execute the Trollope Ploy." Dean Rusk also endorsed the myth in his 1994 memoir as did Robert McNamara in *The Fog of War*, except that they both insisted that Ambassador Llewellyn Thompson was the first to propose it. In fact, Adlai Stevenson appears to have been the first to mention it in his October 17 memo to President Kennedy (see Chapter 8).[6]

President Kennedy himself immediately seized on the political benefit in this simple and dramatic explanation of the settlement of the crisis. Only hours after Khrushchev publicly agreed to remove the missiles, JFK phoned former presidents Eisenhower, Truman, and Hoover—and deliberately misinformed them. He accurately reported that Khrushchev, on Friday, had privately suggested withdrawing the missiles in exchange for an American promise not to invade Cuba; but on Saturday, the Kremlin leader had sent a public message offering to remove the missiles if the U.S. pulled its Jupiter missiles out of Turkey. Kennedy informed Eisenhower, "we couldn't get into that deal"; assured Truman that they "accepted the earlier proposal"; and told Hoover that Khrushchev had gone back "to their more reasonable [Friday] position." Eisenhower, who had dealt personally with Khrushchev, asked skeptically if the Soviets had tried to attach any other conditions. "No," Kennedy replied disingenuously, "except that we're not gonna invade Cuba." The surprised former president, aware of only half the truth, concluded, "this is a very, I think, conciliatory move he's made." The Trollope ploy became the key to the administration's cover story, which was indelibly fixed in public consciousness by *Thirteen Days* and by the 1974 television film *The Missiles of October* based on RFK's memoir.

Despite the availability of the ExComm tapes, the Trollope ploy continues to thrive—much like the resilient fable that Lincoln dashed off the Gettysburg Address on the back of an envelope. However, the crisis was not resolved so neatly or melodramatically.

～

At the morning ExComm meeting on Saturday, October 27, barely twelve hours after receiving Khrushchev's Friday evening letter—the first of the two critical messages—JFK read aloud a press statement just handed to him: "Premier Khrushchev told President Kennedy in a message [broadcast over Moscow Radio] today he would withdraw offensive weapons from Cuba if the United States withdrew its rockets from Turkey." The president and the ExComm were clearly startled and puzzled. But JFK speculated, "He may be putting out another letter," and called in press secretary Pierre Salinger. "I read it [the Friday letter] pretty carefully," Salinger asserted, "and it didn't read that way [suggesting a missile swap] to me either." "Well," the president concluded, "let's just sit tight on it." Rusk speculated that this might be a new proposal.

The missile trade suggestion might have been new in the messages from the Soviet side, but Ambassador Stevenson had floated the idea early in the crisis and had endured withering criticism when he backed it again at the October 26 ExComm meeting. Robert McNamara and Llewellyn Thompson had defended a missile trade during the first week of meetings, and the president had been cautiously probing the Turkish option since October 18. "Where are we," the president now asked, "with our conversations with the Turks?" Assistant Defense Secretary Paul Nitze responded firmly, "The Turks say that this is absolutely anathema" and view it "as a matter of prestige and politics." JFK understood the world of prestige and politics as well as anyone in the room, but told Nitze, "Well, I don't think we can" take that position "if this is an accurate [report]."

Bundy argued that if Khrushchev had backed away from the "purely Cuban context" in last night's letter, "There's nothing wrong with our posture in sticking to that line." "Well maybe they changed it overnight," JFK persisted. "He's in a difficult position to change it overnight," Bundy reasoned. "Well now, let's say he has changed it," JFK snapped, "and this is his latest position." "Well, I would answer back," Bundy retorted testily, "saying that 'I would prefer to deal with your interesting proposals of last night.'" Someone egged Bundy on, whispering, "Go for it!"

JFK's reply represents a turning point in the discussions, leaving no doubt about his evolving position: "Well now, that's what we oughta be thinkin' about. We're gonna be in an insupportable position on this matter if this becomes his proposal. In the first place, we last year tried to get the missiles out of there because they're not militarily useful, number one. Number two, it's gonna—to any man at the United Nations or any other rational man, it will look like a very fair trade." "I don't think so," Nitze countered, as someone muttered "No, no, no" in the background. "Deal with this Cuban thing. We'll talk about other things later."

Salinger soon brought in a news ticker report which JFK read aloud, confirming Khrushchev's new public offer on Moscow Radio to link the missiles in Cuba and Turkey. "Now we've known this might be coming for a week," Kennedy repeated impatiently; "This is their proposal." "How much negotiation have we had with the Turks this week?" JFK grumbled; "Who's done it?" "We haven't talked with the Turks," Rusk tried to explain; "The Turks have talked with us." "Where have they talked with us?" JFK demanded. "In NATO," Rusk replied. "Yeah, but have we gone to the Turkish government before this came out this week? I've talked about it now for a week," the president protested again. "Have we got any conversations in Turkey with the Turks?" Rusk reluctantly admitted that there had been no talks.

Under Secretary of State George Ball declared that approaching the Turks on withdrawing the Jupiters "would be an extremely unsettling business." "Well," JFK barked, "this is unsettling now George, because he's got us in a pretty good spot here. Because most people will regard this as not an unreasonable proposal. I'll just tell you that." "But, what 'most people,' Mr. President?" Bundy asked skeptically. The president shot back: "I think you're gonna have it very difficult to explain why we are going to take hostile military action in Cuba . . . when he's saying, 'If you get yours out of Turkey, we'll get ours out of Cuba.' I think you've got a very tough one here." "I don't see why we pick that track," Bundy persisted, "when he's offered us the other track in the last twenty-four hours." JFK interrupted irritably, "Well he's now offered us a new one!" "You think the public one is serious?" General Taylor asked, rather incredulously. "Yes!" the president declared stubbornly. "I think we have to assume that this is their new and latest position, and it's a public one."

Khrushchev, in light of declassified Soviet documents, apparently made the Friday offer because of intelligence predicting an imminent American invasion of Cuba. He hoped to head off the invasion first and deal later with the Jupiters in Turkey. Only hours later he received reports that the invasion scare was erroneous and sent another message introducing a Turkish missile withdrawal. "Pride and arrogance again took the upper hand over prudence: he could not look weak in the eyes of his subordinates." Vassily Kuznetsov, the Soviet Union's first deputy minister of foreign affairs, later declared, "Khrushchev shit his pants."[7]

Ball and Bundy suggested pulling the rug out from under Khrushchev by releasing his private October 26 letter. "Yeah, but I think we have to," the president countered, only partially suppressing an exasperated laugh, "be now thinking about what our position's gonna be on this one, because this is the one that's before us and before the world." JFK noted that Khrushchev's private Friday offer also had "serious disadvantages . . . which is this guarantee of Cuba [against invasion]. But in any case," he repeated yet again, "this is now his official one. We can release his other one, and it's different, but this is the one that the Soviet government obviously is going on."

Nitze tried again to shake the president's determination by suggesting that the Soviets might be pursuing both a private track with Cuba and a public track with the U.S. "to confuse the public scene and divide us with additional pressures." JFK readily admitted, "It's possible." A short time later, when the president was briefly out of the room, Douglas Dillon can be heard muttering irritably, "The United States cannot accept a Turkey-Cuba trade at this point."

Robert Kennedy, in a nominal attempt to stand in for his brother, asked, "Can I throw out some ideas?" He suggested key points for the U.S. negotiating stance. First, the issue of the Cuban missile bases "must be resolved within the next few days. This can't wait" because "the work is continuing despite our protests . . . so therefore it's got to be resolved—and quickly." Second, the quarantine is "an action by all of Latin America countries plus the United States." Third, this situation "has nothing to do with the security of the countries of Europe, which do have their own problems." Nonetheless, he added, "We would obviously consider negotiating the giving up of bases in Turkey if we can assure the Turks and the other European countries for whom these bases were placed" that their own security will be protected. A moment later, however, he acknowledged that he personally did not see how the U.S. could compel the Turks to surrender their own defense as long as Soviet missiles were aimed at Turkey.

The low-key, informal conversations that continued with the president still out of the room exposed the depth and persistence of ExComm hostility to a Cuba-Turkey missile trade. Ball reported that Ambassador Stevenson had called to say there was no disposition among the U.S. delegation to the U.N. to get Turkey involved at all, "that they want to keep it strictly separate—keep the Turkey business out." Stevenson, of course, had boldly defended the missile trade proposal at the ExComm meeting just twenty-four hours earlier. "Attack this Turkish thing hard," Nitze demanded. "Say we're not gonna do that. It's an entirely separate situation. It's not a threat." Taylor agreed that the Turkish missile proposal was "a diversionary tactic."

Rusk speculated that the personal Friday night letter had been sent by Khrushchev "without clearance," and a consensus quickly developed that the Politburo was behind the Saturday message. Bundy insisted that the public Saturday letter should be rejected—publicly. CIA director John McCone, backed by several others, affirmed, "This is exactly right!"

The president had already argued vigorously that Khrushchev's public offer had probably made removal of the Turkish missiles unavoidable and his immediate concern, despite the nearly unanimous resistance of the ExComm, was to prevent the Turks from constricting his options. "Wait just a . . . it seems to me," JFK cut in, breaking his silence for the first time since rejoining the meeting, "the first thing we oughta try to do is not let the Turks issue some statement which is wholly unacceptable." He reiterated that work on the missile sites had to stop "before we talk about anything. At least then we're in a defensible position." The president contended again that the Turks did not realize that if the U.S. took military action in Cuba, the Soviets could retaliate against the Jupiter missiles, exposing Turkey to grave danger. "We gotta have a talk with the Turks because I think they've got to understand the peril that they're going to move into next week if we take some action in Cuba. I think the chances are that he'll [Khrushchev] take some action in Turkey. They oughta understand that. And in fact they [the U.S.S.R.] may even come out and say that once the Turks turn us down. . . . So I think the Turks ought to think a little about it and we oughta try to get them not to respond to this til we've had a chance to consider what action we'll take. Now, how long would it take to get in touch with the Turks?" Nitze, notwithstanding, pushed the president even harder by insisting that emphasizing the differences between Khrushchev's last two messages "looks to the public . . . like a rationalization of our own confusion. I think we've got to take a firmer line than that."

RFK, still ambivalent about his brother's stance on a missile trade, insisted "that we make doubly clear that Turkish NATO missiles were one problem and that Cuba was an entirely separate problem." Roswell Gilpatric agreed, stating "that it was crucial for us to stand on the position that we will not negotiate with the Russians while the Soviet missile threat is growing in Cuba." The president, however, did not retreat, recalling that the United States had considered removing the Jupiter missiles from Turkey more than a year ago: "But we are now in a position of risking war in Cuba and in Berlin over missiles in Turkey which are of little military value. From the political point of view, it would be hard to get support on an air strike against Cuba because many would think that we would make a good trade if we offered to take the missiles out of Turkey in the event the Russians would agree to remove the missiles from Cuba." The Turks, he insisted, must be informed of "the great danger in which they will live during the next week and we have to face up to the possibility of some kind of a trade over missiles." RFK expressed concern about the possible deterioration of the U.S. position if talks with the Soviets dragged on for weeks or even months and the Cubans refused to allow inspections to verify that the missiles were inoperable—but, he conjectured with obvious interest, "we could then decide [after all] to attack the bases by air."

JFK, after the morning discussion, met with the Civil Defense Committee of the Governors' Conference. California's Edmund Brown, a Democrat, asked bluntly, "Mr. President, many people wonder why you changed your mind about the Bay of Pigs and aborted the attack. Will you change your mind again?" "I chose the quarantine," Kennedy retorted coldly, "because I wondered if our people are ready for the bomb." At a small meeting held at the State Department that afternoon, RFK again urged full preparation for air attacks on Cuba by Monday or Tuesday (October 29–30). As the group was about to leave for the full ExComm meeting at 4:00 P.M., McNamara learned that a U-2 was missing and that low-level reconnaissance flights had been fired on over Cuba.

No one in Washington knew that in the early morning hours Fidel Castro had sent an emotional letter to Khrushchev, essentially arguing that the situation was deteriorating very rapidly and if Cuba was to avoid receiving the first strike, if an attack was inevitable, then the Soviet Union should instead launch a first strike against the U.S. "It became clear to us," Khrushchev later wrote, "that Fidel totally failed to understand our purpose. We had installed the missiles not for the purpose of attacking the United States, but to keep the United States from attacking Cuba." He later replied to his Cuban ally, "you proposed that we be the first to carry out a nuclear strike against the territory of the enemy. You, of course, realize where that would have led. Rather than a simple strike, it would have been the start of a thermonuclear world war. Dear Comrade Fidel Castro, I consider this proposal of yours incorrect, although I understand your motivation." Castro's letter "may well have influenced Khrushchev's decision to proceed with a settlement with the United States."[8]

When the ExComm reconvened late that afternoon, President Kennedy essentially took charge of the discussion: if the U.S. rebuffed Khrushchev's message on Turkey, he reasoned, "then where are we gonna be? Tomorrow he'll come back and say the United States has rejected this proposal he's made. . . . So I think we oughta be able to say that the matter of Turkey and so on, in fact all these matters can be discussed if he'll cease work. Otherwise he's going to announce that we've rejected his proposal." He paused dramatically for some six seconds before reiterating darkly, "And then where are we? . . . That's our only, it seems to me, defense against the appeal of his trade. I think our message oughta be that we're glad to discuss this [Turkey] and other matters but we've gotta get a cessation of work."

Ball, who had resisted the trade idea earlier in the meeting, now buttressed

JFK's argument by revealing that the Soviet U.N. ambassador had told Secretary General U Thant that Khrushchev's private Friday letter had been "designed to reduce tension." But, "so as far as he was concerned," the public Saturday message, just as the president had been arguing, "contained the substantive proposal." Bundy continued to resist and boldly warned the president that accepting the Turkish trade proposal would wreck the NATO alliance. Sorensen too noted that "practically everyone here would favor the private [Friday] proposal."

Rusk then proposed new language for JFK's message to Khrushchev, concluding: after the crisis in Cuba is resolved, "'we can make progress on other and wider issues.'" President Kennedy recognized immediately that Rusk's wording contradicted his own stance on pursuing a Turkey-Cuba trade. "It's rejecting the tie-in [on Turkey]," Dillon affirmed; "But, we've got to do that." President Kennedy responded vigorously. "We're *not* rejecting the tie-in."

"Now that they've taken a public position," the president emphasized again, "I think the best position now with him and publicly is to say 'we're glad to discuss this matter' [Turkey] . . . [once] they have ceased their work in Cuba." A more flexible stance "puts us in a much stronger world position because most people will think his offer is rather reasonable . . . But I think that if we don't say that, he's gonna say that we rejected his offer and therefore he's gonna have public opinion with him . . . Therefore we're in much better shape to put our case on that, than rather that Turkey's irrelevant."

Ambassador Thompson warned that if the U.S. accepted the trade, the Russian military base would remain in Cuba with everything (SAM sites, bombers, military and technical personnel, etc.) except the nuclear missiles. President Kennedy replied with practical and determined logic: "But our technicians and planes and guarantees would still exist for Turkey. I'm just thinking about what we're gonna have to do in a day or so, which is five hundred [air] sorties in seven days and possibly an invasion, all because we wouldn't take missiles out of Turkey." Perhaps recalling his own wartime experience, JFK continued, "And we all know how quickly everybody's courage goes when the blood starts to flow and that's what's gonna happen in NATO." If the Soviets "grab Berlin, everybody's gonna say, 'Well, that was a pretty good proposition.' Let's not kid ourselves, that's the difficulty." President Kennedy had clearly made up his mind, notwithstanding ExComm opposition, to accept some arrangement involving the Turkish missiles as the price for averting "the final failure" of nuclear war.

If the Turks were adamant, JFK continued, then the U.S. ought to get NATO to "put enough pressure on them. I just tell you," he lectured, "I think we're better off to get those missiles out of Turkey and out of Cuba because I think the way of getting 'em out of Turkey and out of Cuba is gonna be very, very difficult and very bloody, one place or another."

Sorensen also pressed the president to delay replying to Khrushchev's public Saturday offer and instead respond privately to the secret Friday letter: "There's always a chance that he'll accept that. . . . We meanwhile won't have broken up NATO over something that never would have come to NATO." "The point of the matter is," President Kennedy snapped again, "Khrushchev's gonna come back and refer to his thing this morning on Turkey. And then we're gonna be screwing around for another forty-eight hours. . . . He'll come back and say, 'Well we're glad to settle the Cuban matter. What is your opinion of our proposal about Turkey?' So then we're on to Monday afternoon, and the work goes on. . . . He can hang us up for three days while he goes on with the work." "For three weeks!" Dillon muttered irritably.

"Let's start with our letter," JFK finally agreed; but he nonetheless had no illusions about Khrushchev's response to U.S. pressure to go back to Friday's proposal, "which he isn't gonna give us. He's now moved on to the Turkish thing. So we're just gonna get a letter back saying, 'Well, he'd be glad to settle Cuba when we settle Turkey.'" The president also cautioned, "It's got to be finessed. We have to finesse him."

Ambassador Thompson repeated that Khrushchev might still accept the Friday deal since he could still say that he had removed the U.S. threat to Cuba. "He must be very undecided," RFK pointed out, "or he wouldn't have sent the [Friday] message to you in the first place." "That's last night!" JFK retorted impatiently. "But it's certainly conceivable," RFK countered, "that you could get him back to that. I don't think that we should abandon it." The president conceded that nothing would be lost by trying, but insisted yet again that the real question remained "what are we gonna do about the Turks?"

"Actually, I think Bobby's formula is a good one," Sorensen observed; "we say, 'we are accepting your offer of your letter last night and therefore there's no need to talk about these other things.'" The president seemed willing to go along with this scheme on the slim chance that Khrushchev would at least agree to a cessation of work, but he clearly remained unconvinced and unenthusiastic: "As I say, he's not gonna [accept] now [after his public offer on Turkey]. Tommy [Thompson] isn't so sure. But anyway, we can try this thing, but he's gonna come back on Turkey." Bundy jumped on the bandwagon as well: "That's right, Mr. President. I think that Bobby's notion of a concrete acceptance on our part of how we read last night's telegram is very important."

After news arrived that a U-2 had been shot down over Cuba by a Soviet surface-to-air missile, the president tried to placate the opponents of a Turkish deal by reiterating that "first we oughta try to go the first route which you suggest and get him back [to the Friday offer]. That's what our letter's doing." At the same time, he again underscored his lack of conviction about that strategy and made clear that he was still determined to pursue the Turkish option: "Then it seems to me we oughta have a discussion with NATO about these Turkish missiles." He was ready to move ahead on a Turkey-Cuba deal, either bilaterally or through NATO: "It's going to look like we're caving in," he admitted candidly. But, if necessary, "To get it done, probably you have to do it bilaterally, to take all the political effects of the cave-in of NATO." Political fallout, the president recognized, was preferable to nuclear fallout.

The unrelenting pressure continued, however, as Rusk, McNamara, Bundy, Thompson, and RFK urged the president to reject any proposal that included removing the Jupiter missiles from Turkey. Dillon, summing up the nearly unanimous view in the room, pressed the president to avoid "a lot of talk" and just take out a SAM site immediately as a reprisal for the loss of the U-2: "Don't say anything. Just do that." JFK, once again, cut through the determined ExComm opposition to make his views unmistakably plain: "We can't very well invade Cuba, with all its toil and blood there's gonna be, when we could have gotten 'em [the missiles in Cuba] out by making a deal on the same missiles in Turkey. If that's part of the record, then you don't have a very good war." He paused for some six seconds before concluding, "But other than that, it's really a question now of what we say to NATO."

The European allies must be prepared, he stressed yet again, "for a disaster to NATO later in the week in Berlin or someplace . . . the reason we're consulting with them is that the situation's deteriorating [in Cuba] and if we take action we think there will be reprisals." Khrushchev's public offer, from JFK's perspective, had made a deal on the Turkish missiles diplomatically, militarily, and politically inescapable. The only other choice was to take military action against Cuba and risk Soviet retaliation in Berlin and even further escalation.

In between the late afternoon and evening ExComm meetings, McNamara, Deputy Defense Secretary Roswell Gilpatric, Ball, Bundy, RFK, Rusk, Sorensen, and Thompson joined President Kennedy, at his invitation, in the Oval Office. JFK revealed that he was about to send his brother Bobby to meet with Ambassador Anatoly Dobrynin and solicited advice on what to tell the Soviet diplomat. The group quickly agreed that RFK should warn Dobrynin that military action against Cuba was imminent and make clear, consistent with Khrushchev's Friday letter, that the U.S. was prepared to pledge not to invade Cuba if the missiles were withdrawn.

But the president continued to press urgently for a deal on the Turkish missiles. Dean Rusk, finally recognizing JFK's determination, suggested that RFK should advise the ambassador that a public quid pro quo for the missiles in Turkey was unacceptable but the president was prepared to remove them once the Cuban crisis was resolved. The proposal was promptly accepted and the eight advisers pledged to secrecy. Robert Kennedy was also instructed to tell Dobrynin that any Soviet reference to this secret proposal would make it null and void.[9]

JFK definitely had no confidence in the strategy of accepting Khrushchev's Friday offer and ignoring his public Saturday message. Instead, in addition to offering the secret concession on the Turkish missiles, he also endorsed an emergency fall-back plan, the so-called Cordier ploy (see Chapter 5). The president was prepared to gamble that if the U.S., as a last resort, publicly announced its acceptance of this supposedly neutral U.N. plan, it would be madness for the Soviets to reject it.

The October 27 meeting tapes prove that ExComm participants and scholars have read far too much cunning and coherence into their discussion of the so-called Trollope ploy. President Kennedy, as the tapes document, stubbornly and persistently contended that Khrushchev's Saturday offer could not be ignored, precisely because it had been made public. In fact, JFK's eventual message to Khrushchev did *not* ignore the Saturday proposal on Turkey, but left the door open to settling all broader international issues once the immediate danger in Cuba had been neutralized. JFK ultimately offered the Kremlin a calculated blend of Khrushchev's October 26 and 27 proposals: the removal of the Soviet missiles from Cuba, an American noninvasion pledge (contingent on U.N. inspection), a willingness to talk later about NATO-related issues, and a secret commitment to withdraw the Jupiters from Turkey.

Robert Kennedy and most of the other ExComm members tirelessly pressed the president not to give up on Khrushchev's Friday proposal. JFK, although skeptical and reluctant, finally agreed to try this scheme despite repeatedly predicting that the Soviet leader would inevitably return to his public offer on the Turkish missiles. The president had no illusions about forcing Khrushchev to settle for the terms in his earlier message and assented to this strategy largely to placate unyielding ExComm opposition. In fact, as revealed by RFK's instructions for the meeting with Dobrynin and the steps taken later that evening to create a secret, fail-safe strategy, JFK was not going to pass up what might be the last chance to avert nuclear catastrophe. As he had reminded the gung ho Joint Chiefs on October 19, an attack on Cuba could prompt the firing of nuclear missiles against American cities and result in 80–100 million casualties—"you're talking about the destruction of a country."

The tapes prove that the diplomatic subterfuge known as the Trollope ploy was little more than a superficial concession to the full ExComm. But it did serve later as a plausible public smokescreen for the secret deal (even kept from half the ExComm) that peacefully resolved the Cuban missile crisis.

10 Lyndon Johnson and the Missile Crisis: An Unanticipated Consequence?

You know, a mad dog, he tastes a little blood...

—Lyndon Johnson, October 27, 1962

VICE PRESIDENT LYNDON B. JOHNSON was a member of the Ex-Comm and attended both meetings on the first day, October 16, but missed several subsequent discussions because he was campaigning in the West for the midterm congressional elections. Once he had returned to Washington, he appears to have attended several of the remaining White House meetings. The problem is that he was uncharacteristically silent, so much so that his presence is often nearly impossible to verify. For example, he attended JFK's contentious meeting with the leaders of Congress on October 22, but never said a word. His presence can be confirmed only because he specifically referred to an episode from that meeting in a later discussion.

LBJ was normally assertive, domineering, and articulate, but he seemed oddly passive and reticent in President Kennedy's presence. His former aide, George Reedy, told the author that JFK and LBJ were the two most charismatic men he had ever known. But he also observed that Johnson's commitment to being a loyal vice president, in addition to his sense of inadequacy in the presence of the "Harvards" in JFK's favored circle, prompted his very uncharacteristic passivity and silence. LBJ, Reedy believed, all but deactivated his own charisma when JFK was present.[1]

If Johnson had not become president a year later, his views at the missile crisis meetings would not be of great interest to historians. The most important fact about LBJ and the crisis, oddly enough, is a negative one: he was excluded from the rump meeting in the Oval Office on the evening of Saturday, October 27, at which the secret deal on the Jupiter missiles in Turkey was finally agreed upon. As a result, several historians have speculated that the vice president absorbed the wrong lesson from the missile crisis. He believed that JFK had prevailed over the Soviet Union by standing firm and demonstrating a willingness to use American military power. In fact, Kennedy had cut a secret deal and compromised despite the opposition of essentially the entire ExComm.[2]

LBJ appears to have subsequently applied that false conclusion to the deteriorating situation in Vietnam. He was convinced that if he showed any willingness to seek a political solution in Southeast Asia, the Cold Warriors in the Democratic party, led inevitably by his bête noire, Robert Kennedy, would denounce him for repudiating JFK's legacy of strength and toughness. In December 1964, for example, the hawkish columnist Joseph Alsop challenged LBJ to live up to the alleged lesson of the missile crisis: "For Lyndon B. Johnson, Vietnam is what the second Cuban crisis was for John F. Kennedy. If Mr. Johnson ducks the challenge, we shall learn by experience about what [it] would have been like if Kennedy had ducked the challenge in October, 1962." President Johnson was livid about Alsop's remarks, but if he had known the full truth, he might have responded instead "with a shrug, or a caustic remark about Alsop's ignorance."[3]

LBJ's contributions to the October 27 meetings, however, demonstrate that he was wavering back and forth between seeking a negotiated compromise and using military force—and was particularly inconsistent on the decisive and divisive issue of the Turkish missile trade. It is simply impossible to draw any reliable conclusions about his later stance in Vietnam based solely on the contradictory positions he took, largely on that one crucial day. It is nonetheless striking that his key advisers—Robert McNamara, McGeorge Bundy, Dean Rusk, and others (all inherited from the Kennedy administration)—consciously kept him unaware *after* November 22, 1963, of the full story of how the missile crisis had actually been settled.

In *Thirteen Days*, not surprisingly, Lyndon Johnson is barely mentioned. RFK, whose personal dislike of the vice president is well documented, merely lists him as a member of the ExComm but says nothing about his role in the meetings, which was in fact quite limited until Black Saturday.

$\sim$

At the first meeting on October 16, JFK turned to Johnson and asked for his thoughts. LBJ declared that the U.S. should take any action recommended by the JCS to safeguard its security and warned that "the country's blood pressure is up, and they are fearful, and they're insecure, and we're gettin' divided." But the politically shrewd Texan admonished the president not to expect strong support from the OAS or the NATO allies—or the Congress: "I realize it's a breach of faith not to confer with them," the once-powerful Senate majority leader admitted. But "we're not gonna get much help out of them." Later that day, JFK again asked Johnson for his thoughts and the vice president, rather passively, replied that he had nothing essential to add.

On October 23, when the president was orchestrating a public relations offensive to build support for the blockade, he sent CIA director John McCone to brief key members of Congress recommended by LBJ. After that, Johnson remained essentially silent until the final day of meetings on October 27.

The vice president finally spoke up during the marathon (nearly four-hour) ExComm meeting that began at 4 P.M. on Black Saturday. He had obviously watched with great interest as the president pressed for acceptance of Khrushchev's missile trade proposal against nearly unanimous opposition. But Johnson was not asked for his views and said nothing until the president was temporarily out of the room. LBJ then urged breaking the impasse over Khrushchev's Friday and Saturday offers by simply informing the Soviet leader, as JFK had argued, that the United States would be willing to discuss issues involving the security of NATO "as soon as the present Soviet-created threat [in Cuba] has ended." "There it is! That's the proposal to 'em, sayin we can and will just as soon as you get rid of these bases." We are ready to talk about Turkey, he insisted, rapping the table for emphasis, "soon as you stop the work."

Johnson appeared to reject Robert McNamara's arguments against a straight-out missile trade: "Bob," he asked sharply, "if you're willin' to give up your missiles in Turkey [to prevent a Soviet attack on them], think you oughta give these [Jupiters], why don't ya say that to him [Khrushchev] and say we're tradin'. Save all the invasion, lives, everything else." LBJ also speculated about the likely Turkish reaction to a missile deal:

Why, if you were prime minister of Turkey, say that we're gonna hit Cuba. . . . He's got a big red light on each one of these Jupiters. We want to take 'em out. We're gonna give you more protection than ever, with Polaris, with less advertising. And it's gonna make it less likely you'll get hit. Why wouldn't he buy that? . . . What would you do about it? Wouldn't you rather have Polaris in there? I think the reason he wouldn't buy it would be a fear that that meant that we were through and we wouldn't come [to Turkey's defense].

The vice president continued to think out loud during JFK's absence, later insinuating that the administration had been retreating "gradually from the President's speech" and that the American people, as he had suggested on the first day of meetings, were becoming more insecure. As proof, he claimed that Soviet "ships are comin' through" the blockade. Robert Kennedy reacted angrily: "No! The ships aren't coming through. They all turned back . . . 90 percent of them." But Johnson stuck to his guns: "I don't think . . . at this moment, that it looks like we're as strong as we were on the day of the President's announcement." This exchange, providing only a tantalizing hint of the bitter enmity between Bobby Kennedy and LBJ, petered out, and the attorney general soon left the Cabinet Room. Johnson continued to talk and laugh with several ExComm colleagues, and repeated his charge that the public was becoming disenchanted with the administration's lack of resolve: "I don't say it's wise. I just say that's the temperature—it's 101 degrees."

Several minutes later, treasury secretary Douglas Dillon speculated about the possible impact of night surveillance with flares and the vice president made his opposition clear:

> I've been afraid of those damned flares ever since they mentioned them. . . . Imagine some crazy Russian captain . . . the damn thing [the flare] goes "blooey" and lights up the skies. He might just pull a trigger. ["Right," Rusk murmurs in the background.] Looks like we're playin' Fourth of July over there or somethin'. I'm scared of that. . . . You know they're workin' at night and you can see 'em workin' at night. Now what do you do? Psychologically you scare 'em, well, hell. . . . If you're gonna try and psychologically scare them with a flare, you're liable to get your bottom shot at.

LBJ had come remarkably close to describing the impending shooting down of a U-2 over Cuba.

Dean Rusk asked Johnson whether he thought the U.S. would soon be forced to act militarily. "I think you're at that point," the vice president replied. "I think you're gonna have a big problem right here, internally, in a few more hours in this country" because the public would soon demand more action. "'Where have you been? What are you doin'? The President made a fine speech. What else have you done?'" He repeated his claim, disputed earlier by RFK, that ships were going through the blockade: "There's a great feeling of insecurity," he cautioned, spreading across the nation.

The secretary of state also tried to gauge LBJ's views on the national reaction to "accepting the Turkish aspect," but the vice president admitted candidly, "I don't know." He suggested telling the Turkish prime minister directly: "'Now you've got these Jupiters and they're lighted up there. The searchlight's on 'em and everybody knows about 'em. They're not worth a damn. And we'll take that old T-Model out, we'll give you Polaris, a much better job.'" He wondered again, however, whether the Jupiter missiles provided the Turks with a physical sense of assurance of American support. Rusk then pointed out incredulously, "We've got 17,000 men there!" and Johnson countered, "We've got 20,000 men there." Perhaps, LBJ suggested, the U.S. should "try to sell 'em on that" by telling the Turkish prime minister, "You're more likely to get hit this way [with the Jupiters] than you are the other way [with the Polaris missiles]."

But soon after, the vice president unaccountably appeared to switch sides, arguing that "the weakness of the whole thing is" that if the U.S. gave up Turkey after the Soviets shot down one plane, Moscow might expect the surrender of Berlin if they shot down another plane. "You know, a mad dog, he tastes a little blood..." Dillon and Ambassador Thompson speculated about how many SAM sites should be attacked if another plane were shot down, and LBJ quipped, "You war hawks oughta get together," laughing alone and self-consciously at his own joke. He then predicted gloomily that once night reconnaissance with flares had begun, "I imagine they'll shoot, we'll shoot..."

Thompson reiterated his opposition to even discussing the removal of the Turkish missiles. "Therefore, he's [Khrushchev] really sayin'," Johnson observed with biting sarcasm, "'I'm gonna dismantle the foreign policy of the United States for the last fifteen years in order to get these missiles out of Cuba.'" He paused dramatically for some ten seconds—before harshly rebuking President Kennedy's stance on a Cuba-Turkey deal: "Then we say we're glad, and we appreciate it and we want to discuss it with you." "You just ask yourself" LBJ asserted, "what made the greatest impression on you today, whether it was his [Khrushchev's] letter last night, or whether it was his letter this morning, or whether it's about that U-2 boy's downing." "U-2 boy," Dillon echoed immediately. "That's exactly what did it," the vice president affirmed. "That's when everybody's color changed a little bit and sure as hell that's what's gonna make the impression on him [Khrushchev]—not all these signals that each one of us write. He's expert at that palaver."

When the president returned and explicitly rejected Thompson's position on the missile trade, LBJ, in the most dramatic challenge to JFK's judgment since the stinging attacks by General LeMay and Senators Russell and Fulbright during the first week of meetings (see Epilogue), vigorously disagreed: "It doesn't mean just missiles. He takes his missiles out of Cuba, takes his men out of Cuba and takes his planes out of Cuba—why then your whole foreign policy is gone. You take everything out of Turkey—twenty thousand men, all your technicians, and all your planes, and all your missiles—and crumble."

"How else are we gonna get those missiles out of there then?" JFK replied impassively, again refusing to respond directly to harsh criticism; "That's the problem." "Well, last night he was prepared," Dean Rusk reminded JFK one final time, "to trade them for a promise not to invade." "That's right, now he's got something completely new," the president reiterated yet again. "Somebody told him to try to get a little more," LBJ observed icily. The president did not respond.

$\sim$

We will never know with any degree of certainty, based solely on the vice president's conflicting positions at the ExComm meetings, whether LBJ would have made different decisions about Vietnam had he known the entire truth about the Cuban missile crisis. One thing, however, is indisputable: he should have been informed immediately after becoming president. Indeed, in conversations with McGeorge Bundy in late 1965 and early 1966, Johnson specifically alluded to Kennedy's allegedly tough stand in October 1962, and Bundy made no effort to set the record straight.[4] Instead, Johnson went to his grave in 1973 believing that his predecessor had threatened the use of U.S. military power to successfully force the Soviet Union to back down.

Conclusion: Leadership Matters

JOHN F. KENNEDY and his administration, without question, bore a
substantial share of the responsibility for the onset of the Cuban missile crisis; the secret war against Cuba may have been successfully kept from
the American people, but it was no secret to the leaders of the Soviet Union
and Cuba. JFK even admitted during the crisis that Cuba was "a fixation of
the United States and not a serious military threat" and that the NATO allies
"think that we're slightly demented on this subject." By October 1962 this "fixation" had already led to the Bay of Pigs fiasco, to state-sponsored sabotage and
murder, and ironically had contributed significantly to Khrushchev's decision
to gamble on deploying nuclear missiles in Cuba in the hope of discouraging
further American (or U.S.-sponsored) military action against Castro.

Nonetheless, when faced with the real prospect of nuclear war, President
Kennedy used his intellectual and political skill to steer his advisers and the
two superpowers away from an apocalyptic nuclear conflict. His experience in
the South Pacific had convinced him that war, even without atomic weapons,
was too unpredictable and destructive to be successfully controlled by any
leader or government. A Cold War hawk in public, he distrusted the military,
was skeptical about military solutions to political problems, and horrified by
the prospect of global nuclear war.

"In *all* cases," a prominent revisionist historian argued (before most of the
missile crisis tapes were declassified), "Kennedy *strove to win*" and was committed to "*a strategy of annihilation.*" He reacted to the crisis "*by suspend-*

ing diplomacy in favor of public confrontation," and the nuclear superpowers *"stumbled toward a settlement"* (emphasis added). The ExComm tape recordings prove, on the contrary, that this hard-line, confrontational JFK did not attend the missile crisis meetings.[1] In fact, the president persistently measured each move and countermove with an eye toward averting a nuclear exchange. As he had chided his advisers about Khrushchev's conflicting messages on Black Saturday, "It's got to be finessed. We have to finesse him."

Kennedy's management of the ExComm discussions was understated but remarkably consistent and effective. He never lost his temper and remained all but imperturbable in the face of sometimes severe criticism from the Joint Chiefs, the ExComm, or the leaders of Congress. He was never arrogant or egotistical during those tension-filled thirteen days, never put anyone down harshly, and barely raised his voice even when obviously irritated or angry. JFK was always willing to let people have their say, regardless of whether he agreed with their position, confident that in the end the constitutional authority to decide remained entirely in his hands.

"To keep the discussions from becoming inhibited and because he did not want to arouse attention," Robert Kennedy later claimed, JFK "decided not to attend all the [ExComm] meetings. . . . This was wise. Personalities change when the President is present, and frequently even strong men make recommendations on the basis of what they believe the President wishes to hear."[2] Notwithstanding RFK's perceptive behavioral insight, his assertion about President Kennedy's presence at the ExComm meetings is essentially false. JFK attended all the sessions—except when, in an effort to keep the crisis discussions of the first week secret, he left Washington to campaign in New England (Wednesday, October 17) and in the Midwest (Friday afternoon, October 19, to Saturday afternoon, October 20).

JFK's leadership style rarely comes across in paper records. So much that cannot be captured, even in the most accurate transcript or narrative, is there on the tapes for the listener with a discerning ear: the nuances of his voice and temperament, his impatience, his Cold War blinders and convictions, his apprehension and anxiety, his doubts, his political instincts, his self-control, his persistence, his caution, his skepticism about the gap between military plans and performance, his ironic sense of humor, and above all, his conviction that war was an impossible choice in the nuclear era.

The views of the ExComm members, of course, shifted, evolved, and even reversed direction in response to the changing diplomatic, political, and military situation, their own beliefs and values, and the arguments of their colleagues. Some participants were nearly always diffident and reflective; others were tough and assertive. Some were eager to lead, despite the enormous stakes involved; others were content to follow and say very little.

Only the tapes themselves can fully capture the human reality of these discussions. Imagine, for example, if it suddenly became possible to *hear* a recording of the actual Gettysburg Address. Our understanding of Lincoln's words, meaning, and intent would certainly be changed by exposure to the unique power of the spoken word—especially when heard in its original historical context. It is hard to imagine that anyone would *first* choose to read the speech if the option to actually hear the original presentation existed as well.

It is also essential to understand the importance of the ExComm discussions in helping the president to make up his mind, especially in the final hours of the crisis. There can be no question, after listening painstakingly to these recordings, that the often rough give-and-take with the ExComm played a continuing and decisive role in shaping JFK's perspective and decisions. He clearly understood, for example, the alarming implications of McNamara's confident assurances about using practice depth charges to "harmlessly" force Soviet submarines to surface; or Bundy's self-important claim that everyone in the government involved in alliance problems would be hostile to a Cuba-Turkey missile trade; or Nitze's inflexibility over amending JCS procedures to prevent the firing of the Turkish Jupiter missiles at the Soviet Union (see Epilogue).

In several of these cases, not to mention the taut exchanges with General LeMay and Senators Russell and Fulbright, JFK barely managed to conceal his disdain in the face of inflexibility, doctrinaire thinking, and lack of imagination. Even in the final days and hours of the crisis, the ExComm had an enormous emotional and psychological impact on his commitment to averting nuclear war. Every major option was discussed, frequently in exhaustive and exhausting detail, providing both the context and sounding board for the president in making his final decisions. JFK repeatedly rejected provocative and confrontational advice and never lost sight of the requirement to find a solution short of nuclear war. The White House tape recordings prove, incontrovertibly, that the president was *not* in fact guided by the cumulative wisdom and counsel of the ExComm; on the contrary, he goaded and channeled the discussions toward a negotiated solution which most of his advisers resisted or opposed.

Kennedy's inclination to pursue the Turkish option was actually reinforced by the dogged intractability of his advisers at the October 27 meetings. The ExComm toughened his determination simply by persistently and all but unanimously opposing his preferred course of action. It is a serious mistake for historians to underestimate the importance of these discussions in prodding the president to implement this potential settlement while there was still time to avoid a nuclear catastrophe. The ExComm tape recordings also demonstrate conclusively that the conventional Trollope ploy explanation was a myth and a cover story from the start (see Chapter 9).

Studying history, of course, is not like assembling a neatly cut jigsaw puzzle. Pieces of historical evidence do not have to fit together tidily or logically within fixed and predetermined borders. Indeed, despite the best efforts of historians, they do not have to fit together at all. History defines its own parameters, and real historical figures often defy our assumptions and expectations. Contradictions and inconsistencies are the rule rather than the exception in human affairs. History is not a play. There is no script.

When first listening to the tapes, I had taken for granted that John Kennedy had been a tough and relentless Cold Warrior. In fact, JFK repeatedly tried to rise above the simplistic Cold War rhetoric he had successfully exploited in his October 22 speech announcing the discovery of Soviet missiles in Cuba. And to a remarkable degree, he succeeded—although not without some "help" from Khrushchev and some genuine luck.

The evidence from the missile crisis tapes is anomalous, contradictory, and even surprising, but no less true: President Kennedy often stood virtually alone against warlike counsel from the ExComm, the Joint Chiefs, and the leaders of Congress during those historic thirteen days. Nonetheless, he never abandoned his commitment, even *after* the missile crisis, to undermine the Cuban revolution and get rid of Fidel Castro. More than two decades after the end of the Cold War, the Kennedy administration's covert actions in Cuba can be regarded, with the benefit of 20/20 hindsight, as futile, short-sighted, and counterproductive. It would, of course, have been potentially far more tragic and catastrophic to have also recklessly risked unleashing "the final failure" of global nuclear war.

As JFK told Ambassador John Kenneth Galbraith after the missile crisis, "Ken, you have no idea how much bad advice I received in those days."[3]

Epilogue: What If?

In a century replete with unspeakable disasters, the Cuban missile crisis of October 1962 came terrifyingly close to producing the greatest disaster of them all: nuclear war, "the final failure." The irony of this non-event is that averting it was the most important event of the 20th century. So it is necessary both to learn how and why the United States and the Soviet Union nudged each other to the edge of the nuclear abyss . . . [and] to understand how a suicidal plunge over it was avoided.
—Martin J. Sherwin, 2003[1]

There is no better way of understanding what did happen in history than to contemplate what very well might have happened. Counterfactual history has a way of making the stakes of a confrontation stand out in relief. It can point out the moment that was truly a turning point—or the moment when the shading of an event edged from unfortunate to tragic.
—Robert Cowley, 2001[2]

THE CUBAN MISSILE CRISIS was unique. Never before or since has the survival of human civilization been at stake in barely two weeks of extremely dangerous deliberations (in which reliable information and intelligence were often in short supply), and never before or since have such secret discussions been recorded and preserved. Not surprisingly, these one-of-a-kind tape recordings reveal that a peaceful resolution was far from inevitable; the crisis could easily have ended in catastrophe despite the best intentions of leaders in Washington and Moscow.

If it were possible to rewind and replay the missile crisis, perhaps one hundred times, it is all but certain that nuclear world war would have occurred in a significant number of those reruns. And, of course, each and every replay would turn out differently in some significant way(s). In normal circumstances, the capacity of a single individual to shape history is often quite limited. But the missile crisis was not normal. Over and over again at the secret meetings, options were discussed which could have fundamentally altered the result of the crisis as we know it; for example, if the president had agreed to intense pressure from his advisers to declare war on Cuba when announcing the blockade or to immediately destroy the SAM site that had brought down a U-2 over Cuba on Black Saturday.

A serious discussion of the "what-ifs," or counterfactuals, of the missile crisis can promote a greater understanding of the how and why of what actually happened. "What ifs can lead us to question long-held assumptions. What ifs can define true turning points. They can show that small accidents or split-second decisions are as likely to have major repercussions as the large ones."[3] The president was repeatedly required to make decisions, some of which may have seemed relatively inconsequential at the time; but if made differently, those decisions could have resulted in unanticipated consequences that dramatically and perhaps fatally redirected the course of the entire event—and of human history as well.

Tuesday, October 16

What if President Kennedy had agreed, after viewing the first U-2 photos, to the Joint Chiefs' proposal to immediately bomb the missile sites, airfields, and so on in Cuba?

JCS chairman General Taylor announced that the Joint Chiefs "feel so strongly about the dangers inherent in the limited air strike [against just the missile sites] that they would prefer taking no military action" rather than sacrifice the advantage of surprise and expose American civilians to retaliatory missiles launched from Cuba. JFK firmly disagreed, insisting that "the chances of it becoming a much broader struggle are increased" with each step of military escalation. Once the Cuban airfields were attacked, he contended, "I mean you're right in a much more major operation, therefore the dangers of the worldwide effects, which are substantial to the United States, are increased."

The president, clearly maneuvering "to get this thing under some degree of control," chided Taylor: "Let's not let the Chiefs knock us out on this one, General"—a striking thing to say to the chairman of the Joint Chiefs. "If you go into Cuba in the way we're talking about, and taking out all the planes and all the rest," he continued, "then you really haven't got much of an argument against invading." Taylor, a veteran of the bloody invasion of Italy in World War II, asserted: "My inclination is all against the invasion, but nonetheless trying to eliminate as effectively as possible, every weapon that can strike the United States." Kennedy put the JCS chairman on the spot with a transparently leading question: "But you're not for the invasion?" and got the answer he appeared to want: "I would not at this moment, no sir."

Taylor feared that if the U.S. got involved in a major invasion of Cuba, the Soviets would have an open road to seize Berlin. His concerns appear to have been justified since at its height the plan for invading Cuba called for using 100,000 army and 40,000 marine combat troops, 579 navy and air force combat aircraft, 175 navy ships, and 8 aircraft carriers. On the first day, 14,500 paratroopers were to be used, "comparable to the force dropped during the invasion of Normandy. Potential casualties were estimated at some 18,500 in ten days of combat."[4]

Thursday, October 18

What if the Soviet Union had responded to a U.S. attack on Cuba by sending in Red Army troops to drive the allies out of West Berlin?

The discussion focused on whether the Soviet Union should be warned in advance if the president decided to bomb the missile sites in Cuba. The president predicted that Khrushchev would "grab Berlin anyway" and that the allies would feel that the U.S. had "lost Berlin because of these missiles [in Cuba], which as I say, do not bother them."

"What do we do when really ... I think he moves into Berlin?" RFK asked.

"Well, when we're talking about taking Berlin," McNamara asked, "what do we mean exactly? Do they take it with Soviet troops?"

"That's what I would see, anyway," JFK responded grimly.

"I think there's a real possibility of that," McNamara agreed. "We have U.S. troops there. What do they do?"

"They fight," General Taylor asserted.

"They fight," McNamara agreed; "I think that's perfectly clear."

"And they get overrun," JFK predicted.

"Yes, they get overrun, exactly," McNamara concurred.

"Then what do we do?" RFK queried.

"Go to general war," Taylor pronounced, "assuming we have time for it."

"You mean nuclear exchange?" the president remarked grimly.

"Guess you have to," Taylor concluded.

October 18

What if the U.S. blockade proclamation had included a declaration of war on Cuba?

Support for a naval blockade, which at least postponed the dangers inherent in any military action against Cuba, had been increasing since the first meetings on October 16. "Now, to get a blockade on Cuba," the president surmised, "would we have to declare war on Cuba?" A cacophony of responses followed, unanimously declaring yes for diplomatic, legal, military, and political reasons. But the president made his opposition clear: "I think we shouldn't assume we have to declare war. . . . Because it seems to me if you're gonna do that, . . . it doesn't make any sense not to invade. . . . We do the message to Khrushchev and tell him that if work continues, etc., etc. At the same time, launch the blockade. If work continues, then we go in and take them out. We don't declare war," he pronounced firmly, because it would increase domestic pressure for an invasion and present an unnecessarily aggressive posture to the Soviets. Khrushchev might easily overreact—particularly in Berlin.

A blockade without a declaration of war, George Ball insisted, was illegal, and Bundy characterized it as "an act of aggression against everybody else." "Including our allies," Ball interjected. JFK retorted sharply, "I don't think anybody who gets excited because their ships are stopped under these conditions—they're not very much help to us anyway." Ambassador Thompson also contended that a declaration of war could be justified as a necessary step to eliminate a threat to the U.S., which is "a little different from saying that we're going to war to destroy" Cuba. The president reiterated that a blockade without a declaration of war would not immediately raise the escalation stakes "as high as it would be under other conditions." Later that evening he noted, "I was most anxious that we not have to announce a state of war existing, because it would obviously be bad to have the word go out that we were having a war rather than it was a limited blockade for a limited purpose."

Friday, October 19

What if the president had agreed to the Joint Chiefs' recommendation to launch an air, sea, and ground invasion of Cuba?

The president met with the Joint Chiefs of Staff to reveal his decision to blockade Cuba. If the U.S. attacked the island, he explained, it would give the Soviets "a clear line to take Berlin." The U.S. would then be regarded by the NATO allies, since "they think we've got this fixation about Cuba anyway," as "the Americans who lost Berlin. . . . [because] we didn't have the guts to endure a situation in Cuba. After all, Cuba is five or six thousand miles from them. They don't give a damn about Cuba. But they do care about Berlin and about their own security. . . . I must say, I think it's a very satisfactory position from their point of view." A quick air strike might neutralize the missiles, but if the Soviets take Berlin in response, that "leaves me only one alternative, which is to fire nuclear weapons—which is a hell of an alternative."

General Curtis LeMay, the air force chief of staff, countered that the United States doesn't have "any choice except direct military action." LeMay turned Kennedy's Berlin argument on its head: "I don't share your view that if we knock off Cuba they're gonna knock off Berlin." On the contrary, the Soviets "are gonna push on Berlin and push real hard" only if the U.S. failed to take military action in Cuba, since they would then feel "they've got us on the run." A skeptical JFK interrupted to ask, "What do you think their reprisal would be" if the U.S. attacked Cuba? There would be no reprisal, LeMay asserted without missing a beat, as long as you tell Khrushchev again, "If they make a move [in Berlin], we're gonna fight. . . . So, I see no other solution. This blockade and political action I see leading into war. I don't see any other solution for it. It will lead right into war. This is almost as bad as the appeasement at Munich. . . . I just don't see any other solution except direct military intervention, right now."

The JCS must have held their collective breath waiting for a reaction from the president. The general had gone well beyond disagreeing with his commander in chief. He had taken their generation's ultimate metaphor for shortsightedness and cowardice, the 1938 appeasement of Hitler at Munich, and flung it in the president's face. And everyone at the table knew that JFK's father, Joseph P. Kennedy, had been a supporter of Neville Chamberlain's policy of appeasement when he served as ambassador to England between 1938 and 1940.[5]

After several seconds of awkward silence the discussion resumed. Admiral George Anderson, chief of naval operations, asserted: "I agree with General LeMay that this will escalate and then we will be required to take other military action at greater disadvantage to the United States, to our military forces, and probably would suffer far greater casualties within the United States if these fanatics do indeed intend to fire any missiles. I do not see that as long as the Soviet Union is supporting Cuba, that there is any solution to the Cuban problem except a military solution." He acknowledged the danger to Berlin but insisted that only a strong U.S. response would deter the Soviets from aggression against that divided city.

General Earle Wheeler, army chief of staff, increased the pressure by endorsing surprise bombing, a blockade, plus an invasion. He warned that because the Soviets had only limited numbers of ICBMs targeted at the U.S., "this short-range missile force gives them a sort of a quantum jump in their capability to inflict damage on the United States. And so as I say, from the military point of view, I feel that the lowest-risk course of action is the full gamut of military action by us. That's it."

Finally, the marine corps commandant, General David Shoup, warned the president that Khrushchev might have deployed missiles so close to America so that Cuba could inflict damage on the U.S. while the Soviets "keep out of it." The longer the U.S. waited to eliminate this threat on its doorstep, he claimed, the greater the forces that would be required to do it. Despite dismissing Cuba as "that little pip-squeak of a place," Shoup argued that these missiles "can damage us increasingly every day." To head off these contingencies, Shoup urged, "you'll have to invade the place," banging the table for emphasis, "and if that decision is made, we must go in with plenty of insurance of a decisive success and as quick as possible."

As to the "political factor," LeMay interjected, "that's not quite in our field . . . but you invited us to comment on this. . . . I think that a blockade and political talk would be considered by a lot of our friends and neutrals as bein' a pretty weak response to this. And I'm sure a lot of our own citizens would feel that way too. In other words, you're in a pretty bad fix at the present time," the general declared, almost taunting the president. "What'd you say?" Kennedy asked matter-of-factly. "I say, you're in a pretty bad fix," LeMay repeated smugly. "You're in with me," Kennedy replied, with an derisive chuckle, "personally."

General Taylor insisted that the Soviet base in Cuba was rapidly becoming more threatening than anyone had believed even earlier in the week. But the president again insisted that the Cuban missiles did not substantially alter the Soviet nuclear threat. He acknowledged that Soviet ICBMs might not be completely reliable, but they still had enough fire power to strike American cities, with or without Cuba, resulting in 80 to 100 million casualties: "you're talkin' about the destruction of a country! . . . The logical argument," the president persisted, "is that we don't really have to invade Cuba. That's just one of the difficulties that we live with in life, like you live with the Soviet Union and China." The president grimly acknowledged that "the existence of these missiles adds to the danger, but doesn't create it. . . . I mean, hell, they can kill, especially if they concentrate on the cities, and they've pretty well got us there anyway." "I appreciate your views," the president finally told the JCS, "as I said, I'm sure we all understand how rather unsatisfactory our alternatives are." But he repeated that the potential advantage of the blockade "is to avoid, if we can, nuclear war by escalation or imbalance. . . . We've got to have some degree of control." JFK soon left the meeting.

LeMay, Shoup, and Wheeler remained behind to talk as the door closed. The hidden tape recorder, of course, continued to turn. Shoup lauded LeMay for challenging the president: "You pulled the rug right out from under him."

"Jesus Christ!" LeMay responded disingenuously, "What the hell do you mean?"

Shoup explained that he supported his air force colleague "a hundred percent" and mocked President Kennedy: "he's finally getting around to the word 'escalation.' . . . When he says 'escalation,' that's it. If somebody could keep 'em from doing the goddamn thing piecemeal, that's our problem. You go in there and friggin' around with the missiles. You're screwed. You go in and friggin' around with little else. You're screwed." "That's right," LeMay exclaimed. "You're screwed, screwed, screwed," Shoup fulminated; "He could say, 'either do the son of a bitch and do it right, and quit friggin' around.' . . . You got to go in and take out the goddam thing that's gonna stop you from doin' your job." The discussion soon trailed off, and the tape ran out just as the last JCS participants left the Cabinet Room.

After the meeting, the president told an aide that he was stunned by LeMay's cocky certainty that Khrushchev would do nothing if the U.S. bombed the missile sites and killed a lot of Russians. "These brass hats have one great advantage in their favor," JFK fumed. "If we listen to them and do what they want us to do, none of us will be alive later to tell them that they were wrong."[6] And we now know what JFK and the ExComm did not know: nuclear warheads were in Cuba and Soviet forces were preparing to obliterate the Guantánamo naval base with a tactical cruise missile if the U.S. attacked the island nation.

Monday, October 22

What if the Soviet Union had attacked the Jupiter missiles in Turkey in response to U.S. military action against Cuba?

Paul Nitze, assistant secretary of defense for international security affairs, was interrupted by the president during a briefing on the Berlin situation. Two days earlier, JFK had told Nitze to make certain that the Joint Chiefs issued new orders to American personnel on the Jupiter bases in Turkey not to fire their missiles at the U.S.S.R., even if attacked, without specific presidential authorization. Nitze reported that "the Chiefs came back with a paper saying that those instructions are already out."[7]

JFK was obviously not satisfied: "Well, why don't we reinforce 'em because, as I say, we may be attacking the Cubans and a reprisal may come on these. We don't want them firing [the nuclear missiles] without our knowing about it. . . . Can we take care of that then, Paul? We need a new instruction out." Nitze muttered a sullen and barely audible reply: "All right. I'll go back and tell them." "They object to sending a new one out?" JFK asked, and Nitze reiterated that the Chiefs objected to a new order because "to their view, it compromises their standing instructions."

He then revealed that the JCS had also made another point in their response—a startling point: "NATO strategic contact [a nuclear attack from the U.S.S.R.] requires the immediate execution of EDP in such events." "What's EDP?" Kennedy asked. "The European Defense Plan," Nitze answered chillingly, "which is nuclear war." "Now that's why," the president interjected vigorously, "we want to get on that, you see." But Nitze tried again to explain, "No, they said the orders are that nothing can go without the presidential order."

The commander in chief's reservations about the military were obvious in his reply. "They don't realize there is a chance there will be a spot reprisal, and what we gotta do is make sure these fellows [at the Jupiter sites] do know, so that they don't fire 'em off and think the United States is under attack. I don't think," he asserted flatly, "we ought to accept the Chiefs' word on that one, Paul." "All right," Nitze mumbled grudgingly.

But Nitze tried again to defend the JCS position: "But surely these fellows are thoroughly indoctrinated not to fire," he bristled, banging on the table. Kennedy cut him off with a temperate but firm order: "Well, let's do it again, Paul." The president's response was clear: his orders would be carried out, regardless of JCS rules and procedures. "I've got your point, we'll do it again," Nitze finally agreed. Some strained laughter broke out, and Bundy relieved the tension in the room by telling Nitze, in a tongue-in-cheek tone, "Send me the documents, and I will show them to a doubting master." The laughter briefly grew even louder.

Within an hour, General Taylor sent an urgent message to the NATO commander which was to remain secret from the Turks and Italians: "Make certain that the Jupiters in Turkey and Italy will not be fired without specific authorization from the President. In the event of an attack, nuclear or nonnuclear . . . U.S. custodians are to destroy or make inoperable the weapons if any attempt is made to fire them." Not surprisingly, Nitze did not mention this exchange with President Kennedy in his published memoirs.[8]

October 22

What if the views of Senators Richard Russell and J. William Fulbright had prevailed?

President Kennedy met with the leaders of Congress just hours before his speech to the nation revealing the crisis in Cuba. "If we invade Cuba," he underscored, "we have a chance that these missiles will be fired—on us." Khrushchev would likely seize Berlin, and the unity of NATO would be shattered because "Europe will regard Berlin's loss . . . as having been the fault of the United States by acting in a precipitous way." The president then announced his decision: "In order not to give Mr. Khrushchev the justification for imposing a complete blockade on Berlin, we're going to start with a blockade on the shipment of offensive weapons into Cuba." Plans for an invasion, he revealed, were still going forward. But "if we invade Cuba, there's a chance these weapons will be fired at the United States." And "if we attempt to strike them from the air, then we will not get 'em all because they're mobile. ... So after a good deal of searching, we decided this was the place to start." But, he candidly admitted, "I don't know what their response will be. ... If there's any strong disagreements with what at least we've set out to do, I want to hear it."

Richard Russell of Georgia, chairman of the Senate Armed Services Committee, suddenly lashed out: "Mr. President, I could not stay silent under these circumstances and live with myself. I think that our responsibilities to our people demand some stronger steps than that." The U.S., he maintained, would never be stronger or in a better position: "It seems to me that we're at the crossroads. We're either a first-class power or we're not." The Georgian tried to hoist the president on his own petard:

> You have warned these people time and again, in the most eloquent speeches I have read since Woodrow Wilson, as to what would happen if there was an offensive capability created in Cuba. ... And you have told 'em not to do this thing. They've done it. And I think that we should assemble as speedily as possible an adequate force and clean out that situation. The time's gonna come, Mr. President, when we're gonna have to take this gamble ... for the nuclear war. I don't know whether Khrushchev will launch a nuclear war over Cuba or not. I don't believe he will. But I think that the more that we temporize, the more surely he is to convince himself that we are afraid to ... fight.

Secretary McNamara tried to explain how the blockade would be enforced, but Russell became even more agitated: "Mr. President, I don't wanna make a nuisance of myself, but I would like to complete my statement. My position is that these people have been warned." Delaying an invasion, he contended, would give the Soviet fighter planes in Cuba a chance "to attack our shipping or to drop a few bombs around Miami or some other place," and when we do invade, "we'll lose a great many more men than we would right now."

"But Senator," JFK patiently explained, "we can't invade Cuba," because it would take several days to assemble and deploy the ninety thousand-plus men required for an invasion. "Well, we can assemble 'em," Russell retorted sharply. "So that's what we're doing now," Kennedy replied impatiently. But the Georgian would not relent: "This blockade is gonna put them on the alert" and divide and weaken our forces, he sputtered, "around the whole periphery of the free world."

President Kennedy, perhaps hoping to isolate Russell by appealing for support from the other congressional leaders, laid out the stark choices on the table: "If we go into Cuba, we have to all realize that we are taking a chance that these missiles, which are ready to fire, won't be fired. So is that really a gamble we should take? In any case, we're preparing to take it. I think, fact is, that is one hell of a gamble." JFK's appeal seemed to make Senator Russell even more combative: "We've got to take a chance somewhere, sometime, if we're gonna retain our position as a great world power."

Russell finally backed off: "I'm through. Excuse me. I wouldn't have been honest with myself if I hadn't. . . . So I hope you forgive me, but I . . . you asked for opinions."

"Well, I forgive you," Kennedy broke in defensively, obviously trying to control his exasperation, "but it's a very difficult problem we're faced with. I'll just tell you that. It's a very difficult choice that we're facing together." "Oh, my God! I know that," Russell exclaimed, not even letting the president finish. "Our authority and the world's destiny will hinge on this decision. But it's comin' someday, Mr. President. Will it ever be under more auspicious circumstances? . . . I assume this blockade will be effective for a while til they make up their minds to try to force their way through." JFK attempted a reply, but Russell cut him off again: "You know, the right of self-defense is pretty elemental, and you relied on that in that very telling statement you made. You relied on that, the right of self-defense, and that's what we'd be doin'."

Suddenly, another influential southern Democrat, J. William Fulbright, chairman of the Senate Foreign Relations Committee, weighed in against the president's chosen course of action. Kennedy had seriously considered asking Fulbright to serve as secretary of state but decided against it because the Arkansas senator had signed the "Southern Manifesto" opposing the Supreme Court's unanimous 1954 ruling on school desegregation. Fulbright contended that an invasion was less risky than a blockade: "I mean legally. I mean it's just between us and Cuba. I think a blockade is the worst of the alternatives because if you're confronted with a Russian ship, you are actually confronting Russia." An invasion against Cuba "is not actually an affront to Russia. . . . They're [Cuba] not part of the Warsaw Pact."

The president tried again to raise the specter of the "immediate seizure of Berlin," but Fulbright persisted that it would be better to try for a solution at the U.N. or to invade Cuba: "A blockade seems to me the worst alternative." McNamara intervened to remind the Arkansas senator that the missile sites were occupied by Russians; an invasion would first require two thousand air sorties directly against some eight thousand Soviet military personnel. Finally, his patience clearly strained, JFK asked, "What are you in favor of, Bill?" "I'm in favor," Fulbright asserted, "on the basis of this information, of an invasion, and an all-out one, and as quickly as possible."

"You can't have a more confrontation than invasion of Cuba," JFK objected. But the senator pressed on: "They're Cuban sites. They're not Russian sites," and "firing against Cuba is not the same as firing against Russia. I don't think a blockade is the right way at all. . . . An attack on a Russian ship," he reiterated, "is really an act of war against Russia. It is not an act of war against Russia to attack Cuba."

Clearly frustrated, the president reminded the senator that the Soviet missiles in Cuba might be fired at the U.S. in response to an invasion; American forces would be directly attacking eight thousand Russians: "We are gonna have to shoot them up. And I think that it would be foolish," JFK challenged the former Rhodes Scholar, "to expect that the Russians would not regard that as a far more direct thrust. . . . And I think that the inevitable result will be immediately the seizure of Berlin. . . . But I think that if we're talkin' about nuclear war, then escalation ought to be at least with some degree of control."[9] Of course, JFK acknowledged, it was offensive to the Russians to have their ships stopped, but "When you start talking about the invasion, it's infinitely more offensive." "But not to the Russians, it seems to me," Fulbright persisted doggedly. "They have no right to say that you've had an attack on Russia."

"I don't know where Khrushchev wants to take us," the president admitted: "Some people would say, 'well, let's go in with an air strike.' You'd have those bombs [nuclear warheads] go off and blow up fifteen cities in the United States. And they would have been wrong. . . . The people who are the best off," he reflected fatalistically, "are the people whose advice is not taken because whatever we do is filled with hazards." "I'll say this to Senator Fulbright: we don't know where we're gonna end up on this matter. . . . We just tried to make good judgments about a matter on which everyone's uncertain. . . . And I quite agree with Senator Russell, Khrushchev's gonna make the strongest statements, which we're gonna have to just ignore, about everything: if we stop one Russian ship, it means war! If we invade Cuba, it means war! There's no telling—I know all the threats are gonna be made." "Now just wait, Mr. President," Senator Russell interjected again, "the nettle is gonna sting anyway." "That's correct," Kennedy acknowledged. "Now I just think at least we start here, then we see where we go. . . . I gotta go and make this speech."

Saturday, October 27

What if the president had followed through on his earlier agreement to attack the SAM site(s) in Cuba immediately if a U-2 plane were shot down?

News arrived late that afternoon that a U-2 plane had been brought down by a Soviet SAM missile in Cuba—and the pilot killed. "How do we interpret this?" the president asked. McNamara admitted, "I don't know how to interpret it." "How can we send a U-2 fellow over there tomorrow," JFK acknowledged, "unless we take out all the SAM sites?" "This is exactly correct," McNamara declared; "I don't think we can." "They've fired the first shot," Nitze pointed out stridently. "We should retaliate against the SAM site," Taylor demanded, "and announce that if any of 'em have any other planes fired on we will come back and attack it." He also reminded the president that a military response to the shooting down of a U-2 by a SAM had already been agreed to several days earlier. JFK had also reiterated that commitment just hours earlier at the morning ExComm meeting. He therefore instructed that an announcement should be made that "action will be taken to protect our aircraft."

The president, despite McNamara's insistence that "we want an excuse to go in tomorrow and shoot up that SAM site," still seemed hesitant about making a public announcement about the U-2 without confirmation. "I'd like to find out," Kennedy added, "whether Havana says they did shoot it down." "To have a SAM site, with a Russian crew, fire," Roswell Gilpatric asserted, "is not any accident." Douglas Dillon warned that domestic American political pressure for reprisals would intensify in the wake of the U-2 loss.

Declassified Soviet sources have confirmed that the launch of the SAM missile against the U-2 was ordered by Russian air defense officers without permission from General Pliyev in Cuba or from the Soviet air command headquarters in Moscow. "Castro's joy was indescribable," but Khrushchev was furious and ordered that no firings take place without his direct order: "No independent initiatives. Everything is hanging by a thread as it is."[10]

President Kennedy, however, focused his attention again on removing the missiles from Turkey rather than speeding up the bombing of the missiles in Cuba: "Therefore, we gotta move. That's why I think we gotta have a NATO meeting tomorrow." McNamara recommended telling NATO: "'We may have to attack Cuba. If we attack Cuba, they're holding Turkey as a hostage and they're likely to attack Turkey.'" Therefore, taking the missiles out of Turkey allows us to act in Cuba "without endangering you, the alliance. This is the theme we're gonna put it on." JFK, however, was clearly thinking of the Turkish missile trade, not in terms of McNamara's politically cunning diplomatic/public-relations scheme to make an attack on Cuba seem less objectionable to NATO, but rather as a bold stroke to resolve the crisis entirely without using military force at all.

The president kept the Turkish issue front and center for the remainder of the long and grueling meeting. The issue of bombing the SAM site(s) came up again briefly toward the end of the discussion. JFK responded warily, "But we don't know whether that plane was shot down yet, do we?" He was advised that there was no firm evidence "on our side" to confirm that it was shot down, but that Havana radio had announced that the plane had been destroyed by antiaircraft fire. "Oh, I'm sorry. I didn't know that yet," the president admitted. However, he again brushed aside the issue of retaliating against the SAM site(s) and resumed discussing Khrushchev's proposal for a Cuba-Turkey missile deal.

The delay in attacking the SAM site(s), as it fortuitously turned out, made it much less politically awkward for Khrushchev to announce the next morning that he had chosen to withdraw Soviet missiles from Cuba. President Kennedy's decision reached the Pentagon just in time to head off a retaliatory air strike on the SAM site believed responsible for knocking the U-2 out of the sky. "The White House, realizing that there was a standing order for the immediate destruction of a firing SAM site," ordered LeMay "not to launch the aircraft until he received direct orders from the President." The air force chief of staff hung up in disgust: "He chickened out again. How in hell do you get men to risk their lives when the SAMs are not attacked?" An aide offered to wait for the president's call; LeMay contemptuously predicted, "It will never come!"[11]

The United States and the Soviet Union each conducted atmospheric nuclear tests on that climactic Saturday, October 27, 1962. The American test was code-named CALAMITY.

Refererence Matter

Notes

Chapter 1

1. Strobe Talbott, ed. and trans., *Khrushchev Remembers* (Boston: Little, Brown, 1970), 492–94; Sergei Khrushchev, *Nikita Khrushchev and the Creation of a Superpower* (University Park: Pennsylvania State University Press, 2000), 484; Barton J. Bernstein, "Reconsidering the Missile Crisis: Dealing with the Problems of the American Jupiters in Turkey," in James A. Nathan, ed., *The Cuban Missile Crisis Revisited* (New York: St. Martin's, 1992), 65–67.

2. Ernest R. May and Philip D. Zelikow, *The Kennedy Tapes: Inside the White House During the Cuban Missile Crisis* (Cambridge, Mass: Harvard University Press, 1997); Philip Zelikow, Timothy Naftali, and Ernest May, eds., *The Presidential Recordings: John F. Kennedy, Volumes 1–3, The Great Crises* (New York: W. W. Norton, 2001); Sheldon M. Stern, *Averting 'The Final Failure': John F. Kennedy and the Secret Cuban Missile Crisis Meetings* (Stanford, Calif.: Stanford University Press, 2003).

3. David Talbot, *Brothers: The Hidden History of the Kennedy Years* (New York: Free Press, 2007), 170; Michael Dobbs, *One Minute to Midnight: Kennedy, Khrushchev, and Castro on the Brink of Nuclear War* (New York: Knopf, 2008), 151.

4. Dobbs, *One Minute to Midnight*, 304.

5. McGeorge Bundy, *Danger and Survival: Choices About the Bomb in the First Fifty Years* (New York: Random House, 1988).

6. Ted Sorensen, *Counselor: A Life at the Edge of History* (New York: Harper, 2008).

7. Seymour Hersh, *The Dark Side of Camelot* (New York: Little, Brown, 1997), 7–8, 351; Zachary Karabell, "Roll Tape…Inside the White House with JFK, LBJ—and Overhearing Everyone Else," *Boston Globe*, October 19, 1997, 1, 5; Gil Troy, "JFK: Celebrity-in-Chief or Commander-in-Chief?" *Reviews in American History 26* (1998), 634; May and Zelikow, *Kennedy Tapes*, 691.

8. William Safire, *New York Times*, October 12, 1997, Section 4, 15.

9. For example, in the infamous recorded call between Monica Lewinsky and Linda Tripp.

10. Ernest R. May and Philip D. Zelikow, "Camelot Confidential," *Diplomatic History* 22 (Fall 1998), 649; Zelikow et al., *Presidential Recordings*, v. 3, xxiii.

11. Hugh Sidey, "Introduction," in Deirdre Henderson, ed., *Prelude to Leadership: The European Diary of John F. Kennedy—Summer 1945* (Washington, D.C.: Regnery, 1995), xxiv.

12. Ibid., xxiv–xxv, xxix.

13. Ibid., xvi, xx, xxviii; Arthur M. Schlesinger Jr., *A Thousand Days: John F. Kennedy in the White House* (Boston: Houghton Mifflin, 1965), 426.

14. Sidey, "Introduction," xx.

15. John F. Kennedy, Editorial, *Harvard Crimson*, October 9, 1939.

16. John F. Kennedy to Inga Arvad, no date, spring 1943, Nigel Hamilton Research Materials [hereafter NHRM], Massachusetts Historical Society [hereafter MHS]. Some of JFK's letters were typed; he often used three dots in place of commas or periods.

17. Ibid., John F. Kennedy to Rose and Joseph Kennedy, September 12, 1943, Personal Papers [hereafter PP], John F. Kennedy Library [hereafter JFKL]; John F. Kennedy to Inga Arvad, no date, spring 1943, NHRM, MHS; Herbert S. Parmet, *Jack: The Struggles of John F. Kennedy* (New York: Doubleday, 1980), 111–12.

18. John F. Kennedy to Inga Arvad, September 26, 1943, NHRM, MHS.

19. Henderson, *Prelude to Leadership*, 5, 7, 88. There was a great deal of speculation about the atomic bomb, dropped on Hiroshima on August 6, but it is unlikely that Kennedy actually knew about the Manhattan Project.

20. John F. Kennedy, "Aid for Greece and Turkey," *Record of the House of Representatives*, April 1, 1947.

21. Charles Bohlen Oral History Interview, 1964, JFKL, Oral History Collection [hereafter OHC]; Richard Goodwin, *Remembering America: A Voice from the Sixties* (Boston: Little, Brown: 1988), 218; Geoffrey Perret, *Jack: A Life Like No Other* (New York: Random House, 2001), 326.

22. John F. Kennedy, Review of B. H. Liddell Hart, *Deterrent or Defense*, *Saturday Review*, September 3, 1960.

23. Sorensen, *Kennedy*, 513.

24. JFK and J. William Fulbright, Tape 26B.5, August 23, 1963, President's Office Files [hereafter POF], Presidential Recordings Collection [hereafter PRC], JFKL.

25. Stern, *Averting 'The Final Failure,'* 100, 122, 399.

26. Ibid., 122, 127, 167.

27. Talbott, *Khrushchev Remembers*, 493–94.

28. Bundy, *Danger and Survival*, 436.

29. There was no recording device at the State Department; summaries of those meetings are based on written minutes.

30. The weekend meetings (October 20–21) were held at the State Department or in the White House living quarters and were not recorded.

31. All the remaining meetings were recorded.

32. Bundy, *Danger and Survival*, 432–33; Barton J. Bernstein, "Understanding Decisionmaking: U.S. Foreign Policy and the Cuban Missile Crisis," *International Security* 25 (Summer 2000), 160–61.

Chapter 2

1. Stern, *Averting 'The Final Failure,'* 402.

2. Robert F. Kennedy, *Thirteen Days: A Memoir of the Cuban Missile Crisis* (New York: W. W. Norton, 1969).

3. Richard E. Neustadt and Graham T. Allison, Afterword to *Thirteen Days* (New York: W. W. Norton, 1971), 121.

4. Arthur M. Schlesinger Jr., *Robert Kennedy and His Times* (New York: Houghton Mifflin, 1978), xii–xiii; Adam Clymer and Don Van Natta Jr., *New York Times*, July 12, 2011.

5. Schlesinger, *Robert Kennedy and His Times*, 507, 531.

6. Timothy Naftali, "The Origins of 'Thirteen Days,'" *Miller Center Report* 15 (Summer 1999), 23–24. George Dalton, a junior naval officer detailed to the White House, prepared these early transcripts. However, Dalton was unfamiliar with the voices of the participants and the issues discussed; his extremely inaccurate and fragmentary transcripts have never been released.

7. Conversation with Dan H. Fenn Jr., a member of the Kennedy White House staff and founding director of the JFK Library, June 18, 2011.

8. Sir Lawrence D. Freedman, "Review of *The Week the World Stood Still*," *Foreign Affairs* (May–June 2005).

9. Phillip Brenner, "Thirteen Months: Cuba's Perspective on the Missile Crisis," in Nathan, *Cuban Missile Crisis Revisited*, 187–219.

10. Stern, *Averting 'The Final Failure,'* 98.

11. Ibid., 134, 254.

12. Ibid., 86, 399.

13. Aleksandr Fursenko and Timothy Naftali, *"One Hell of a Gamble": Khrushchev, Castro, and Kennedy, 1958–1964* (New York: W. W. Norton, 1997), 274–75.

14. Cited in Bruce J. Allyn, James G. Blight, and David A. Welch, eds., *Back to the Brink: Proceedings of the Moscow Conference on the Cuban Missile Crisis, January 27–28, 1989* (Lanham, Md.: University Press of America, 1992), 92–99.

Chapter 3

1. Roswell Gilpatric Oral History Interview, JFKL, OHC, 1970, 50; U. Alexis Johnson Oral History Interview, JFKL, OHC, 36–37. Journalist Joseph Alsop remarked in 1964 that "Bobby never diverged for one instant from his brother's views, nor did he ever really consider anything except his brother's interest" (Joseph Alsop, OHI, JFKL). The ExComm tapes prove that the first part of Alsop's observation is wrong. Notwithstanding, RFK's loyalty to JFK always prevailed.

2. Laurence Chang and Peter Kornbluh, eds., *The Cuban Missile Crisis, 1962: A National Security Archive Documents Reader* (New York: New Press, 1998), 5; Phillip Brenner, "Thirteen Months," in Nathan, *Cuban Missile Crisis Revisited*, 189; Minutes of the First Operation Mongoose Meeting with Attorney General Robert Kennedy, December 1, 1961, and Brig. General Edward Lansdale, The Cuba Project, February 20, 1962, in Chang and Kornbluh, *Cuban Missile Crisis*, 20–37; Raymond L. Garthoff, *Reflections on the Cuban Missile Crisis*, rev. ed. (Washington, D.C.: Brookings, 1989), 32; Raymond L. Garthoff, "The Cuban Missile Crisis: An Overview," in Nathan, *Cuban Missile Crisis Revisited*, 42.

3. James G. Blight and Peter Kornbluh, eds., *The Politics of Illusion* (Boulder, Colo.: Lynne Rienner, 1998), 53, 118, 124–25.

4. Ted Sorensen Oral History Interview, JFKL OHC, 1964, 68.

5. *Foreign Relations of the United States: American Republics, 1961–1963, XII* (Washington, D.C.: United States Government Printing Office, 1998), 634–41.

6. Robert Lovett Oral History Interview, JFKL OHC, 1964.

7. Leonard Meeker, Minutes of the October 19, 1962, Meeting at the State Department, in Chang and Kornbluh, *Cuban Missile Crisis*, 133–37.

8. Nikita Khrushchev to John F. Kennedy, October 26, 1962, in David L. Larson, ed., *The Cuban Crisis of 1962: Selected Documents, Chronology and Bibliography* (Lanham, Md.: University Press of America, 1986), 175–80.

9. Jim Hershberg, "Anatomy of a Controversy: Anatoly F. Dobrynin's Meeting With Robert F. Kennedy, Saturday, 27 October 1962," *Cold War International History Project Bulletin* (Spring 1995), 75–80.

10. For an account of RFK's "blatant falsification of the historical record" and a copy of his deceptive October 30 memo to Rusk, see Jim Hershberg, "More on Bobby and the Cuban Missile Crisis," *Cold War International History Project Bulletin 8–9* (Winter 1996–1997), 274, 344–47.

11. For a summary of the November postcrisis meetings, issues, and negotiations, see Epilogue in Stern, *Averting 'The Final Failure,'* 403–12.

Chapter 4

1. RFK, *Thirteen Days*, 91.

2. Bruce Kuklick, *Blind Oracles: Intellectuals and War from Kennan to Kissinger* (Princeton, N.J.: Princeton University Press, 2006), 146.

3. Fred Kaplan, "The Evasions of Robert McNamara: What's True and What's a Lie in *The Fog of War*," *Slate*, December 19, 2003.

4. Tape 120, November 8, 1963, JFKL, PRC (released on January 24, 2012). McNamara had clearly not forgotten his angry exchange with Anderson during the missile crisis, when the admiral declared that he was planning to fire warning shots at Soviet ships approaching the quarantine line if they refused to stop. McNamara had replaced Anderson as chief of naval operations in mid-1963 (see Stern, *Averting 'The Final Failure,'* 233–34).

5. http://errolmorris.com/film/fow_transcript.html, accessed March 20, 2011.

6. Fursenko and Naftali, *"One Hell of a Gamble,"* 274–75; William Taubman, *Khrushchev: The Man and His Era* (New York: W. W. Norton, 2003), 569–70.

7. Fursenko and Naftali, *"One Hell of a Gamble,"* 272–73; Taubman, *Khrushchev,* 572–73.

8. RFK, *Thirteen Days,* 27.

9. RFK, *Thirteen Days,* 53–54.

10. Alexander Mozgovoi, *Kubinskaya Samba Kvarteta Fokstrotov* (Cuban samba of the fox-trot quartet), not yet translated into English; *Boston Globe,* June 22, 2002; also see Fursenko and Naftali, *"One Hell of a Gamble,"* 247; press release, October 2002 Havana Conference, October 11, 2002; *Boston Sunday Globe,* October 20, 2002.

11. Ball and McCone vacillated later in the meeting after a U-2 was shot down over Cuba.

Chapter 5

1. Arthur M. Schlesinger Jr., *Journals: 1952–2000* (New York: Penguin, 2008), 98.

2. Schlesinger, *Thousand Days,* 435.

3. RFK, *Thirteen Days,* 36.

4. Schlesinger, *Robert Kennedy and His Times,* 507 (citation is to an article by Acheson about *Thirteen Days* in the February 1969 *Esquire*).

5. RFK, *Thirteen Days,* 25.

6. Robert F. Kennedy Oral History Interview, JFKL OHP, 1965, 6.

7. David Rusk to Sheldon M. Stern, May 20, 2011.

8. Only Cordell Hull, 1933–44, served longer.

9. Schlesinger, *Robert Kennedy and His Times,* 507 (citation is to an 11/30/62 memo in the RFK papers).

10. Bundy, *Danger and Survival,* 433.

11. *Boston Sunday Globe,* October 20, 2002.

12. Philip Nash, *The Other Missiles of October: Eisenhower, Kennedy and the Jupiters, 1957–1963* (Chapel Hill: University of North Carolina Press, 1997), 95; Bernstein, "Reconsidering the Missile Crisis," 57–60.

13. Nash, *Other Missiles of October,* 95–102.

14. Raymond L. Garthoff, *Intelligence Assessment and Policymaking: A Decision Point in the Kennedy Administration* (Washington, D.C.: Brookings, 1984), 30.

15. Harlan Cleveland Oral History Interview, JFKL OHC, 1978, 34.

16. Dean Rusk Oral History Interview JFKL OHC, 1970, 134.

17. RFK, *Thirteen Days,* 45.

18. Fursenko and Naftali, *"One Hell of a Gamble,"* 259–60; Talbott, *Khrushchev Remembers,* 497.

19. Chang and Kornbluh, *Cuban Missile Crisis,* 385.

20. Nikita Khrushchev to John F. Kennedy, October 26, 1962, in Larson, *Cuban Crisis,* 175–80.

21. Dean Rusk, as told to Richard Rusk, *As I Saw It* (New York: W. W. Norton, 1990), 240–41; James G. Blight, Joseph S. Nye Jr., and David A. Welch, "The Cuban

Missile Crisis Revisited," *Foreign Affairs 66* (Fall 1987), 178–79; Bernstein, "Reconsidering the Missile Crisis," 100–101, 127; Chang and Kornbluh, *Cuban Missile Crisis*, 391. For discussion of an earlier and also unused "Cordier ploy" to call for "a U.N. commission to monitor the status of the missiles in Cuba and Turkey," see Garthoff, "Documenting the Cuban Missile Crisis," 298.

22. Dean Rusk, *As I Saw It,* 231.

23. David Rusk to Sheldon M. Stern, May 2, 2011.

24. Ibid.

Chapter 6

1. RFK, *Thirteen Days*, 89; Rusk Oral History, 126.

2. Schlesinger, *Robert Kennedy and His Times*, 507.

3. Errol Morris, dir. *The Fog of War: Eleven Lessons from the Life of Robert S. McNamara* (Sony Pictures Classics, 2003).

Chapter 7

1. RFK notes, 10/31/62, cited in Schlesinger, *Robert Kennedy and His Times*, 507.

2. Schlesinger, *Thousand Days*, 208–9.

3. Bundy, *Danger and Survival*, 429.

4. Ibid., 684–85.

5. Bernstein, "Reconsidering the Missile Crisis," 60–64; Sorensen Oral History, 65.

6. Fursenko and Naftali, *"One Hell of a Gamble,"* 241.

7. JFK's knee-slapping is vividly captured in Robert Drew's 1963 *cinéma-vérité* documentary, *Crisis: Behind a Presidential Commitment*, about the struggle with Governor George Wallace over the desegregation of the University of Alabama.

8. Bundy, 1964 memo, in Kai Bird, *The Color of Truth: McGeorge Bundy and William Bundy: Brothers in Arms* (New York: Simon & Schuster, 1998), 234.

9. Chang and Kornbluh, *Cuban Missile Crisis,* 385.

10. Nikita Khrushchev to John F. Kennedy, October 26, 1962, in Larson, *Cuban Crisis*, 175–80.

11. Bernstein, "Understanding Decisionmaking," 157.

12. Bundy, *Danger and Survival*, 429–31.

13. Ibid., 434.

Chapter 8

1. Stewart Alsop and Charles Bartlett, "Eyeball to Eyeball," *Saturday Evening Post,* December 1962.

2. Adlai Stevenson to John F. Kennedy, October 17, 1962, in Chang and Kornbluh, *Cuban Missile Crisis*, 129–30.

3. RFK, *Thirteen Days*, 57–59.

4. Paul H. Nitze, *From Hiroshima to Glasnost: At the Center of Decision, A Memoir* (New York: Grove Weidenfeld, 1989), 227.

5. Dictabelt 38.1, Cassette K, POF, PRC, JFKL.

Chapter 9

1. Ted Sorensen, *Counselor*, 1–2.

2. Ibid., 3, 8.

3. Ibid., xvi.

4. RFK, *Thirteen Days*, 77.

5. Schlesinger, *Thousand Days*, 828; Theodore C. Sorensen, *Kennedy (New York:* Harper & Row, 1965), 714–15.

6. James G. Blight and David A. Welch, *On the Brink*: *Americans and Soviets Reexamine the Cuban Missile Crisis* (New York: Noonday Press, 1990), 162, 179, 369; Evan Thomas, *Robert Kennedy: His Life* (New York: Simon & Shuster, 2000), 438; Robert W. Merry, *Taking on the World: Joseph and Stewart Alsop—Guardians of the American Century* (New York: Viking Press, 1996), 389; Graham Allison, *Essence of Decision: Explaining the Cuban Missile Crisis (Boston:* Little, Brown, 1971), 227; David A. Welch and James G. Blight, "The Eleventh Hour of the Cuban Missile Crisis: An Introduction to the ExComm Transcripts," *International Security* (Winter 1987/88), 16; Adlai Stevenson to John F. Kennedy, in Chang and Kornbluh, *Cuban Missile Crisis*, 129–30.

7. Vladislav Zubok and Constantine Pleshakov, *Inside the Kremlin's Cold War: From Stalin to Khrushchev* (Cambridge, Mass.: Harvard University Press, 1996), 266–67.

8. Sergei Khrushchev, *Nikita Khrushchev*, 628. Nikita Khrushchev to Fidel Castro, October 30, 1962, in Blight et al., *Cuba on the Brink*, 481–91; Jorge E. Domínguez, "The @#$%& Missile Crisis: (Or, What Was Cuban About U.S. Decisions During the Cuban Missile Crisis?)," *Diplomatic History 24* (Spring 2000), 313; Taubman, *Khrushchev*, 569–73.

9. Jim Hershberg, "Anatomy of a Controversy: Anatoly F. Dobrynin's Meeting with Robert F. Kennedy, Saturday, 27 October 1962," *Cold War International History Project Bulletin 5* (Spring 1995), 75, 77–80.

Chapter 10

1. George Reedy, *Lyndon B. Johnson: A Memoir* (Kansas City, Mo.: Andrews McMeel, 1982).

2. See the analyses in Eric Alterman, *When Presidents Lie: A History of Official Deception and Its Consequences* (New York: Viking Press, 2004); and Max Holland and Tara Marie Egan, "What Did LBJ Know About the Missile Crisis? And When Did He Know It?" *Washington Decoded*, October 19, 2007, http://www.washingtondecoded.com/site/2007/10/what-did-lbj-kn.html.

3. Ibid.

4. Ibid.

Conclusion

1. "John F. Kennedy's Quest," in Thomas G. Paterson, ed., *Kennedy's Quest for Victory: American Foreign Policy, 1961–1963* (New York: Oxford University Press, 1989), 5, 7, 20; "When Fear Ruled: Rethinking the Cuban Missile Crisis," *New England Journal of History 52* (Fall 1995), 26.

2. RFK, *Thirteen Days*, 26–27.

3. John Kenneth Galbraith, *Name-Dropping: From FDR On* (Boston: Houghton Mifflin, 1999), 105.

Epilogue

1. Martin J. Sherwin, review of Sheldon M. Stern, *Averting 'The Final Failure': John F. Kennedy and the Secret Cuban Missile Crisis Meetings*, History Book Club (November 2003).

2. Robert Cowley, ed., *What If? Eminent Historians Imagine What Might Have Been* (New York: G. P. Putnam's Sons, 1999), 399.

3. Cowley, *What If?*, xiii–xiv.

4. Garthoff, *Reflections on the Cuban Missile Crisis*, 73–74.

5. The first time I heard this tape, in 1981, I was astonished by LeMay's personal attack and expected President Kennedy to defend himself; instead, he chose to avoid a confrontation. Tension between JFK and LeMay was hardly new. Roswell Gilpatric recalled that whenever the president had to confer with LeMay,

> he ended up in sort of a fit. I mean he just would be frantic at the end of a session with LeMay because, you know, LeMay couldn't listen or wouldn't take in, and he would make what Kennedy considered, and we all considered, perfectly, you know, outrageous proposals that bore no relation to the state of affairs in the 1960s. And the President never saw him unless at some ceremonial affair, or where he felt he had to make a record of having listened to LeMay, as he did on the whole question of an air strike against Cuba. And he had to sit there. I saw the President right afterwards. He was just choleric. He was just beside himself. (Roswell Gilpatric Oral History Interview, OHC, JFKL, 116)

On the other hand, Kennedy admired candor, once remarking to Hugh Sidey, "I like having LeMay head the Air Force. Everybody knows how he feels. That's a good thing" (Schlesinger, *Thousand Days*, 912).

6. Kenneth O'Donnell and David Powers, *Johnny We Hardly Knew Ye* (Boston: Little, Brown, 1970), 318. Scholars have justifiably dismissed this book as hagiography. However, this remark is strikingly similar to one JFK made three days later when he told the National Security Council that if we make a wrong choice, we won't have "the satisfaction of knowing what would have happened if we had acted differently" (Stern, *Averting 'The Final Failure,'* 150).

7. Barton J. Bernstein has contended, "In simply strategic terms, these 'soft' IRBMs, vulnerable to a sniper's bullet and taking hours to fire, were useful only for a

first strike. They never could have been used in retaliation, because they would have been easily wiped out in a first strike." However, as General Taylor had conceded during the October 16 discussion about bombing the Cuban missiles, no first strike could ever be 100 percent effective.

8. May and Zelikow, *Kennedy Tapes,* 223; Nitze, *From Hiroshima to Glasnost,* 214–38.

9. The Kennedy administration's estimate of the number of Soviet military personnel in Cuba highlights one of the most egregious and dangerous American intelligence failures of the missile crisis. General Anatoli I. Gribkov confirmed at the January 1992 Havana Conference that more than 42,000 Soviet troops had already been brought secretly to Cuba by the time of President Kennedy's October 22 speech. JFK's estimate of 8,000 troops was consistent with the latest intelligence reports, although that number was revised to 12,000 to 16,000 by November 19. When U Thant visited Cuba in late October to try (unsuccessfully) to arrange for U.N. inspection of the removal of the missiles, he was told that only 5,000 Soviet troops were on the island (James G. Blight, Bruce J. Allyn, and David A. Welch, *Cuba on the Brink: Castro, the Missile Crisis, and the Soviet Collapse* [New York: Pantheon, 1993], 58–61; Garthoff, *Reflections on the Cuban Missile Crisis,* 18–20, 35–36).

10. Sergei Khrushchev, *Nikita Khrushchev,* 609.

11. Brugioni, *Eyeball to Eyeball,* 463–64; Fursenko and Naftali, *"One Hell of a Gamble,"* 258.

Bibliography

Archives

John F. Kennedy Library, Boston, Mass. [JFKL]
John F. Kennedy Personal Papers [PP]
John F. Kennedy Presidential Papers, 1961–1963:
  National Security Files [NSF]
  Oral History Collection [OHC]
  President's Office Files [POF]
  Presidential Recordings Collection [PRC]
Nigel Hamilton Research Materials, Massachusetts Historical Society, Boston, Mass.
  [NHRM, MHS]

Secondary Sources

Allison, Graham. *Essence of Decision: Explaining the Cuban Missile Crisis*. Boston: Little, Brown, 1971.
Allison, Graham, and Philip Zelikow. *Essence of Decision: Explaining the Cuban Missile Crisis*, second edition. Boston: Addison Wesley Longman, 1999.
Allyn, Bruce J., James G. Blight, and David A. Welch, eds. *Back to the Brink: Proceedings of the Moscow Conference on the Cuban Missile Crisis, January 27–28, 1989*. Lanham, Md.: University Press of America, 1992.
Alterman, Eric. *When Presidents Lie: A History of Official Deception and Its Consequences*. New York: Viking Press, 2004.
Amuchastegui, Domingo. "Cuban Intelligence and the October Crisis." In Blight, James G., and David A. Welch, eds., *Intelligence and the Cuban Missile Crisis*. London: Frank Cass, 1998, 88–119.
Bernstein, Barton J. "Commentary: Reconsidering Khrushchev's Gambit—Defending the Soviet Union and Cuba." *Diplomatic History 14* (Spring 1990), 231–239.

Bernstein, Barton J. "Reconsidering the Missile Crisis: Dealing with the Problems of the American Jupiters in Turkey." In Nathan, James A., ed., *The Cuban Missile Crisis Revisited*. New York: St. Martin's, 1992, 55–130.

Bernstein, Barton J. "Understanding Decisionmaking: U.S. Foreign Policy and the Cuban Missile Crisis." *International Security* 25 (Summer 2000), 134–164.

Bird, Kai. *The Color of Truth: McGeorge Bundy and William Bundy: Brothers in Arms*. New York: Simon & Schuster, 1998.

Blight, James G., Bruce J. Allyn, and David A. Welch. *Cuba on the Brink: Castro, the Missile Crisis and the Soviet Collapse*. New York: Pantheon, 1993.

Blight, James G., and Phillip Brenner. *Sad and Luminous Days: Cuba's Struggle with the Superpowers After the Cuban Missile Crisis*. Lanham, Md.: Rowman and Littlefield, 2002.

Blight, James G., and Peter Kornbluh, eds. *The Politics of Illusion*. Boulder, Colo.: Lynne Rienner, 1998.

Blight, James G., Joseph S. Nye Jr., and David A. Welch. "The Cuban Missile Crisis Revisited," *Foreign Affairs* 66 (Fall 1987), 178–79.

Blight, James G., and David A. Welch. *On the Brink: Americans and Soviets Reexamine the Cuban Missile Crisis*. New York: Noonday Press, 1990.

Blight, James G., and David A. Welch. "The Cuban Missile Crisis and Intelligence Performance." In Blight, James G., and David A. Welch, eds., *Intelligence and the Cuban Missile Crisis*. London: Frank Cass, 1998, 173–217.

Blight, James G., and David A. Welch. "What Can Intelligence Tell Us About the Cuban Missile Crisis, and What Can the Cuban Missile Crisis Tell Us About Intelligence?" In Blight, James G., and David A. Welch, eds., *Intelligence and the Cuban Missile Crisis*. London: Frank Cass, 1998, 1–17.

Brenner, Philip. "Thirteen Months: Cuba's Perspective on the Missile Crisis." In Nathan, James A., ed., *The Cuban Missile Crisis Revisited*. New York: St. Martin's, 1992, 187–219.

Brugioni, Dino. *Eyeball to Eyeball: The Inside Story of the Cuban Missile Crisis,* edited by Robert F. McCort. New York: Random House, 1991.

Bundy, McGeorge. *Danger and Survival: Choices About the Bomb in the First Fifty Years*. New York: Random House, 1988.

Chang, Laurence. "The View from Washington and the View from Nowhere: Cuban Missile Crisis Historiography and the Epistemology of Decision Making." In Nathan, James A., ed., *The Cuban Missile Crisis Revisited*. New York: St. Martin's, 1992, 131–160.

Chang, Laurence, and Peter Kornbluh, eds., *The Cuban Missile Crisis, 1962: A National Security Archive Document Reader*. New York: New Press, 1998.

Cowley, Robert, ed. *What If? Eminent Historians Imagine What Might Have Been*. New York: G. P. Putnam's Sons, 1999.

Dobbs, Michael. *One Minute to Midnight: Kennedy, Khrushchev and Castro on the Brink of Nuclear War*. New York: Knopf, 2008.

Domínguez, Jorge E. "The @#$%& Missile Crisis: (Or, What Was Cuban About U.S.

Decisions During the Cuban Missile Crisis?)." *Diplomatic History 24* (Spring 2000), 305–315.

Flank, Lenny. *At the Edge of the Abyss: A Declassified History of the Cuban Missile Crisis.* St. Petersburg, Fla.: Red and Black, 2010.

Foreign Relations of the United States [FRUS], Vols. V–XVI. Washington, D.C.: United States Government Printing Office, 1994–1998. state.gov/r/pa/ho/frus/kennedyjf/

Frankel, Max. *High Noon in the Cold War: Kennedy, Khrushchev and the Cuban Missile Crisis.* New York: Presidio Press, 2004.

Fursenko, Aleksandr, and Timothy Naftali. *"One Hell of a Gamble": Khrushchev, Castro and Kennedy, 1958–1964.* New York: W. W. Norton, 1997.

Fursenko, Aleksandr, and Timothy Naftali. "Soviet Intelligence and the Cuban Missile Crisis." In Blight, James G., and David A. Welch, eds., *Intelligence and the Cuban Missile Crisis.* London: Frank Cass, 1998, 64–87.

Garthoff, Raymond L. *Intelligence Assessment and Policymaking: A Decision Point in the Kennedy Administration.* Washington, D.C.: Brookings, 1984.

Garthoff, Raymond L. *Reflections on the Cuban Missile Crisis,* rev. ed. Washington, D.C.: Brookings, 1989.

Garthoff, Raymond L. "U.S. Intelligence in the Cuban Missile Crisis." In Blight, James G., and David A. Welch, eds., *Intelligence and the Cuban Missile Crisis.* London: Frank Cass, 1998, 18–63.

Garthoff, Raymond L. "Documenting the Cuban Missile Crisis." *Diplomatic History 24* (Spring 2000), 297–303.

Goodwin, Richard. *Remembering America: A Voice from the Sixties.* Boston: Little, Brown, 1988.

Gribkov, Anatoli I., and William Y. Smith. *Operation ANADYR: U.S. and Soviet Generals Recount the Cuban Missile Crisis.* Chicago: Edition Q, 1994, 3–76.

Henderson, Deirdre, ed. *Prelude to Leadership: The European Diary of John F. Kennedy—Summer 1945.* Washington, D.C.: Regnery, 1995.

Hershberg, James G. "Before 'The Missiles of October': Did Kennedy Plan a Military Strike Against Cuba?" *Diplomatic History 14* (Spring 1990), 163–198; also in different form in Blight, James G., and David A. Welch, eds., *Intelligence and the Cuban Missile Crisis.* London: Frank Cass, 1998, 237–280.

Hershberg, Jim. "Anatomy of a Controversy: Anatoly F. Dobrynin's Meeting With Robert F. Kennedy, Saturday, 27 October 1962." *Cold War International History Project Bulletin* 5 (Spring 1995). Also: http://www.gwu.edu/~nsarchiv/nsa/cuba_mis_cri/moment.htm.

Hershberg, Jim. "More on Bobby and the Cuban Missile Crisis." *Cold War International History Project Bulletin* 8–9 (Winter 1996–1997), 274–277.

Holland, Max, and Tara Marie Egan. "What Did LBJ Know About the Missile Crisis? And When Did He Know It?" *Washington Decoded,* October 19, 2007, http://www.washingtondecoded.com/site/2007/10/what-did-lbj-kn.html.

Kennedy, Robert F. *Thirteen Days: A Memoir of the Cuban Missile Crisis.* New York: W. W. Norton, 1969.

Khrushchev, Sergei. *Nikita Khrushchev and the Creation of a Superpower.* University Park: Pennsylvania State University Press, 2000.

Kuklick, Bruce. *Blind Oracles: Intellectuals and War from Kennan to Kissinger.* Princeton, N.J.: Princeton University Press, 2006.

Larson, David L. *The Cuban Crisis of 1962: Selected Documents, Chronology and Bibliography.* Lanham, Md.: University Press of America, 1986.

Mastny, Vojtech. *The Cold War and Soviet Insecurity.* New York: Oxford University Press, 1997.

May, Ernest, and Philip D. Zelikow. *The Kennedy Tapes: Inside the White House During the Cuban Missile Crisis.* Cambridge, Mass.: Harvard University Press, 1997.

May, Ernest, and Philip D. Zelikow. "Camelot Confidential," *Diplomatic History* 22 (Fall 1998).

McCauliffe, Mary S., ed. *CIA Documents on the Cuban Missile Crisis, 1962.* Washington, D.C.: Central Intelligence Agency, 1992.

Merry, Robert W. *Taking on the World: Joseph and Stewart Alsop—Guardians of the American Century.* New York: Viking Press, 1996.

Munton, Don, and David A. Welch. *The Cuban Missile Crisis: A Concise History.* New York: Oxford University Press, 2011.

Naftali, Timothy. "The Origins of 'Thirteen Days.'" *Miller Center Report* 15 (Summer 1999), 23–24.

Nash, Philip. *The Other Missiles of October: Eisenhower, Kennedy and the Jupiters, 1957–1963.* Chapel Hill: University of North Carolina Press, 1997.

Neustadt, Richard E., and Graham T. Allison. "Afterword." In *Thirteen Days.* New York: W. W. Norton, 1971, 101–45.

Nitze, Paul H. *From Hiroshima to Glasnost: At the Center of Decision, A Memoir.* New York: Grove Weidenfeld, 1989.

O'Donnell, Kenneth and David Powers. *Johnny We Hardly Knew Ye.* Boston: Little, Brown, 1970.

Parmet, Herbert S. *Jack: The Struggles of John F. Kennedy.* New York: Doubleday, 1980.

Paterson, Thomas G., ed. *Kennedy's Quest for Victory: American Foreign Policy, 1961–1963.* New York: Oxford University Press, 1989.

Paterson, Thomas G. "When Fear Ruled: Rethinking the Cuban Missile Crisis." *New England Journal of History* 52 (Fall 1995), 12–37.

Perret, Geoffrey. *Jack: A Life Like No Other.* New York: Random House, 2001.

Polmar, Norman, and John D. Gresham. *Defcon-2: Standing on the Brink of Nuclear War During the Cuban Missile Crisis.* New York: Wiley, 2006.

Rabe, Stephen G. "After the Missiles of October: John F. Kennedy and Cuba, November 1962 to November 1963." *Presidential Studies Quarterly* 30 (December 2000), 714–26.

Reedy, George. *Lyndon B. Johnson: A Memoir.* Kansas City, Mo.: Andrews McMeel, 1982.

Rusk, Dean, as told to Richard Rusk. *As I Saw It.* New York: W. W. Norton, 1990.

Schechter, Jerrold, ed. and trans. *Khrushchev Remembers: The Glasnost Tapes.* Boston: Little, Brown, 1990.

Schlesinger, Arthur M., Jr. *A Thousand Days: John F. Kennedy in the White House.* Boston: Houghton Mifflin, 1965.

Schlesinger, Arthur M., Jr. *Robert Kennedy and His Times.* New York: Houghton Mifflin, 1978.

Schlesinger, Arthur M., Jr. *Journals: 1952–2000.* New York: Penguin, 2008.

Sorensen, Ted. *Counselor: A Life at the Edge of History.* New York: Harper, 2008.

Sorensen, Theodore C. *Kennedy.* New York: Harper & Row, 1965.

Stern, Sheldon M. *Averting 'The Final Failure': John F. Kennedy and the Secret Cuban Missile Crisis Meetings.* Stanford, Calif.: Stanford University Press, 2003.

Stern, Sheldon M. *The Week the World Stood Still: Inside the Secret Cuban Missile Crisis.* Stanford, Calif.: Stanford University Press, 2005.

Talbot, David. *Brothers: The Hidden History of the Kennedy Years.* New York: Free Press, 2007.

Talbott, Strobe, ed. and trans. *Khrushchev Remembers.* Boston: Little, Brown, 1970.

Talbott, Strobe, ed. and trans. *Khrushchev Remembers: The Last Testament.* Boston: Little, Brown, 1974.

Taubman, William. *Khrushchev: The Man and His Era.* New York: W. W. Norton, 2003.

Thomas, Evan. *Robert Kennedy: His Life.* New York: Simon & Shuster, 2000.

Topping, Seymour. *On the Front Lines of the Cold War: An American Correspondent's Journal from the Chinese Civil War to the Cuban Missile Crisis and Vietnam.* Baton Rouge: Louisiana State University Press, 2010.

Welch, David A., and James G. Blight. "The Eleventh Hour of the Cuban Missile Crisis: An Introduction to the ExComm Transcripts." *International Security* 12.3 (Winter 1987/88), 5–29.

White, Mark. "Robert Kennedy and the Cuban Missile Crisis: A Reinterpretation." *American Diplomacy* (September 2007).

Zelikow, Philip, Timothy Naftali, and Ernest May, eds. *The Presidential Recordings: John F. Kennedy, Volumes 1–3, The Great Crises.* New York: W. W. Norton, 2001.

Zubok, Vladislav, and Constantine Pleshakov. *Inside the Kremlin's Cold War: From Stalin to Khrushchev.* Cambridge, Mass.: Harvard University Press, 1996.

Index

In this index an "f" after a number indicates a separate reference on the next page, and an "ff" indicates separate references on the next two pages. A continuous discussion over two or more pages is indicated by a span of page numbers, e.g., "57–59." *Passim* is used for a cluster of references in close but not necessarily consecutive sequence.

Stanford Nuclear Age Series

General Editor, Martin J. Sherwin

ADVISORY BOARD

Barton J. Bernstein and David Holloway

The Struggle Against the Bomb: Volume Two, Resisting the Bomb, A History of the World Nuclear Disarmament Movement, 1954–1970
By Lawrence S. Wittner. 1997

James B. Conant: Harvard to Hiroshima and the Making of the Nuclear Age
By James G. Hershberg. 1993

The Struggle Against the Bomb: Volume One, One World or None, A History of the World Nuclear Disarmament Movement Through 1953
By Lawrence S. Wittner. 1993

A Preponderance of Power: National Security, the Truman Administration, and the Cold War
By Melvyn P. Leffler. 1992

The Wizards of Armageddon
By Fred Kaplan, with a new foreword by Martin J. Sherwin. 1983, reissued 1991

Robert Oppenheimer: Letters and Recollections
Edited by Alice Kimball Smith and Charles Weiner, with a new foreword by Martin J. Sherwin. 1980, reissued 1995

The Advisors: Oppenheimer, Teller, and the Superbomb
By Herbert F. York, with a new preface and epilogue historical essay by Hans A. Bethe. 1976, reissued 1989

The Voice of the Dolphins and Other Stories
By Leo Szilard. 1961, expanded in 1991 with an introduction by Barton J. Bernstein

Atomic Energy for Military Purposes
By Henry D. Smyth, preface by Philip Morrison. 1945, reissued with new foreword, 1989